Gavin Mortimer has been writing about sport since 1996, contributing articles to a wide range of national newspapers and magazines. Gavin writes regularly on football for *The Week*. In addition he is the author of *Fields of Glory: the extraordinary lives of 16 warrior sportsmen*, *The Great Swim*, the story of the first woman to swim the English Channel that was dramatized on BBC Radio Four, and *A History of Cricket in 100 Objects* (Serpent's Tail). Born in North London, Gavin chose Barnet over Arsenal and Tottenham, a decision he continues to regret.

A complete catalogue record for
this book can be obtained from the
British Library on request

The right of Gavin Mortimer to be
identified as the author of this work
has been asserted by him in accordance with the Copyright, Designs and
Patents Act 1988

First published in this edition in
2014 by Serpent's Tail
First published in 2012 by
Serpent's Tail,
an imprint of Profile Books Ltd
3A Exmouth House
Pine Street
London EC1R 0JH
website: www.serpentstail.com

ISBN 978 1 84668 930 7
eISBN 978 1 84765 905 7

Designed and typeset by Jade Design
Printed and bound in Great Britain
by CPI Group (UK) Ltd, Croydon
CR0 4YY

10 9 8 7 6 5 4 3 2 1

A HISTORY OF

FOOTBALL

IN 100

OBJECTS

Gavin Mortimer

SERPENT'S TAIL

For my dad, and his touchline support, then and now.

Introduction

How do you narrate the history of football in 100 objects? A bit like supporting England these past forty years – it hasn't been easy; fewer missed penalties but just as many selection dilemmas.

The toughest challenge lay not in compiling the list but in cutting it. Ideally the book would have been titled *The History of Football in 117 Objects*, but as my editor pointed out, that lacked a certain *je ne sais quoi*, as Arsène Wenger might say.

The selection criteria were simple: we wanted objects that represented the convoluted, colourful and controversial history of football over the past 150 years, but we also wished to provoke and stimulate. A book full of shirts, badges and silverware wouldn't have been much fun. Oh, and all objects had to be inanimate. The thought of Maradona jostling for space with Jose Mourinho didn't bear thinking about.

We accept our history is a little Anglo centric but then the English invented football, formulated the rules, fine-tuned the style, and then graciously consented to be beaten by the rest of the world on a regular basis.

We accept, too, that not everyone will be satisfied with our 100 objects – why have you included this and omitted that? – but then isn't that the essence of football? It satisfies and frustrates, it excites and it exasperates, but above all it endures.

Next year is 2013, 150 years since the birth of the Football Association and the start of modern football as we know it. Of course the game today is virtually unrecognisable from the one first played on the green and pleasant fields of England in 1863. But there does remain one crucial constant: the team that wins is still the one that scores the most goals.

Happy reading and happy 150th, football!

School bench

We begin with a bench. Not a pitch-side bench on which to park a substitute's bottom, but a school bench, hard and unforgiving, as football was in its formative years when it was played with unbridled ferocity by the English elite.

Forget all that baloney about football being the invention of the Chinese. It wasn't, and nor was the game – as we know it today – played in the Middle Ages, whether in Florence or London. All our forebears did was use a ball for amusements. Modern football began in England in the early nineteenth century, though not on the streets of Derby in one of the city's annual Shrove Tuesday thrashes. The Derby game was really a riot with a ball and no wonder the army was called out in 1846 to restore order.

No, football has its origins not on the backstreets of Derby or the lanes of Lancashire but in altogether more salubrious surrounds – the hallowed walls of the English public school.

At the turn of the nineteenth century the English public school was not a place for the faint-hearted. Rosy-faced cherubs saying their prayers and singing their hymns were thin on the ground; instead the sort of pupil causing mayhem at Harrow, Eton or Winchester was the arrogant offspring of an aristocrat with an innate sense of superiority and a wilful disdain for anyone not of blue blood. As Richard Sanders writes in *Beastly Fury: The Strange Birth of British Football*: "The boys had very little interest in learning. The bald fact was this: if you were born an aristocrat in the eighteenth century you were going to run the country no matter how useless and incompetent you were."

Riots were not uncommon in English public schools at this time with the militia frequently called in to quell the adolescent rebels. When the occasion arose, soldiers arrived, as they did in the Cheapside district of London in 1811, when schoolboys from Merchant Taylors and St Paul's fought running battles in the capital. When they weren't fighting the boys liked to hunt, using stones, catapults and bows and arrows to kill birds, rabbits, squirrels and dogs.

A form of football was played, one which initially bore a passing resemblance to the Derby Game, but which evolved in the first decades of the nineteenth century as the strong asserted their dominance over the weak in bringing some vague form of rules to proceedings. *The History of Marlborough College*, published in 1923, recalled the football boys played in the 1840s:

> Piles of coats supplied the first goalposts, between which was stationed some shivering small boy who suffered dire physical woe for any unhappy dereliction of duty. The ball – for the school boasted but a solitary specimen – was a small round one. The rules, such as they were – and there were none in particular – were somewhat similar to those of the present Association game; for no handling of the ball was permitted, except in the case of a fair catch, which gave the right to a free kick off the ground. 'Off side' was unknown. Indeed the whole game was played in a senseless, unscientific manner, and attracted but few supporters.

There were more supporters watching Eton's Field Game, and at Winchester where the football was based around "charging". At Charterhouse they preferred to dribble with the ball while at Rugby and Shrewsbury there was no rule against handling.

The man credited with bringing order to the "senseless, unscientific" games played in public schools was Thomas Arnold, headmaster of Rugby from 1828 to 1842. No great lover of sport himself, Arnold nonetheless saw how it could help boys channel their energies and shape their character. More importantly, organised games would distract a boy's mind from the Unholy Trinity of Victorian vices: drinking, gambling and masturbation. As Percy Young wrote in *A History of British Football*, none of these habits were "conducive to corporate character at which the nineteenth century 'public' school aimed, nor convenient to accommodate. Sport, therefore, became and remained at once a means of sublimation and correction. It also afforded pious headmasters suitable analogies wherewith to imbue their less intelligent charges with a basic philosophy."

By the middle of the nineteenth century hundreds of young men were taking this philosophy up to Oxford and Cambridge Universities – and there a problem arose. There were no common rules. The football played at Eton was different to that played at Harrow or Shrewsbury or Marlborough. "The result was dire confusion," reflected Henry Malden, studying classics at Cambridge in 1848. "Every man played the rules he had been accustomed to at his public school. I remember how the Eton men howled at the Rugby men for handling the ball."

In exasperation Malden and a group of former public schoolboys called a meeting to agree upon a set of uniform rules. The meeting began at 4 p.m. and ended five minutes before midnight, by which time the weary men had drawn up the "Laws of the University Foot Ball Club". Although the original document has been lost, an 1856 revision of the laws is held in the library of Shrewsbury School:

   1. The Club shall be called the University Foot Ball Club.

2. At the commencement of play, the ball shall be kicked off from the middle of the ground; after every goal there shall be a kick off in the same way or manner.

3. After a goal, the losing side shall kick off; the sides changing goals unless a previous arrangement be made to the contrary.

4. The ball is out when it has passed the line of the flag-posts on either side of the ground in which case it shall be thrown in straight.

5. The ball is "behind" when it has passed the goal on either side of it.

6. When the ball is behind, it shall be brought forward at the place where it left the ground no more than ten paces and kicked off.

7. Goal is when the ball is kicked through the flag posts and under the string.

8. When a player catches the ball directly from the foot, he may kick it as he can without running with it. In no other case may the ball be touched with the hands except to stop it.

9. If the ball has passed a player and has come from the direction of his own goal, he may not touch it till the other side has kicked it, unless there are more than three of the other side before him. No player is allowed to loiter between the ball and the adversaries' goal.

10. In no case is holding a player, pushing with the hands or tripping up allowed. Any player may prevent another from getting to the ball by any means consistent with this rule.

11. Every match shall be decided by a majority of goals.

In a letter dated 1897, Malden recalled that the students, after a good night's sleep, pasted the laws the following day on a noticeboard on Parker's Piece. "And very satisfactorily they worked," added Malden. Alas, the passing of time had clearly dimmed Malden's memory, for the Laws of the University Foot Ball Club worked to virtually no one's satisfaction. So by the early 1860s football was still as disorganised as ever and in desperate need of an authority figure. As we shall see from our next object, that man was Charles Alcock.

Cricket bat

Before we are introduced to Charles Alcock we should see how football was evolving outside the confines of England's public schools and leading universities. The short answer is that it wasn't, which is why our next object is a cricket bat.

Organised football was still an alien concept to the English working class, as was rugby. Cricket was the only team sport with which they were familiar. If a football was seen on the streets it was normally being chased by scores of excited young men, bloodied and bruised, such as those who rampaged through Derby in 1846. There was, however, an exception – in South Yorkshire. It was in the hill country to the north of Sheffield that football began to evolve, with matches organised between villages that were more than just shambolic kickabouts. There were rules.

As early as 1843 a report in the journal *Bell's Life* described how "an excellent match of football took place at Thurlstone [north of Sheffield] lately, between six of the celebrated players of that place and six from Totties, which ended with neither party getting a goal."

In Sheffield itself cricket was still God. But that began

to change in 1855, the year that the Sheffield Cricket Club moved into its new premises in Bramall Lane. One of the members brought along a football so they could have kickabouts before the cricket began. Two of the team, William Prest and Nathaniel Creswick, agreed that forming a football team might be a good way for the boys to stay in shape over the winter.

On 24 October 1857, the world's first club, Sheffield FC, came into existence with, according to FIFA, "its headquarters located in a potting shed and green house. Creswick was appointed captain and secretary and he and Prest went about establishing a set of rules that would allow for the activity's progression."

Creswick was still alive when Sheffield celebrated its Golden Jubilee in 1907. In a speech to mark the occasion he recalled that he'd drawn up the rules by studying the football laws used by the various schools. What he regarded as good laws he incorporated into the Sheffield rules and what he viewed as absurd he discarded. These rules (which were sold at auction in July 2011 for £881,250) were published at the club's first annual general meeting in October 1858, and were as follows:

The kick off from the middle must be a place kick.

Kick out must not be more than 25 yards out of goal.

A fair catch is a catch from any player provided the ball has not touched the ground or has not been thrown from touch and is entitled to a free kick.

Charging is fair in case of a place kick (with the exception of a kick off) as soon as a player offers to kick, but he may always draw back unless he has actually touched the ball with his foot.

Pushing with the hands is allowed but no hacking or tripping up is fair under any circumstances whatever.

No player may be held or pulled over.

It is not lawful to take the ball off the ground (except in touch) for any purpose whatever.

> The ball may be pushed or hit with the hand, but holding the ball except in the case of a free kick is altogether disallowed.
>
> A goal must be kicked but not from touch nor by a free kick from a catch.
>
> A ball in touch is dead, consequently the side that touches it down must bring it to the edge of the touch and throw it straight out from touch.
>
> Each player must provide himself with a red and dark blue flannel cap, one colour to be worn by each side.

With the laws in place, football in Sheffield underwent a surge in popularity. Montague Shearman, writing in 1887, described how "after 1860 there was a great football 'boom' at Sheffield, and several fresh clubs sprang up, and indeed from that time for the next fifteen years the Sheffielders could put an eleven into the field able to meet any other eleven in the kingdom."

By 1862 Sheffield boasted fifteen clubs and though in time these gave football the crossbar, the free kick and the corner they persisted in using smaller goals (roughly the size of hockey goals) so that scores were never high. When Sheffield played Hallam at Bramall Lane in the world's first derby match, neither side scored in nearly three hours of football. What there was, however, was a mass brawl involving players and public, sparked by a rash challenge from a Hallam player called Waterfall on Nathanial Creswick. One local paper commented the next day that the game was the moment when "the waistcoats come off & the fighting began."

Eleven months after the Sheffield Derby, in November 1863, representatives from eleven football clubs in the London area assembled at the Freemason's Tavern in Great Queens Street. They were there to decide upon a universal set of football rules. None of the Sheffield clubs were invited, an oversight that would take years to remedy and would require the diplomacy of Charles Alcock.

Freemason's Tavern

Why the representatives of the eleven clubs decided to meet in the Freemason's Tavern on the evening of 26 October 1863 isn't known. Perhaps one or more of them were pigeon fanciers and knew of the tavern's large hall, where pigeon shows had been held throughout the 1850s. Or perhaps the tavern, the third object in our cornucopia of footballing history, simply served the best beer in town.

Not that they had much opportunity to sample the ale. From the outset the discussion was frank. Charles Alcock wasn't there but his brother John was in his capacity as secretary of the Forest Club in north-east London. Initially, wrote Charles Alcock later, relying on the testimony of his brother, "every-thing augured favourably for the formation of a body which would secure the adhesion of football players of every sect." By sect he meant those clubs who viewed the game as one of "dribbling" and those who favoured running with the ball in hand and "hacking" an opponent, or, to put it more bluntly, giving him a kick in the shins.

Francis Campbell of the Blackheath Club was all for hack-ing, warning that if it was outlawed "you will do away with all the courage and pluck of the game, and I will be bound to bring over a lot of Frenchmen who would beat you with a week's practice."

The meeting broke up with no firm agreement, so on 10 November they reconvened – again choosing the Freemason's Tavern. This time it was decided that Ebenezer Morley, the honorary secretary, would draft a set of twenty three provisional rules for ratification at a later date.

Charles Alcock was cautiously optimistic that progress was being made, noting that "running with the ball in the case of a fair catch or on the first bound was allowed, and even the worst features of the Rugby game, hacking and tripping when running with the ball, were duly provided for."

But this still didn't go far enough for the five clubs – led by Blackheath – that Alcock described as the "rugby clubs". Finally, at the sixth meeting at the Freemason's Tavern on December 8, Francis Campbell withdrew the support of the Blackheath Club and the other four "rugby clubs" followed suit. It was all very cordial. Campbell agreed to remain as treasurer until the next general meeting, but within a few years Blackheath was one of the twenty one clubs to form the Rugby Football Union.

Undeterred, the remaining clubs formed the Football Association and published its first set of rules (see appendix). And barely anyone paid them a blind bit of notice.

It took the FA another three years after its formation to hold another general meeting, by which time only four new members had joined. By 1866 Charles Alcock had replaced his brother on the committee and he now set about implementing a clear set of rules. Richard Sanders in *Beastly Fury* describes how the FA, cajoled by Alcock at their 1866 general meeting at the Freemason's Tavern, agreed to introduce a tape "a height of eight feet between the posts and stipulated the ball must pass beneath this for a goal. They removed the right to a shot on goal, or conversion, following a touchdown (although they kept the touchdown). They removed the right to a free kick following a clean catch. And, most importantly, they introduced Westminster's three-man offside rule."

In addition Alcock, a northerner by birth, reached out to the Sheffield clubs, still happily abiding by their own set of rules, and challenged them to a match in Battersea Park. Alcock, a bruising player in his own right, played in the match and remarked afterwards that the success of the occasion "had contributed in no small measure to increase the popularity of the Association game in London, and the effects were visible in a considerable addition to the number of clubs which declared allegiance to the Association."

There was a further streamlining of football's rules at the 1867 annual meeting including the abolition of the touchdown. The following year the FA had twenty eight member clubs, each of which paid an annual subscription of five shillings. In 1870 Alcock became honorary secretary of the FA and he used his increasing influence to lure the Sheffield Association further into the fold, "the only step required to realize the long-expected hope of one code of rules acknowledged by Association players throughout the kingdom."

It had taken seven years since that first meeting in the Freemason's Tavern, but the Football Association was finally in a position to take the game to the people.

A football

OBJECT 4

Ever since man first learned to walk upright he has enjoyed kicking something, be it the head of a woolly mammoth, the bladder of a cow or a ball made of cloth. It's said that 2000 years ago the Chinese played a game called "tsu chu" in which balls made from animal skins were kicked at targets by players, although this in no way gives credence to Sepp Blatter's outlandish claim that China and not England is the birthplace of football. Balls to the FIFA president and that's what our next object is.

By the Middle Ages villages in Britain were amusing themselves with an inflated pig's bladder, and over the course of time these 'balls' were covered in leather to prolong their lifespan. One such ball, estimated to date from between 1540 and 1570, is housed in the Smith Museum in Stirling, Scotland. The small grey ball was discovered during an excavation project inside Stirling Castle in the mid-1970s, concealed behind the thick oak-panelled walls of the bed chamber once occupied by Mary Queen of Scots. It's believed it was used for a kickabout in the castle's courtyard by soldiers and staff, although how it ended up in Mary's boudoir is a mystery.

Balls barely changed between the death of Mary and the coronation of Queen Victoria in 1837. The year before Victoria's accession, Charles Goodyear began experiments with vulcanised rubber, though financial problems meant it was nearly another twenty years before he designed the first vulcanised rubber football with panels that were glued together. The ball was used in a game between a side from Oneida, the first organised team in the USA, and a Boston XI in November 1863, a month after London's Freemasons' Tavern had hosted the first meeting of the nascent Football Association.

It wasn't to Goodyear that the FA turned, however, as their supplier of balls, but rather to Richard Lindon, a Warwickshire manufacturer who had been supplying egg-shaped balls to local schools for several years. As the official Richard Lindon website explains their founding father "introduced India rubber inner-tubes and because of the pliability of vulcanised rubber the shape for a soccer ball could finally be spherical. First attempts were made using 7 panels of leather with a leather 'button' at each end which was reasonably spherical, only slightly egg-shaped, and proved a huge success... for the first time in the history of the inflatable ball a template for leather panels could be made and balls be replicated time over to an exacting standard."

Though the FA had neglected to address the specifications of the ball in drawing up their first set of rules in 1863, they did stipulate in a revision of the rules of 1872 that footballs "must be spherical with a circumference of 27 to 28 inches." Those dimensions remain the same 140 years on, though what has changed is the weight (up from 13–15 ounces to 14–16 ounces) and the materials used in the manufacture of footballs.

In the first half-century or so after the formation of the FA, most balls were made from tanned leather with eighteen sections stitched together by hand. The bladder was inserted through a small slit and, once inflated, this slit was laced back up. Rain made these balls heavy and cumbersome.

Come the 1930 World Cup the eighteen sections had been reduced to twelve but this failed to satisfy either of the finalists. Hosts Uruguay wanted to use their ball, reportedly slightly larger than that of their opponents Argentina, who wanted to play with theirs. A compromise was reached and the Argentine ball was used in the first half and the Uruguayan in the second. Argentina led 2-1 at half-time but Uruguay's ball propelled them to a 4-2 victory in the inaugural World Cup final.

Twenty years later, when Brazil hosted the World Cup, 12-panel balls were still in vogue, although, as the FIFA website notes, the balls had "curved edges to create less stress on the seams." Although white balls were introduced into English football in the early 1950s and synthetic materials began to be used in ball manufacture from the 1960s onwards, the ball for the 1966 World Cup in England was still of tanned leather. It was made by Malcolm Wainwright, the star designer for sports firm Slazenger, who later recalled: "I made about 20 balls all told. They were 24-panel balls, which meant that there were six panels made up of three long strips of leather but the centre panels of these three strips had a further seam at right angles just to give more strength."

The 1966 World Cup was the last in which a ball was just a ball. Since the 1970 tournament Adidas has been the official supplier to FIFA, designing balls with names that get sillier every four years. In 1970, when the 32-panel leather ball consisted of white hexagons and black pentagons, they called it the "Telstar"; in 1978 the "Tango" and in 1986 (the first World Cup ball to be made entirely of synthetic material in layers) the "Azteca". The ball used for the 2010 World Cup in South Africa was the "Jabulani" and according to FIFA its design celebrated "two of the most important facets of the South African nation – diversity and harmony – as it is these principles that make it such a colourful and welcoming nation." "This ball will unify us in this country," declared World Cup organising chief executive Danny Jordaan, adding: "It carries a lot of hope for the future of this country."

The ball for the 2014 World Cup in Brazil is the first to be named by the fans, with over one million Brazilians casting their vote in 2012. The winning name – chosen by seventy per cent – was 'Brazuca' which, as Fifa explained, is an informal term used by Brazilians to describe pride in their way of life which "symbolises emotion, pride and goodwill to all".

With all that pressure on the ball, at least they won't need a pump.

FA Cup

OBJECT 5

You'll remember that we last encountered Charles Alcock in 1870 as he sought to bring the Sheffield Association into the Football Association's fold to further unify the football "kingdom". Alcock's next step to establish football as the people's game was the launch of the first national competition. More than 140 years later the competition is still going strong and the cup for which clubs play is object number five.

On 20 July 1871 Alcock chaired a meeting at the London office of the *Sportsman*, the newspaper for which he wrote. The outcome of the meeting was a declaration by the FA that "it is desirable that a Challenge Cup should be established in connection with the Association, for which all clubs should be invited to compete."

The idea was ratified at a subsequent meeting in October, and the FA Cup was born. Not everyone was pleased. The northern clubs complained that they had already arranged fixtures for that season so wouldn't be entering into the following year's competition; a number of southern clubs, on the other hand, regarded competitive football as they did the newly proclaimed German Empire – both dangerous and not to be trusted. As Alcock wrote subsequently:

> There has been, and still is, a large section, even of the best friends and supporters of football, who take exception to Cup competitions... their contention is, in the main, that Cup competitions give rise to an excessive rivalry. According to their notions the stimulus they give is not conducive to the real interests of the game. On the contrary, the desire to secure possession of, or even to gain a prominent place in the struggle for, the Cup, they impute, introduces an unhealthy feeling which tends to lower the general standard of morality among those who compete.

Alcock pressed on. Fifteen clubs entered the inaugural FA Cup, though only two of those sides came from the north of Hertfordshire. One, Queen's Park, hailed from north of the border, a feature of the competition until 1887, after which Scottish clubs were no longer allowed to compete.

Wanderers were the first winners of the FA Cup, defeating the Royal Engineers 1-0 in March 1872 at the Kennington Oval for a cup that measured 18 inches and cost just £25. "The game was well contested, the men being well matched," wrote one Fleet Street paper, the *Sun and Central Press*. "But the Wanderers had evidently the best throughout. The play was capital, and the goal was won the by Wanderers; Chequer kicking the ball home [A. H. Chequer was the alias of Morton Betts]."

Hardly a comprehensive match report but then who was interested? Only 2,000 spectators were at the Kennington Oval to see the match; in contrast, cricket matches were pulling in crowds of 20,000-plus, and the first rugby international – between England and Scotland – in 1871 had attracted 4,000 fans to Edinburgh.

But by the time of the 1889 FA Cup a crowd of around 25,000 was squeezed into the Oval. The reason for this increase? The finalists – Preston North End and Wolverhampton Wanderers – were two clubs from the north, and it was in this region that the FA Cup found the greatest approval.

The FA Cup gained little momentum in its early years. The southern clubs entered with barely concealed distaste for a competition which rugby clubs dismissed as "pot hunting". The Rugby Football Union would never stoop so low, and it was this attitude that ultimately helped football become the game of the English working classes. The lack of competitive rugby matches didn't sit well with the public, particularly in the north of England, so people switched their allegiance to football. The FA Cup was the chance for towns such as Blackburn and Darwen to put themselves on the map, and their clubs enjoyed good cup runs in the late 1870s.

Blackburn Olympic's 2-1 defeat of Old Etonians in the 1883 final was the first time a club from the north had won the FA Cup; a southern side wouldn't get their hands on the trophy again until Tottenham beat Sheffield United in 1901. That 1883 final was also the last time a team of gentleman amateurs appeared in English football's showpiece event.

The north of England loved the FA Cup. It helped forge an identity among towns, pitting West Bromwich Albion against Preston, or Wolves against The Wednesday of Sheffield. In 1895 the FA Cup Final switched to Crystal Palace to accommodate the growing crowds, and for the last final of the century a record crowd of 74,000 saw Sheffield United hammer Derby County 4-1.

Charles Alcock couldn't help but sound a little smug when, in 1906, he reflected on his baby in his book *Football: The Association Game*:

> So far, at least as the experience of over thirty years goes, the trial of the Football Association Cup has been a complete refutation of the arguments of those who were opposed to its inception for the reasons referred to. The disadvantages have been few; the advantages, on the other hand, many and undeniable... the extraordinary development of the Association game during the last fifteen years is beyond all doubt attributable in a very great measure to the influence of the Cup.

That influence has steadily declined in recent years in the face of the financial juggernaut that is modern football. Manchester United notoriously withdrew from the competition in 1999/2000 to play in some worthless Club World Championship in Brazil, a decision foisted on them by the FA and the government. It was hoped that United's participation in the tournament would help England win the right to host the 2006 World Cup. No chance. Instead, all United's withdrawal did was damage the prestige of the oldest club knockout competition in the world. As for the Club World Championship, it lasted one whole season (although it was re-launched several years later).

But still the football authorities continue to undermine the FA Cup. In 2011, for the first time in the competition's history, a number of Premier League matches were held on the same day as the final, diminishing its "showpiece" feel. The following season Kenny Dalglish took Liverpool to the final of both the League Cup and the FA Cup, winning the former and losing the latter to Chelsea. His reward was to be sacked because Liverpool had only finished eighth in the Premier League.

Yet though the FA Cup's stature has shrunk in recent

decades, to the players involved the final remains a special occasion. As Chelsea defender John Terry said after becoming the first captain to lift the cup four times with the same club in 2012: "It's fantastic. This is what we live for, what we play football for."

Queen's Park team photo

Hands up who knows their Latin? And we're not talking America. Old style Latin, or to be exact: "*Ludere causa ludendi*", which means "to play for the sake of playing."

A worthy sentiment, and one which is embossed on the club badge of Queen's Park, the Scottish Third Division club who pride themselves on the fact that none of their players has ever been paid.

The team photo of the 1873 Queen's Park XI is our next object, a tribute not just to the way the club influenced Scottish football but also to the impact they had further south, among the "auld enemy".

On the evening of 9 July 1867, ten young Glaswegian businessmen assembled with one purpose in mind, as the minutes of their meeting recorded: "Tonight at half past eight o'clock a number of gentlemen met at No. 3 Eglinton Terrace for the purpose of forming a football club."

The club they formed was called Queen's Park, and most of the men present had played a form of football before. Most, too, were familiar with the rules laid out by the Football Association. But few agreed with the English interpretation of the offside law, revised in 1866 to permit a forward pass as long as at least three defenders were between the player and the opposition goal when the ball was passed.

The Scots were of the opinion that a player was offside only if he were in front of the penultimate man, and in the final 15 yards of the pitch. Consequently Queen's Park's style of play encouraged players to pass and not to dribble (as was the wont of the English).

Having formed a team, reinterpreted the offside rule and agreed upon a club motto, the men of Queen's Park next fixed training nights for Mondays, Wednesdays and Saturdays.

Of course one problem for the newly-formed club was a lack of opponents. They were the only football club, not just in Glasgow but also in Scotland. But with an increasing number of young neophytes turning up at training, Queen's Park arranged matches in-house. Writing in the club's official fiftieth anniversary history (1920), Richard Robinson explained how "sides were arranged – North v. South of Eglinton Toll, Reds v. Blues, Light v. Heavy Weights, President's Team v. J. Smith's Team (a series of six games), and Clerks v. The Field, etc. In these games the dribbling and passing, which raised the Scottish game to the level of a fine art, were developed."

A year after the formation of Queen's Park, other football clubs began appearing on the scene. In the summer of 1868 Queen's Park secretary Robert Gardner wrote to Glasgow Thistle (the letter is on display in the Scottish Football Museum), challenging them to a match, which Queen's Park won, and the following year there was a game against Hamilton Gymnasium.

The difficulty encountered by Queen's Park in these matches was that no one could agree on the rules, not even the number of players on a team. It had been 20-a-side against Thistle and 15-a-side in the easy win over Hamilton. Increasingly exasperated by the incoherence in Scottish football, Queen's Park applied for membership of the Football Association in the autumn of 1870. The insightful secretary of the FA, Charles Alcock, was only too happy to have Queen's Park. Word had already reached him that they "were the first to demonstrate the possibilities of combination." By combination, Alcock meant teamwork, passing the ball from player to player instead of the more 'individualistic' approach of the English where the tendency was for one player to dribble the ball downfield oblivious of his teammates.

Despite this innovation neither Alcock nor any other Englishman expected Queen's Park to put up much of a show at the Oval on 4 March 1872. They were facing the mighty Wanderers in the semi-final of the inaugural FA Cup, a side that was bigger, fitter and supremely confident. But after ninety minutes of fast-paced football the scores were goalless. Though the Scots couldn't afford to return to London for the replay (they withdrew and Wanderers went on to beat the Royal Engineers in the final) the impression they left behind was immense. "They dribble little, and convey the ball by a series of long kicks, combined with a judicious plan of passing on," wrote the *Field*.

The upshot of Queen's Park performance was the staging of the first international football match on November 30 1872. This time it was the English who had to take the train, journeying to the West of Scotland Cricket Ground in the Partick suburb of Glasgow. The English side reflected the growing popularity of the game in the country, with players from northern clubs such as Notts County and The (Sheffield) Wednesday, and southern sides like Crystal Palace and Harrow Chequers. The Scotland XI, on the other hand, was Queen's Park in disguise.

Once more the match finished goalless and again the English press couldn't conceal their surprise and admiration of the Scottish style. "Individual skill was generally on England's side," wrote the *Graphic*. "The Southrons, however, did not play to each other so well as their opponents, who seem to be adepts in passing the ball."

The result and the manner of the Scots' performance

captured the country's imagination, and Queen's Park were soon touring Scotland and playing exhibition matches. Rugby, hitherto the dominant sport in Scotland, began to lose ground, except in the Borders – the one region where Queen's Park never toured. Everywhere else, including Edinburgh, football took hold and in 1873 the Scotland Football Association was formed.

Being so much smaller than England, and with football concentrated in the area between Glasgow and Edinburgh, Scotland adopted only one style – the short passing game invented by Queen's Park. When Charles Alcock sat down in 1906 to write *The Association Game*, England had won just eleven of its thirty four internationals against Scotland, and he had no doubt who was responsible for this dominance. "The development of the Association game in Scotland was indeed extraordinary," he wrote, "and in the course of a few years the enthusiasm of the Queen's Park club had worked such a wonderful effect... and enabled Scotland to show a much greater advantage in its international matches with England."

Ref's whistle

Once upon a time there was no need for our next object on a football field – a referee's whistle.

When the Football Association promulgated its Laws of Football in December 1863 it made no mention of the referee.

Instead there were two umpires, one supplied by each team, whose job it was to patrol along the touchline of one half of the field in much the same manner as today's assistants. The pair were almost superfluous to what occurred on the field of play. Football was, after all, a game played by gentlemen who could be relied upon to adhere most singularly to the spirit of the game. What hastened the change to a more officious approach to controlling matches was the advent of the Football Association Cup in 1871–72. Now there was something at stake and winning suddenly became more important. Recognising this, the FA issued some rules for all cup ties, one of which stated: "The Committee shall appoint two umpires and a referee to act at each of the matches in the Final Ties. Neither the umpires nor the referee shall be members of either of the contending Clubs and the decision of the umpires shall be final except in the case of the umpires disagreeing when an appeal shall be made to the referee, whose decision shall be final."

There was a further stipulation to the FA's rule: referees would be neutral.

For twenty years the referee and his two umpires officiated matches. Montague Shearman in his 1887 book *Athletics and Football* explained how the system worked:

Each side has its own umpire, who is armed with a stick or flag; the referee carries a whistle. When a claim for infringement of rules is made, if both umpires are agreed, each holds up his stick, and the referee calls the game to a halt by sounding his whistle. If one umpire allows the claim, and the referee agree with him, he calls a halt as before; if the other umpire and the referee agree that the claim be disallowed, the whistle is not sounded. Two of the three officials must therefore agree in allowing the claim or the whistle is silent, and players continue the game until the whistle calls them off. Both umpires and referee, therefore, must lose no time in arriving at a decision, or so much play is wasted.

The exact year referees began to whistle isn't known with certainty, though Nottingham Forest claim it all began with them. In December 1872 the club secretary-treasurer, Walter Roe Lymbery, noted in his account book an outlay of fivepence "for an umpire's whistle". In the same year R.M. Ruck, a member of the Royal Engineers XI, recalled that if the ball hit a player's arm "it was considered the correct thing if challenged... [if] he at once threw up his hand and acknowledged it without waiting for the umpire's whistle."

Not all clubs welcomed the whistle-blowers. In 1886 the secretary of Bangor FC wrote to the FA to enquire "whether it is correct for umpires to have whistles" and the reply, apparently, confirmed that it was not.

But five years later, in 1891, the FA decided three officials was a crowd. Umpires were told to concentrate on running the line while the referee would be the sole arbitrator of the game's laws. It appears this diminution of the umpires' powers wasn't well received in all quarters for when the FA released its amended laws in 1891 it stated that "two linesmen shall be appointed, whose duty (subject to the decision of the Referee) shall be to decide when the ball is out of play, and which side is entitled to the comer-kick, goal-kick, or throw-in; and to assist the Referee in carrying out the game in accordance with the Laws. In the event of any-undue interference or improper conduct by a Linesman, the Referee shall have power to order him off the field of play and appoint a substitute."

That wasn't the only additional power attributed to the referee. He was now able to award a free kick for a foul (and from 1891 a penalty kick) without waiting for an appeal to be made by a player. As the referees became more influential and important to the game so they became the target of spectators' wrath. John Lewis, who officiated three FA Cup finals in the 1890s, recalled that: "For myself, I would take no objection to hooting or groaning by the spectators at decisions with which they disagree. The referee should remember that football is a game that warms the blood... and that unless they can give free vent to their delight or anger, as the case may be, the great crowds we now witness will dwindle rapidly away."

Spectators may have occasionally become a little boisterous, but players still behaved impeccably at the tail end of the nineteenth century, as they did for the first half of the century that followed.

A Sheffield steel knife

OBJECT 8

Officialdom wasn't the only thing sneaking insidiously into football during the 1870s. So was professionalism, the paying of players by clubs desperate to secure the services of the country's best footballers. The practice began in the mid-1870s as the northern clubs began to emerge from the shadow of the southern clubs. The latter were populated by well-to-do gents, most of whom were of "independent means" and regarded payment for playing with the same distaste they reserved for referees: unnecessary, unwanted and not the hallmark of a gentleman's game.

But in Scotland, Lancashire and Yorkshire football was predominantly the preserve of the working-classes, men from low-income families who saw football as a way out of their humdrum existence. Sound familiar? Professionalism began with clubs reimbursing the travelling expenses of players but soon the clubs wanted something more binding.

The man regarded as football's first professional is James Lang, a Glaswegian striker who began his career with Clydesdale. He appeared for the club in the inaugural Scottish

FA Cup Final of 1874 against Queen's Park and was subsequently selected for a Glasgow XI who played a team from Sheffield. Present at that match were representatives from The Wednesday Club (later renamed Sheffield Wednesday) and they liked the look of the 25 year-old Lang.

Undeterred by the fact that Lang had only one eye (the result of a shipyard accident in 1869), Wednesday made him an offer: come and play for us and we'll make sure you never have to work in the shipyards again. Lang jumped at the chance and arrived in Sheffield for the start of the 1876–77 season. "I am not going to say that I crossed the border to play for nothing," Lang later remarked in an interview, "because you would not believe me if I did."

Lang, who had made his Scotland debut earlier in 1876, was given a job in a local knife works owned by one of Wednesday's directors. The firm manufactured bayonets, blades and knives, but Lang's time "was chiefly devoted to football and reading the news of the day in the papers." Perhaps a newspaper would have been a more suitable object for this entry...

A trickle of other players followed Lang's example, prompting the *Football Annual* to make a sly reference to the practice in its 1878 edition: "What was ten or fifteen years ago the recreation of a few has now become the pursuit of thousands," proclaimed the football bible, "an athletic exercise, carried on under a strict system and, in many cases, by an enforced term of training, almost magnified into a profession."

The Lancashire clubs became more brazen in their efforts to attract Scotland's finest players. Fergie Suter, a Partick stalwart, was lured south to Blackburn Rovers by the offer of £100, a startling sum in those days, and by 1882 little attempt was made to conceal what was going on.

The advert placed in the *Scotsman* newspaper in October 1882 – "Football player (a good full-back) wanted for a club in Northeast Lancashire, to act as captain" – was typical of many such notices paid for by northern English clubs.

Belatedly the FA acted, singling out Preston North End as the worst culprits of the professional scourge sweeping Lancashire and Yorkshire. On 18 January 1884, Charles Alcock wrote to Preston in his capacity as honorary secretary informing them that they had violated Article 15 of the FA's charter that stated no club should remunerate its players.

Preston – and not just the club – was furious. The local paper, the *Preston Herald*, pointed out that just about every club in the county had imported players from far afield to boost their ranks. Why had they been picked on?

In Preston chairman Billy Sudell (see object 10) the FA had taken on a formidable personality, a man who Alcock admired for his commitment to the club and to football as a whole.

Faced with a possibly catastrophic rupture between the southern and northern clubs, Alcock once again showed his brilliance as an administrator. A month after writing to Preston North End he told the FA that in his opinion "the time has come for the legalisation of professionalism." He pointed at the example of cricket (Alcock was also secretary of Surrey Cricket Club) and said football could learn from their example of accommodating amateurs and professionals.

But others disagreed, and violently, with Alcock's motion. The FA turned on itself and for months the arguments raged, and then, just as Alcock and his supporters were on the brink of defeat, in stepped the clubs on his behalf.

In October 1884, nine northern clubs announced they were going to break away from the FA and form the professional British Football Association. Within a matter of days the nine had become twenty five and the FA had a full-blown crisis on its hands.

On 19 January 1885 the FA held a general meeting at the Freemason's Tavern in London, the same venue where the association had been born twenty two years earlier. Lancashire and the northern clubs sat on one side of the table and the southern and Midlands clubs on the other. Alcock proposed the motion that professionalism should be legalised, and

Charles Crump of Birmingham opposed it, saying "the introduction of professionalism will be the ruin of the pastime."

It went to the vote and Alcock's motion was carried – but only by 113 votes to 108, short of the two thirds majority that he needed. Two months later the FA tried again but once more didn't garner enough support. Finally, on 20 July 1885, Alcock's motion was carried, and the FA voted for the professionalisation of football.

There were restrictions and codicils, and much harrumphing about how the sport had sold its soul, but Billy Sudell was elated. "Professionalism must improve football," he declared, "because men who devote their entire attention to the game are more likely to become good players than the amateur who is worried by business cares."

Crossbar

They've been rattled, shaken, struck, grazed and clipped, but still the crossbar comes back for more. For services to football in the face of adversity, therefore, the crossbar is a worthy entrant to our pantheon of objects.

When the FA published the Laws of Football on 8 December 1863 they decreed that "the maximum length of the ground shall be 200 yards, the maximum breadth shall be 100 yards, the length and breadth shall be marked off with flags; and the goal shall be defined by two upright posts, 8 yards apart, without any tape or bar across them." But as every back garden footballer knows, a goal without a crossbar is an invitation to argue.

"That was a goal."

"No it wasn't."

"Yes it was." *Ad infinitum.*

So it was that in 1865, a length of tape began to be stretched across the goal from one post to the other at a height of 8 feet (2.4m), and when the FA published a revised set of laws in 1872 they stated that a goal was scored when the ball "passes between the goalposts under the tape, not being thrown, knocked on, or carried."

The first three FA Cup finals had tape for transversals until, in 1875, the Football Association ordered the introduction of the crossbar at a similar height to the tape, a move that was standard practice by 1882.

Nine years later the Football Association updated the laws of the game, stating that from then on the goals "shall be upright posts fixed on the goallines, equidistant from the corner flagstaffs, 8 yards (7.32m) apart, with a bar across them 8 feet from the ground. The maximum width of the goal posts and the maximum depth of the cross bar shall be 5 inches. Lines shall be marked 6 yards from each goalpost at right angles to the goal lines for a distance of 6 yards, and these shall be connected with each other by a line parallel to the goal lines; the space within these lines shall be the goal."

But still no sign of the net, though it was on its way. Its creator, a civil engineer called John Alexander Brodie, had realised the need on 26 October 1889 when a match between Everton and Accrington ended acrimoniously after a disputed goal. Watching from the stands, Brodie decided a net would solve such quarrels in the future. The following year he took out a patent for his invention and the first "Brodie Goal Net" was trialled at a match on the Crosby Cricket ground in Merseyside. Such was the success of the net that it was used in the 1892 FA Cup Final at the Kennington Oval between Aston Villa and West Bromwich Albion.

Now that they had a proper goal to defend, goalkeepers began to assume more prestige. A change to the laws in 1894 outlawed the shoulder charge on the goalkeeper unless he was playing the ball. In the same year Bill "Fatty" Foulkes made his debut for Sheffield United. Foulkes was 6ft 2in and eventually ballooned to around 20 stone, an asset in an age where it was still permissible for goalkeepers to be barged over the line as they caught the ball. Fatty Foulkes was unbargeable. The *Liverpool Post* described how, during a game in 1898, Foulkes had been charged by Liverpool striker George Allan and "the big man, losing his temper, seized him by the leg and turned him upside down." Thanks to Fatty Foulkes, United won the First Division title in 1897–98 and the FA Cup in 1899 and 1902.

Nearly a century after Foulkes became the most famous footballer in England, FIFA proposed a change to the dimensions of the goal, arguing that because goalkeepers were getting bigger fewer goals were being scored. In an interview with a German magazine in January 1996, FIFA General Secretary Sepp Blatter revealed they were considering widening the goal by 50cm (the circumference of two balls) and increasing its height by 25cm (one ball). The new goals would therefore be 7.82m wide and 2.69m in height.

Howls of protest greeted the announcement, former England and Liverpool goalkeeper Ray Clemence one of many who told FIFA to get a grip: "People don't want to see goals just for the sake of goals being scored. They want to see good goals," said Clemence, adding: "You see great goals being scored and, just as importantly, goalkeepers making great saves. That's all part of the glamour of football. If you make the goals too big and keepers have a nigh on impossible job of making those saves, it will take something away from it."

FIFA backed down and the crossbar was left where it was, to be rattled, shaken, struck, grazed and clipped. But not raised.

Preston mill

We saw with our eighth object how Preston chairman Billy Sudell faced down the Football Association in 1885. We left him boasting that "professionalism must improve football," and boy was he right. Within four years the Football League had been formed and its first champions were Sudell's Preston North End. They were dubbed the "Invincibles" and that's how Sudell must have felt at the end of a decade when he bestrode English football like a colossus. Alas, he would soon be brought down to earth, and Preston, too, but the legacy of Billy Sudell lives on more than a century later.

But why a mill? Because that's how Sudell rose from relatively humble beginnings to a position where he was able to take on the football establishment. He was born in Preston in 1850, the son of a warehouse manager who was determined the youngest of his four children would make his mark on this world. Young Billy was privately educated and upon leaving school found employment in the cotton mill of John Goodair.

Sudell worked hard and by his late thirties was managing both of Goodair's mills, earning a good wage and living in a grand house with two servants and a flash carriage parked in the driveway. Material possessions weren't enough for Sudell, who no doubt had a complex about his humble origins. He enlisted in the local militia, became treasurer of the cricket club and joined William Gladstone's Liberal Party.

In 1874 he became chairman of Preston North End and soon the club had eclipsed the town's rugby club as the preeminent sports team. Next Sudell set out to make Preston the biggest club in all the county. He moved Preston to Deepdale, the ground they still occupy, and over the next decade they conquered Lancashire. Then it was time for the next stage of Sudell's grand masterplan.

Travelling to Edinburgh Sudell did what several northern clubs had been doing for years – he enticed some of Scotland's best players across the border, among them the great Hearts' captain and full back Jack Ross. Soon there were ten "Scottish Professors" (as they were euphemistically labelled) in the Preston XI, and when they entered the FA Cup in 1883–84 for the first time they destroyed all before them. The FA was outraged and expelled them from the competition (see object 8) on the eve of their fourth round tie against Upton Park, the upshot of which was Sudell's protracted but ultimately successful fight to legalise professionalism.

With that done, in the summer of 1885 Sudell resumed his scheme for nationwide supremacy. By now he was more than just chairman of Preston North End; he was manager in all but name, creating a cult of personality within the club that wouldn't be seen again inside a British football club until Herbert Chapman took charge of Arsenal in the mid-1920s. Neil Carter of the International Centre for Sport, History and Culture, says that Sudell was "the game's first professional manager... In the early days of the professional game, teams were picked and recruited by a committee rather than by one man but at Preston Sudell was the committee."

Sudell pioneered the paternalistic approach to football management, taking care of the players' welfare and scolding them if they drank too much. He studied opponents, devised team tactics and espoused the short passing game of the Scots. The results were impressive. Though they lost the 1888 FA Cup Final to West Bromwich Albion, Preston were triumphant the following year, the same season in which they claimed the inaugural Football League title. They didn't just win it, they ran away with it, winning eighteen and drawing four of their twenty two matches to finish 11 points clear of second place Aston Villa. Newspapers hailed the achievement as "Sudell's great victory" rather than Preston's, and the squad was accorded a civic reception. In front of Preston Town Hall Sudell gave a rousing speech that was greeted with great acclaim.

Preston won the league title again in 1890 and finished runners up in the three seasons that followed. Then came the fall. Ironically, considering Sudell's role a decade earlier, it was professionalism that did it for Preston North End. Larger, richer clubs, those from big cities such as Liverpool, Birmingham, Sheffield and Nottingham, had more financial clout than smaller clubs like Preston. Jack Ross was lured to Everton with the promise of higher wages and Sunderland were soon paying players £5 a game. Sudell tried to keep pace but he couldn't, at least not legally.

On 20 March 1895 Sudell was arrested and charged with embezzlement. When the case came to court he was found guilty of divesting the Goodairs' mills of £5,326 – not for his own enrichment, but for Preston North End's.

He was sentenced to three years imprisonment and upon his release, such was Sudell's shame, he emigrated to South Africa, where he became a sports reporter. He died in 1911, five years after Charles Alcock had paid a generous tribute to his part in creating a Preston team that played "consistently fine football."

Yet Sudell's greatest achievement wasn't to produce a side that played attractive football but to help transform the image of football, turning it from a pastime played by southern gentlemen into a sport that was the lifeblood of the northern working class. He alluded to this shifting of English football's tectonic plates during the speech he gave at Preston Town Hall at the end of their Double-winning season of 1888–89. In words that were paraphrased by a local paper, Alcock told Preston fans that "he did not know a single amusement out of which the operative classes had got so much amusement at such a cheap rate as that of football... the richer classes could have their hunting, shooting, fishing and boating."

Automatic telegraph receiver

Were it not for the fact we already have a tavern in our list, object number 3 might well have been the Cotton Tree, the pub owned by Jack Hunter, the Blackburn Olympic and England centre half. It was here that half of Blackburn gathered on the day of the 1883 FA Cup Final between Olympic and the Old Etonians, drinking pints of porter and stout as they waited anxiously for telegrams updating them on the score.

As the afternoon wore on the wait for the telegrams grew more agonising. Finally, word came through that it was one apiece at the end of full-time; a goal in extra-time from Jimmy Costley decided the match in Blackburn's favour.

If Costley's winning goal was a watershed for English football, creating a northern winner of the FA Cup for the first time, so the dawn of a new age was about to break in Britain. The electric telegraph, certainly as far as journalism was concerned, was soon to become obsolete, replaced by the end of the 1880s with a new, faster system of relaying news – the telephone.

A year after Blackburn's FA Cup triumph, London's first trunk telephone line, to Brighton, was opened. By 1890 the British capital was connected with cities in the Midlands and the north of England, and within seven years the country had its first automatic telephone system.

The consequences for British football were immense. Results and reports could now be relayed in seconds, a revolution that prompted an explosion in sports reporting. Saturday evening Pink 'Uns and Green 'Uns appeared in towns and cities throughout the country, with the *Birmingham Saturday Night* credited as the first "football special". James Catton, one of the pioneers of this journalistic genre, began his career covering football for the *Preston Herald* in 1875. By the early 1900s he would recall that "in days long ago when Association football players wore beards and breeches... the reports were brief, and there were none of the personal paragraphs, garrulous items, and more or less sensational news which are now part not only of weekly periodicals, but of morning and evening newspapers."

In his day football was relegated to a few paltry paragraphs in *Bell's Life* or the *Field*, underneath effusive reports about the cricket and the horse racing. The telephone changed all that, and a slew of new titles dedicated to popular sport appeared, foremost among them the *Athletic News*. Between 1891 and 1893 – helped no doubt by the introduction of the Football League (see object 13) – its circulation doubled from 50,000 to 100,000. By the time of the First World War its readership was just under 200,000, a phenomenal increase considering the competition: among those jostling for space on the news stand were *Football Field*, *Football Chat*, *Football Post*, *National Football News*, *Sporting World* and the *Sporting Herald*, not to mention the extensive sports coverage in 170 provincial daily papers.

To keep one step ahead of the opposition, the *Athletic News* became an innovator in the world of sports reporting. For the 1904 FA Cup Final between Manchester City and Bolton Wanderers, the *News*'s editor, James Catton, hired a hot-air balloon tethered to the ground and then ordered one of his cub reporters, known only as "Balloonatic", to get a bird's eye view of the match at Crystal Palace. It probably seemed liked a great idea at the time; less so when the wind buffeted the balloon as if it were a defender marking a striker in the penalty box. "I saw the glittering Crystal Palace float past," wrote Balloonatic, "and then I got a glimpse at the footballers, and then a tree tried to scratch my face off."

Scotland football badge

A question for you: what links Mary Queen of Scots, Sir Walter Scott and Gordon Ramsey? (And it's not bad language.) The answer is they're all – or were – Scots with a fondness for football.

As we mentioned when describing our fourth object, a small grey football was found hidden in Mary's bedchamber in Stirling Castle, while TV chef Ramsey once had a trial with Glasgow Rangers. As for Sir Walter, he wrote an ode to the game having been present at a match between two rival villages in 1815, ending his verse with the line: "There are worse things in life than a tumble on heather / And life is itself but a game at football."

Football, or a rough and tumble version of it, had been played in Scotland for centuries, but as we have seen it was the Queen's Park club who knocked the game into shape and spread the "Association Game" throughout the country.

Queen's Park's revolutionary "passing" game supplanted the English "dribbling" game by the mid-1880s, and it was this style of football that the Scots exported across the world. Charles Miller, the son of a Scotsman, introduced football to Brazil in the 1890s, while Scot William Leslie Poole did likewise in Uruguay; Argentina have the Glasgow-born schoolteacher Alexander Watson Hutton to thank for their footballing prowess after he began teaching the locals in the 1880s.

Even the English were increasingly beholden to the Scottish influence: draper William McGregor was the driving force behind the formation of the Football League in 1888, and a decade or so later the Glaswegian architect Archibald Leitch embarked on a programme of stadium-building for most of the top English clubs. Admittedly, Leitch didn't design the original Wembley Stadium in 1923; that was done by Maxwell Ayrton, another Scot.

Richard Sanders was spot on when he wrote in *Beastly Fury* that "everywhere you turn in the early history of football you bump into a Scot... [and] almost as late as 1910 almost a quarter of all English First Division players were Scottish."

Leaders off the pitch in the first fifty years of football, Scotland was also dominant on it, despite the fact their playing resources were dwarfed by those of their English neighbours. The Scottish Football League was launched with the inaugural 1890–91 season and featured eleven clubs; it was still this number in 1900, albeit with a second division comprising ten clubs. England, in contrast, now boasted thirty six clubs, split into a first and a second division.

On the international field, however, there was little to separate the two countries. Eleven years after England and Scotland contested football's first international match they sat down with representatives from the Welsh and Irish Associations to discuss a number of points: firstly they agreed to all play by one set of rules; then they formed the International Football Association Board to oversee these rules; and then they agreed to stage football's inaugural international tournament – the British Home Championship.

The first match in Championship history took place in Belfast on 24 January 1884. Scotland, sporting dark blue jerseys with the Lion Rampant as their badge, thrashed Ireland 5-0. Next the Scots beat England 1-0 in Glasgow before demolishing Wales 4-1 a fortnight later to become the first winners of an international football tournament.

They were winners again in 1885, and the following year shared the title with England before again winning the Championship outright in 1887 and 1889. In 1890 it was decided to change the Scotland badge to a thistle (the emblem of the national rugby team) but twelve years later the Lion Rampant returned and has been on shirts ever since.

This on-pitch success was reflected in the size of the crowds flocking to matches. To keep up with demand the Scotland Football Association organised a series of rebuilding programmes so that by the turn of the century Glasgow had the three biggest football stadiums in the world: Celtic Park, Ibrox Park and Hampden Park, which in 1908 hosted 121,452 spectators as Scotland drew 1-1 with England.

These years constituted the Golden Age of Scottish football, when the game – like the lion on their badge – was rampant. Scots were at the forefront of exporting football to the world, yet in doing so they hastened their eventual decline. The nadir came in May 1931 when Scotland were humbled 5-0 by the Austrian *Wunderteam*, a side coached by Hugo Meisl and his English sidekick Jimmy Hogan.

Hogan had played a season for Fulham in his youth on a side packed with Scots. They'd taught Hogan the "Scottish passing game" and he in turn passed it on to the Austrians. The Scots had been beaten at their own game.

Fountain pen

The problem for football by the late 1880s was that it was a victim of its own success. It had codified its rules, introduced its first competition, the FA Cup, which was going from strength to strength, and it had legalised professionalism. Rugby Union had been usurped as the country's number one winter sport and the Football Association was master of all it surveyed.

Or so thought the FA. The clubs, however, and not for the last time, were of a different opinion. Professionalism brought with it wage bills – some players were on as much as £2 a game – and a handful of FA Cup matches in a season otherwise sown with meaningless friendlies wasn't going to do much for clubs' coffers.

Fortunately a Scottish draper called William McGregor arrived on the scene, along with his pen. McGregor had been born in Perthshire in 1847, a poorly child who later admitted that he tried football "once when I was very young, and had to take to bed for a week". He moved to Birmingham in his twenties to run the family drapers' shop and started following Aston Villa. A regular churchgoer, teetotaller and member of the Liberal Party, the Villa board were only too happy to appoint him to their committee in 1877.

As McGregor made his way up Villa's chain of command, eventually becoming club chairman, so he developed more of an understanding about the parlous nature of their finances. And it wasn't just Villa; every club was struggling to attract supporters to games that meant nothing, or were having to pay players even if an opponent scratched on the day of a match for one spurious reason or another.

Finally in 1887 McGregor wrote to some of the strongest clubs in the country. "I beg to tender the following suggestion," he began, "...that ten or twelve of the most prominent clubs in England combine to arrange home and away fixtures each season."

The response was encouraging and a meeting was held a few weeks later in London, an odd choice considering the power of club football lay in the north of England. Those present were Villa, Derby County, Blackburn Rovers, Notts County, Stoke City, Wolverhampton Wanderers, West Bromwich Albion and Burnley.

A second meeting was held a month later, this time in Manchester, and Accrington, Bolton Wanderers, Everton and Preston North End added their support to the idea. On

17 April 1888, the Football League was formally launched by these twelve founder clubs.

Though the FA Cup continued to provide the glamour in English football, the league gave clubs financial stability, as it did in Scotland when eleven of the top clubs there copied the idea in 1890. As Charles Alcock wrote in his 1906 book *The Association Game*: "What an important part the League system has played in the economy of modern football can hardly be fully discussed in what is primarily a practical treatise on the game... [but] no history of Association football would be complete if full justice were not done to the great influence of the League, and the hundreds of kindred combinations founded on the same lines and carried on with such remarkable success all over the country."

Preston North End were runaway champions in the inaugural league season, winning eighteen and drawing four of their twenty two matches. McGregor's Aston Villa were runners-up, as they were in 1911, the year the founder of the football league died. By then the first division had expanded to twenty teams and was now far more representative of English football: there were clubs as far south as Bristol City and as far north as Newcastle, with Arsenal and Tottenham representing the capital.

In December 2011 a service was held in Birmingham to commemorate the centenary of McGregor's death and to rededicate his restored headstone, on which is engraved: "Founder of the Football League". Lord Mawhinney, chairman of the Football League from 2003 to 2010, told the congregation that McGregor would be "chuffed" to see what his league had become.

Really? In 1909 McGregor had told English football to be on its guard against "the clever, sharp men" increasingly involving themselves in the professional game. "Give me the honest plodder, the straightforward man," he added. "That is the kind of man we want for League football."

It's not our place to speculate on whether that's the kind of man now running English football. But if McGregor's prime motivation in forming the football league was to help the clubs look after each other, distributing money and influence equally, that can hardly be said of the Premier League. As the *Birmingham Evening Mail* commented: "There we were, assembled to pay homage to a man who created a league for the collective benefit of all its members – an aim which it retains today despite having been crassly deserted by the 'big boys' in 1992. Little wonder if some club representatives in the front pews were squirming a little."

McGregor must have been turning in his grave.

The Old Firm

They may have loved their football in Lancashire and London but at the start of the twentieth century no city was quite as mad for football as Glasgow. It had the three grandest stadiums in the world – Hampden Park, Ibrox and Celtic Park – and its football journal, Scottish Referee, boasted a circulation of 500,000 in 1909, not bad for a country of four and a half million.

It was the *Scottish Referee* that five years early had come up with the name to describe what was already a fierce sporting rivalry but has since become acknowledged as the most ferocious in football if not in sport in general – Rangers against Celtic. They dubbed the regular clash of Glasgow's top team clubs as the meeting of the "Old Firm", an occasion when – insinuated the *Referee*

– both sides did their utmost to maximise their profits at the expense of their thousands of supporters. Rather than take offence at the mockery, both sets of supporters rather liked the expression and it entered football folklore. More than 100 years later "Old Firm" encounters remain special affairs – a colourful cacophony often laced with controversy.

Why is this so? As David Goldblatt explains in *The Ball is Round*, it was due to the unique and complex composition of Glasgow's population: the city's "football rivalries were the first to be so intimately connected to the warp and weft of real social divisions and conflicts."

Unlike Glasgow's first club, Queen's Park, which was formed by middle-class businessmen with no sectarian ties, the fan bases of Rangers and Celtic were working-class communities that reflected their people. Glasgow Rangers was formed in 1872 by a group of men who took the name from an English rugby club. Within five years Rangers reached their first Scottish Cup Final, losing 3-2 to Vale of Leven after two replays.

In those early days Rangers was not a club that made much of its religious roots; its supporters came from the predominantly Protestant working-class areas of Govan and they played in blue, but there was no great anti-Catholic sentiment. That changed with the formation, in 1887, of Celtic.

Established in the East End of Glasgow by the Irish Catholic Marist Brother Walfrid, the motivation behind the club was to raise money to help the poor of the district. The thousands of Irish immigrants living in Glasgow took the club to their heart and Celtic's Catholic identity soon defined the side.

In 1888 a match was organised between Rangers and Celtic – what one contemporary newspaper described as a "friendly encounter" – with the newly-formed club thrashing Rangers 5-2. As the 1890s wore on the friendliness remained, even if the rivalry did take on a keener edge.

At the 1898 clash between the two clubs over 50,000 fans packed into Celtic Park, and the febrile atmosphere was such that the match was abandoned after one too many a pitch invasion. There were similar scenes seven years later when Celtic fans attacked the referee with iron railings ripped from the stand, but both these incidents paled into insignificance compared to the events of the 1909 Cup Final replay. Thousands of fans rioted at Hampden Park and battled with police during violence that left scores injured.

On all these occasions religious tensions were non-existent – it was simply the fervour of Britain's most committed football fans. That changed in the 1920s after Ireland gained independence following a bloody civil war, and Northern Ireland consequently came into existence. Exactly how and when exactly Celtic came to be perceived as "the Catholic club" and Rangers "the Protestant club" is a mystery, but Old Firm matches became a manifestation of the bigotry that, alas, has existed for centuries among a small minority on either side of the religious divide.

In recent years both clubs have been largely successful in stamping out sectarianism on the terraces; fortunately the sporting conflict remains as strong as ever. As FIFA noted recently: "there are still precious few matches in world football that can rival the seething passion that will be served up when these old rivals meet."

Penalty spot

OBJECT
15

Were it not for our next object a long list of players – from England's Stuart Pearce to Italy's Roberto Baggio, from David Trezeguet of France to England's Ashley Cole – would never have endured the misery of the penalty shootout. Gareth

Southgate wouldn't have made a mint from a pizza commercial and John Aldridge wouldn't still be the toast of Wimbledon. That they have all suffered is the fault of William McCrum, the man who gave the penalty spot to football in 1891.

There'd been no need for McCrum and his ilk when the Football Association laid down the sport's laws in 1863. Gentlemen, God forbid, never fouled. As late as 1887 Montague Shearman was writing in *Athletics and Football* that "another feature of the rules which an Association player can hardly fail to notice is that there is practically no penalty for breaking any of the rules. It has been found after many years' experience quite unnecessary to inflict one."

Football was, to all intents and purposes, a free-for-all, albeit a refined free-for-all with fouls committed in the most gentlemanly manner. Watching all this mayhem from his position as goalkeeper for Milford FC, a village team in the county of Armagh in Northern Ireland, was William McCrum. According to his great-grandson Robert McCrum "told funny stories, sang songs and loved to play games," much to the displeasure of his father, a prominent and powerful local businessman.

McCrum came up with the idea for a penalty kick, mainly as a way of protecting the goalkeeper from psychotic centre forwards, and submitted his idea to the Irish Football Association, who in turn tabled the proposal with the International Football Board (IFB) in June 1890. It was met with widespread astonishment. Penalties weren't British, thundered the legendary sportsman C. B. Fry, adding that the very notion was a "standing insult to sportsmen to have to play under a rule which assumes that players intend to trip, hack and push opponents and to behave like cads of the most unscrupulous kidney".

Unfortunately "cads" were creeping into the game in the late nineteenth century and a year later, June 1891, the penalty kick was adopted for the 1891–92 season. John Heath of Wolverhampton Wanderers scored the first penalty, slotting the ball past the Accrington keeper in a match on 14 September 1891.

For the first ten years of its life the penalty kick was taken from a spot anywhere along a 12-yard line. Then in 1902 the IFB introduced the penalty area, 18 yards from the goal line and 44 yards wide with a penalty spot at its centre. Then came the 6-yard box in place of a semi-circle in the goalmouth (the 'D' shape at the edge of the penalty area wasn't added until 1937) and with it a whole lot of angst.

Writing in his book *The Association Game*, in 1906 Charles Alcock – the FA secretary credited with creating the FA Cup – declared that "the penalty kick which was introduced in the season of 1891–92 has been a source of great anxiety to those who have to make the laws... It is to be regretted, of course, that a condition of things should have arisen to make such a severely repressive measure as the penalty kick advisable. At the same time one is bound to admit that it has proved to be a necessity, and as its importance cannot be overrated, it looms largely in any outline of the actual play."

What did William McCrum make of his invention? He lived for a further forty years but according to his great-grandson "died alcoholic, penniless and alone in a boarding house in Armagh just before Christmas in 1932."

Miserable as he was when he died, at least McCrum never suffered the agony of the penalty shootout. Who actually came up with the idea of the shootout is disputed: Israeli Yosef Dagan claims he did after seeing his country eliminated from the semi-finals of the 1968 summer Olympics on the toss of a coin. That's not what Karl Wald, a former Bavarian referee, maintained, who said it was he who convinced UEFA to adopt the idea in 1970. FIFA followed suit six years later and the shootout has been with us ever since.

And while it may have shattered the souls of generations of England supporters (with a 14 per cent success rate – one victory in seven shootouts – England have the worst record in penalty showdowns of all the major football nations), the shootout has been a boon for statisticians. In 2002 a trio of economists watched videos of 459 penalties from the French First Division and Italian Serie A as research for their paper "Testing Mixed-Strategy Equilibria When Players are Heterogeneous: The Case of Penalty Kicks in Soccer." They concluded that the "importance of taking into account heterogeneity across actors plays a critical role in our analysis, since even some of the most seemingly straightforward predictions of the general model break down in the presence of heterogeneity."

Which we think, in layman's terms, means "just hit it and hope".

Locomotive

OBJECT 16

"LIVERPOOL FC FANS' TRAVEL HEADACHE OVER FA CUP FINAL RAILWAY CLOSURE!" screamed the headline in the *Liverpool Echo* on 16 April 2012. It was a grim warning to Reds supporters that getting to Wembley the following month might prove a little awkward. Oh well, there's always the motorway… football fans in the nineteenth century would have scoffed (once you'd explained what a motorway is).

When the FA Cup was launched in 1871–72 Britain's rail network was sparse – and expensive. So expensive that in 1872 the Glaswegian club Queen's Park pulled out of their FA Cup semi-final replay against the Wanderers in London because they couldn't afford the fare. But by the end of the century, Britain's rail network was expanding, the cost of fares diminishing, and trains were being specially laid on for supporters.

"Today," wrote Fleet Street turf correspondent L.H. Curzon in 1892, "the railways convey the masses in large numbers to the different seats of sport."

This was particularly true for football. In the two decades after the formation of the Football Association, visiting away fans at football matches were a rare sight, principally because in and around London matches didn't generate tribalism. It was two teams of gentleman amateurs whiling away an agreeable afternoon.

That all changed in the 1880s as football took root in the north of England. As author Mike Huggins explained of Lancashire in *Victorian Sport and the Railways*: "Local railway companies first began to advertise cheap trips to away matches in the mid-1880s. Distances between Darwen, Padiham, Blackburn, Church, Bolton, Burnley and Accrington, the early top Lancastrian teams, were relatively short, and the fares were within the reach of working men. By the 1890s excursions were travelling somewhat further."

Railway companies such as the Lancashire & Yorkshire Railway began laying on football "specials" so fans in Blackburn were able to go and watch their boys play Liverpool. In 1891 two "specials" containing a total of 2,500 fans left Edinburgh station for Glasgow for the Scottish Cup final between Hearts and Dumbarton, while the North East Railway did something similar for Newcastle and Sunderland fans (although the cost of rail travel between Sunderland and the Midlands would actually delay their acceptance into the Football League from 1888 until 1890).

Not everyone was impressed with the innovation and there were numerous complaints to the railway companies about the "yells and general noise" of football supporters on trains, but the travelling supporter marched on regardless.

The other crucial factor in the emergence of the travelling

football fan was the introduction of the half-day holiday on Saturday, which by the end of the 1870s was standard among working-class men. Now they could down tools at Saturday lunchtime and rush down to the station to catch the train to the match.

In an 1892 article titled "Football Mania", Charles Edwards found it "quite odd to see how strongly the people in League districts are smitten by the football fever. Many old people and women are so caught by it that they would not, on any ordinary account, miss a local match. They may be seen, too, wedged in the crowd of youths and young men who patronise the excursion trains to fields of combat fifty or a hundred miles from home."

In London, meanwhile, the mania of which Charles Edwards wrote was spreading throughout the capital. Here too clubs quickly grasped the importance of the railway to their fans and their finances. In 1899 Tottenham Hotspur built their White Hart Lane Stadium next to a station served by the Stoke Newington & Edmonton Railway, while Chelsea's Stamford Bridge Stadium was conveniently close to a station operated by the West London Line. When Arsenal relocated north from Plumstead to Highbury in 1913, chairman Henry Norris chose a plot of ground within walking distance of an underground station – Gillespie Road, renamed Arsenal Station in 1932.

The rail companies weren't slow to grasp the potential for profit. It was all very well catering to the hoi polloi, but the most lucrative market was that new social stratum called the middle class. Wealthier supporters were encouraged to make a day of it, perhaps even a weekend, with the FA Cup the greatest attraction. For the 1923 final – the first at Wembley – British Railways advertised a "Full Day Excursion in London"; for twenty shillings, football fans could enjoy "rail journeys, meals, conducted sightseeing drive and other accommodation". A bargain! No wonder a quarter of a million fans flocked to Wembley that year.

17

FA rule book

They've won the World Cup a record five times, they've played some of the finest football imaginable and they've produced some of the greats of the games, geniuses such as Pelé, Garrincha, Carlos Alberto Torres and Ronaldo. And it all began with our next object, the Football Association rulebook, brought to Brazil in 1894 by Charles Miller. It was packed into Miller's valise, along with a pair of boots and a couple of leather footballs, all souvenirs from the ten years he had spent in England.

Despite the Anglophone name, Miller had in fact been born in São Paulo in 1874 to John Miller, a Scottish railway worker, and Carlota Alexandrina Fox, a Brazilian woman of English extraction. Miller had emigrated to Brazil to help construct the railway that would join the port of Santos to the fertile farming lands of the interior. Money, reportedly, was Miller's prime motivation in crossing the Atlantic, as it was for the thousands of other Britons who arrived in South America in the second half of the nineteenth century to help "modernise" the continent. There they could earn as much as £400 a year, more than double what they could take home in Britain.

Aged 10, Miller was packed off to Britain to receive an education at Banister Court in Southampton, a small private school run by Christopher Ellaby and his three teachers. Ellaby was from the same school of thought as Dr Thomas Arnold, believing that a healthy body equalled a healthy mind, and that sport was the best way to transform boys into men. Football was Ellaby's forte, and Miller found he had a natural flair for the game, more so than two of his contemporaries – Arthur Maundy Gregory, who became a British spy and was implicated in the Zinoviev Letter, which helped defeat the Labour Party in the 1924 General Election, and Harold Davidson, later the Rector of Stiffkey who was defrocked in 1932 for consorting with loose women.

Mark Pitchforth, the archivist at Hampshire Record Office in Winchester, recounts that: "Being a skilled athlete, Charles Miller took to this new game of football instantly and soon became captain of the school team. Slightly-built, he earned himself the nickname Nipper, but his size didn't stop him becoming a prolific centre forward and sprightly winger... He went on to play for and against both the famous Corinthians, a team formed of players invited from public schools and universities, and St Mary's Church of England Young Men's Association, now better known as Southampton Football Club."

In 1894, shortly before his twentieth birthday, Miller boarded the steamer Magdalena for the twenty-day voyage back to Brazil. Stories differ as to why he decided to return home when he had apparently been offered a contract to turn professional. According to some sources he was piqued at having failed to win election to the Hampshire Football Association; others suggest he was concerned at the failing health of his mother. Miller's father was waiting for him when the Magdalena docked at Santos. "What's that?" he asked of his son, as he stepped onto the quayside with his two footballs. "My degree," replied Charles. "Your son has graduated in football."

Miller took his football to the São Paolo Athletic Club, the social hub for the city's expatriate community where cricket had hitherto been the sport of choice. A kickabout was organised between a dozen young men, and within a fortnight there were enough interested members for an eleven-a-side game on a piece of wasteland set aside as a grazing area for mules of the São Paulo Railway Company. The two sides that lined up for the first game of organised football in Brazil were the São Paulo Railways XI against the Gas Works XI. Miller later recalled: "The general feeling at the time was, 'What a great little sport, what a nice little game'."

By the turn of the century, football in Brazil was expanding, though it remained almost exclusively an expatriate sport. There were five teams of mainly German players – including SC Internacional – and a side of American students from Mackenzie College. It left the Brazilians rather nonplussed, one journalist writing of a match he'd seen in Rio de Janeiro between two teams of Britons: "A bunch of maniacs as they all are, get together, from time to time, to kick around something that looks like a bull's bladder. It gives them great satisfaction or fills them with sorrow when this kind of yellowish bladder enters a rectangle formed by wooden posts."

The "maniacs" weren't just confined to Brazil. All across South America – from Argentina (where another Scot, Alexander Watson Hutton was the driving force) to Uruguay to Chile – British expatriates' love of football was taking root.

Back in Brazil, Miller helped establish the country's first league in 1902 and the club for whom he played – São Paulo Athletic Club – won the first three league titles. He also arranged for the Corinthians and St Mary's (now renamed Southampton FC) to tour Brazil, and quickly the game began to spread among the local population. In 1904 Miller wrote an article for the Banister Court school magazine in which he described how "football is the game here. We have no less than sixty or seventy clubs. A week ago I was asked to referee a match of small boys, twenty a side... even for this match 1,500 people turned up. No less than 2,000 footballs have been sold here within the last twelve months; nearly every village has a club now."

The popularity of football spread more rapidly in Brazil than any other South American country. Rich and poor, white and black, all were swept up by this new sport, with teams formed in factories and on farms throughout the country. One of the clubs that sprang up took the name Corinthians, inspired by the touring British side of same name; today Corinthians is the richest football club in Brazil, with a reputation for producing players of the quality of Rivelino and Ronaldo.

With the coming of the First World War, the presence – and influence – of Europeans in South America evaporated. Thousands of men returned home to fight in the trenches, and Britain and Germany were no longer able to flex their economic muscle. At the same time there was a new-found confidence on the continent, which led Argentina and Uruguay to hispanicise the language of the game. Then in 1916, as Europe tore itself apart on the battlefield, South America united on the football field, creating the CONMEBOL (Confederación sudamericana de fútbol) a full forty years before Europe's footballing powers formed UEFA.

Charles Miller remained in Brazil for the rest of his life, marrying the famous pianist Antonietta Rudge and working as an agent for the Royal Mail. He died in 1953 aged 78, three years after Brazil had hosted the World Cup. "It is amazing to think, but Brazil, the country now so synonymous with the beautiful game, didn't even play football until little more than 100 years ago and it was Charles Miller, having learnt to play in Southampton, who started the revolution," writes Mark Pitchforth. "It was not until 1958 that the country won the first of its five titles, but Charles Miller had the satisfaction of seeing the amazing growth of the sport he himself introduced just half a century earlier."

Elgar's piano

What would a football ground be without its chanting and singing? Most probably a rugby ground, devoid of atmosphere and intensity. But thanks in part to our next object football stadiums across the world reverberate to the sound of singing. The piano belongs to Sir

Edward Elgar, arguably England's greatest composer, and the man responsible for the "Enigma Variations" and "Land of Hope and Glory". According to the website of the Elgar Society, the piano was: "restored by his father's business in Worcester in 1867 [and] the instrument was selected by Elgar in 1898 for installation in Birchwood Lodge, the family's summer retreat near Malvern. Close inspection of the soundboard reveals it to be inscribed with the titles of some of the works he composed or completed during his time there, including "Caractacus" (first performed in 1898), "Sea Pictures" (1899) and "The Dream of Gerontius" (1900).

What the website neglects to mention is that it was also the piano on which Sir Edward composed football's first chant, having been inspired by Wolverhampton Wanderers. Elgar's love for Wolves began in 1895 when, as his great friend Dora Penny Powell recorded in her book *Edward Elgar: Memories of a Variation,* he came to visit her family in the city. The young Dora met Elgar at the station and, to her disappointment, realised music was the last thing on his mind. Instead he enquired if "I ever saw the Wolverhampton Wanderers play and when he heard that our house was a stone's throw from the ground he was quite excited.

'Can't we go and see a match today?'

'There isn't one, I'm afraid, it's a Friday.'

'I shall come again on a Saturday'."

Elgar didn't get to see Wolves in action until the autumn of 1896, but the whole spectacle "delighted him". He was particularly struck by crowd's "staccato 'Aw!' at a mishap" and by the predatory powers of the Wolverhampton forward Billy Malpass.

For the next two years Elgar regularly cycled the forty miles from his home in Worcester to watch Wolves in action, and in February 1898 Penny Powell recalled how, at Elgar's request, she sent him a match report from the local newspaper in which the "reporter used a characteristic expression in describing the culmination of a fine piece of tactical work: 'he banged the leather for goal'. This brought a letter from E.E by return of post in which he had set the words to music, so greatly did they take his fancy."

Elgar set the phrase to three bars of music – a vocal line and two stave accompaniment – and altered the words to "we bang'd the leather for goal" with a sforzando on "goal".

For more than half a century Elgar's ode to Wolves was lost to posterity, until it was unearthed in the 1950s by Percy Young, the Wolves' club historian and something of an Elgar buff. In September 2010 "Bang'd the Leather for Goal" received its first known public performance at a charity concert in Wolverhampton, an event gleefully reported in the national press. "OOH AAH... EDWARD ELGAR" was the headline in the *Daily Telegraph*, which really should have known better, while the *Sun* claimed that "terrace chants in praise of their heroes or mocking opponents have been given highbrow praise."

The *Telegraph* wheeled out Professor Steven Mithen, author of *The Singing Neanderthals: The Origins of Music, Language, Mind and Body*, who told the paper that "football chants are a very sophisticated activity. They come from a point in our evolutionary past before language, when we used music and chanting and dance to bond as social groups."

True, there are some clever chants out there (Chelsea fans singing "You're shish, and you know you are" to Turkish club Galatasaray in their 1999 Champions League encounter at Stamford Bridge was one of the more memorable ones), although "the referee's a wanker" and "You're going home in an ambulance" aren't among them. But there was a time when the good professor was right, a period in the 1960s and 1970s, when fan culture, like British culture in general, underwent a great upheaval. Up until then what singing there was had its origins in traditional folk music or the music hall: Newcastle fans adopted "Blaydon Races" as their anthem in the 1930s, Portsmouth's faithful belted out "Play-up Pompey", Spurs had "Glory, glory Tottenham Hotspur" and Birmingham City supporters sang the words from the Harry Lauder hit "Keep Right on to the End of the Road".

Football's soundtrack began to change in the 1960s, a result of two factors. First, the television pictures beamed into British living rooms from the 1962 World Cup in which Brazil fans celebrated their side's victory with chants of "Brazil, cha-cha-cha!", a tune soon copied on British terraces. The second influence, writes David Goldblatt in *The Ball is Round*, emanated from Liverpool, a city more "open to and more connected to the transatlantic currents of Caribbean migration and American music than anywhere outside London. When the market for working-class entertainers in television, music and comedy inched open, Liverpool's heritage of spoken wit and word play gave it a head start."

Not all chants from the supporters in the Kop (the famous stand at Liverpool's Anfield stadium) were directed at supporting their own team; when Leeds' goalkeeper Gary Sprake threw the ball into his own net during a match in 1967 he was serenaded with a rendition of the Des O'Connor hit "Careless Hands".

Such gentle but biting wit has long since been replaced by something altogether more ugly. It began in the later 1970s, as the scourge of hooliganism blighted the English game and fans baited each other across police lines on the terraces. Nothing was off-limits. Leeds fans subjected Manchester United fans to taunts about the 1958 Munich Air Disaster, and Chelsea supporters once infamously mocked Cardiff fans with a chant about the Aberfan disaster of 1966, in which 116 children died. In 2005 Hull City supporters abused Queen's Park Rangers fans about the recent suicide bombings in London.

Individual players have also been routinely targeted in recent years with references to anything from their sexual preferences, to those of their wives, to the state of their mental health. And as for the vitriol directed towards referees...

Writing in the *Sunday Times* in 2008, columnist and football fan Rod Liddle pondered the question of why football chants have descended from supporting one's team to abusing opponents and officials: "Perhaps we are much nastier people these days," wrote Liddle, "or the gulf between players and supporters has become so grotesque that players are no longer viewed as anything other than fair game for an unlimited level of abuse. We pay their obscene wages; they repay us with a total and utter lack of loyalty, so they get what they deserve."

The truth lies somewhere in between. The anonymous age of the internet has coarsened society, emboldening us to heap abuse on others from a distance, safe in the knowledge we'll never be confronted by the object of our bile face-to-face. But the cossetted lifestyle of the modern millionaire player, so removed from their forefathers who lived on the same street as us and earned the same wage, has created in some cases a bitter envy – and not just among supporters. Commenting on the 2010 performance of Elgar's "Bang'd the Leather for Goal", the *Daily Mirror* wondered: "How many Premier League stars, later that night, will be performing the modern-day version called 'He Banged The Slapper' for £1,200?"

So much for pomp and circumstance.

Trinity Road stand

Stand back a bit please: this next object, the Bill Struth Main Stand at Ibrox, is going to take up a wee bit of space.

So we've seen how football began to take shape in the second half of the nineteenth century with the introduction of rules and the establishment of competitions. The telegraph helped fans keep in touch with their team, and the train transported the more adventurous to the ground of their choice. But what awaited the supporter once there? Not much, as David Goldblatt explains in *The Ball Is Round*: "The borrowed cricket grounds, simply fenced fields, rented parkland and tiny pavilions that hosted most football matches in the late 1880s could not have possibly coped with this great wave of humanity. Fifty League clubs moved to new grounds between 1889 and 1910 and initiated an era of stadium building."

In the vanguard of this construction was Archibald Leitch, a Glaswegian architect whose legacy is still with us today. Several of the forty six stands or pavilions he designed remain in use, and two of his buildings – the Bill Struth Main Stand at Ibrox and Fulham's Craven Cottage ground – are listed. Leitch was responsible in some measure for the creation of twenty nine stadiums, from the Art Deco glamour of Arsenal's Highbury to the splendour of Manchester United's Old Trafford, to grounds in the north-east such as Roker Park in Sunderland and Middlesbrough's Ayresome Park.

No one knows Leitch as well as Simon Inglis, author of *Football Grounds of Britain* and *Engineering Archie*. He has written extensively about Leitch and his impact on British football, commenting that "with hindsight it is tempting to think of Archie's early football grounds as basic, primitive affairs. But for their time they were a huge improvement on what had existed before, in the late Victorian era. Archie was the first man, perhaps since the completion of the Coliseum in Rome, to adopt an engineering approach to the building of facilities for mass spectator sport."

And yet Leitch's first design ended in tragedy. In 1899, three years after the 34-year-old had set up his own business (Archibald Leitch Factory Architect and Consulting Engineer), Leitch was commissioned by Rangers to build Ibrox Park. In

December 1899 the ground was open for business.

To boost their chances of hosting international matches, Rangers instructed Leith to construct two large terraces at the western and eastern ends of the ground. Leitch complied, building the terracing out of wood supported on iron pillars. It was passed fit for purpose but in 1902 a section of the terracing collapsed as Scotland played England, leaving twenty five dead and hundreds more injured. Most of the blame fell on the wood supplier (who was tried and acquitted of culpable homicide) and Leitch's reputation remained intact. Rangers didn't seem to mind. They hired him to replace the wooden terraces with earthen ones, and to build the stand that remains today.

Nor did the Ibrox disaster affect Leitch's standing in England. Having built a two-tier stand – seats up top and terracing below – at Sheffield United's Bramall Lane, he was commissioned by Middlesbrough to construct a complete stadium. Ayresome Park was typical Leitch, functional not flashy. Built at a cost of £11,957, the stadium opened in 1903 and was used as one of the eight venues when England hosted the 1966 World Cup. Six of those venues owed some structure or other to Leith's ingenuity.

Leitch's services didn't come cheap, however, as Hearts discovered when they commissioned him to build their Main Stand. The Edinburgh club were told it would cost them £6,000, but when the pitch-length grandstand was opened in 1914 the final bill came to £12,780. Hearts were obliged to sell star striker Percy Dawson to Blackburn for £2,500 to meet the cost of the 4,000-seater stand. The club wasn't happy and for several months there was "strongly worded correspondence" between the two parties.

Simon Inglis writes that going to football matches in the '60s and '70s he soon learned to spot the hand of Leitch in "the criss-cross steelwork balconies of Roker, Goodison, Ibrox, Fratton et al, and the roof-top gables of Hillsborough, Craven Cottage and Ayresome Park." But Inglis also explains that it was Leitch who designed the terracing upon which millions of football fans stood throughout much of the twentieth century. "Every dimension of tread and riser, the sinking of lateral gangways, the provision of barrier configurations, the lowering of the first row to improve the sightlines... all these basic design parameters were drawn up by Archie, making their debut at Craven Cottage and Stamford Bridge in September 1905. If you ever stood on terracing, it is highly likely that at one time or another you have leant against a patented Leitch crush barrier."

What put an end to the terracing was the Hillsborough Disaster of 1989. The Taylor Report that followed ushered in the new all-seater stadium and did away – in the top echelons of the British game at least – with terracing. One of the last of Leitch's creations to go was Chesterfield's Saltergate ground. It bit the dust in 2010, seventy four years after its construction. "This is a lovely football ground, yes," admitted club chairman Barrie Hubbard, a Chesterfield fan for all of his seventy two years. "But we have to do it, for progress."

FIFA logo

At the risk of appearing a bit too "Frederick Wall" (see below) we won't dwell too long on this object: it doesn't portray the British in the best of lights.

And anyway, what is there to say about the FIFA Charter, other than to give a bald account of how it came into this world in 1904? We'll talk more later about the Medusa that FIFA has become, but for now let's content ourselves with its creation.

Like so much of sport's early administration it was a Frenchman responsible for establishing the Fédération Internationale de Football Association, known now by its acronym FIFA. In 1903 Robert Guérin, who as well as being a journalist for *Le Matin* newspaper was also on the committee of the Union Française de Sports Athlétiques, proposed to Frederick Wall, then secretary of the Football Association, that it would be in football's best interests if the leading nations formed a world federation. Guérin wrote later of Wall's response: "His head in his hands, Mr Wall listened to my story. He said he would report back to his council [the FA]. I waited a few months. I travelled to London once more and had a meeting with the FA president Lord Kinnaird. However, that too was of no avail."

Eventually the FA responded to Monsieur Guérin, informing him that they "cannot see the advantages of such a federation". Guérin gave up on the British; negotiations with the Home Unions was "like beating the air".

Guérin pressed ahead with his idea, inviting to Paris representatives from Belgium, Holland, Denmark, Switzerland, Sweden and Spain. The meeting was held at the headquarters of the Union Française de Sports Athlétiques on Rue Saint Honoré, and congeniality reigned. Everyone, to use modern parlance, was singing from the same hymnsheet, and FIFA was formed. Among the statutes enshrined in its founding charter were: "the reciprocal and exclusive recognition of the national associations represented and attending; clubs and players were forbidden to play simultaneously for different national associations; recognition by the other associations of a player's suspension announced by an association; and the playing of matches according to the Laws of the Game of the Football Association."

Each national federation agreed to pay an annual fee of

50 French francs if it wished to become a member of FIFA, and before the meeting at the Rue Saint Honoré broke up a telegram arrived from the Deutscher Fußball-Bund (German Football Federation) confirming their desire to join the embryonic body. From England and the other home unions came only a deafening silence.

Robert Guérin was elected FIFA's first president, and to his credit the Frenchman persevered with the British, finally persuading the Football Association to join in April 1905 with the help of the Belgian sports administrator Baron Edouard de Laveleye. The FA responded better to an aristocrat than a mere 28-year-old journalist like Guérin. England's affiliation was followed by that of Scotland, Wales and Ireland, along with Italy, Hungary, Austria and Germany.

The British weren't happy to see the Germans admitted. Political tensions were beginning to rise across the continent and Britain saw Germany as a threat. To keep the British onside, in 1906 FIFA elected a new president in place of Guérin – an Englishman called Daniel Burley Woolfall who had a long history of football administration. A former tax inspector, Woolfall was described as "thorough in all he did, while urbanity of manner, courtesy and tact, enabled him to deal with difficulty problems."

Woolfall was an inspired choice as the second president of FIFA. He placated the French by agreeing to have their language as the official FIFA tongue, while at the same time ensuring that "the application of the Laws of the Game, strictly established according to the English model, became compulsory."

He extended FIFA beyond Europe, welcoming South Africa in 1909–10, Argentina and Chile in 1912, the United States in 1913, and in his capacity as FIFA president he sanctioned the official introduction of football as an Olympic sport in the 1908 Games.

FIFA, with Woolfall at its head, was moving in the right direction, but that was to all change with the outbreak of war in 1914. Woolfall died in 1918 and he took with him to his grave Britain's commitment to FIFA. When Europe emerged from the wreckage of war, Britain's relationship with FIFA soon fell into ruin.

Pair of old boots

The Football Association were quite clear about it: "No one wearing projecting nails, iron plates, or gutta-percha on the soles or heels of his boots be allowed to play." Gutta-percha, if you're wondering, is a natural rubber produced from a tree found in south-east Asia used in the manufacture of golf balls. It was tough and durable, but not allowed on players' boots when the FA published their set of rules in 1863.

Unlike that other essential object of the game – the ball – the boots worn today are almost unrecognisable from what players' ancestors wore 150 years ago.

In May 2012 German sportswear company Adidas released the latest version of their biggest-selling boots of all time – the Predator. The original boot, designed by former Liverpool player Craig Johnston in 1994 and featuring revolutionary rubber strips attached to the forefoot, has gone through twelve incarnations, the most recent the Lethal Zones boot. Available in lots of colours (except black), the boot boasts five "lethal zones", including a sweet spot like "a sniper who can curve a bullet... take aim, fire, and let the crowds explode."

Tasteful... and a long way from the Ellis Patent Boot Studs designed in 1886 and endorsed by one player who praised their "improvement in making football boots suitable for any weather." Studs were a daring innovation at the time, a radical departure from the thick leather ankle-high boots which were reinforced at the toe – it was common practice for players to kick the ball with this part of the foot and not the instep. Recognising that they could not hold back progress, in 1891 the FA relaxed the rule on footwear, declaring: "A player shall not wear any nails, except such as have their heads driven in flush with the leather, or metal plates or projections, or gutta percha, on his boots, or on his shin guards. If bars or studs on the soles or heels of the boots are used, they shall not project more than half an inch, and shall have all their fastenings driven in flush with the leather. Bars shall be transverse and flat, not less than half an inch in width, and shall extend from side to side of the boot. Studs shall be round in plan, not less than half an inch in diameter, and in no case conical or pointed."

One of the earliest boot manufacturers was William Shillcock, who in 1905 released his "McGregor" boot, on which was woven an image of William McGregor, the man credited with forming the football league. In was from Shillcock's Birmingham shop, incidentally, that the original FA Cup was stolen in 1895 having been loaned by holders Aston Villa.

More than a quarter of a century after the stud came the next great innovation in the football boot – the replaceable stud, a 1920s design from the German brothers Adolf and Rudolf Hassler who went on to call their company Adidas.

But boots were still heavy and uncomfortable, and players

had their own means to break them in. The England and Newcastle United centre forward Jackie Milburn recalled of his playing days in the early 1950s: "I always wore a size six football boot even though my feet were size eight, so I used to break in a new pair by wearing them without socks and soaking them in cold water to mould them to my feet. I always preferred heavier soles to put some clout in my shots."

By the 1960s boots were becoming lighter and more comfortable thanks to the introduction of kangaroo skin in the uppers. They were also low-cut with nylon soles and moulded studs. As more money poured into the game and the likes of George Best, Johan Cruyff and Pelé added a touch of glamour, boot manufacture became big business. A fierce war erupted between Adidas and Puma, the latter owned by Rudolf Hassler following a post-war rupture with his brother. This rivalry reached its climax seconds before the start of the 1970 World Cup Final between Brazil and Italy, when Pelé drew the referee's attention to a problem with his boot. Bending down to retie the lace, Pelé gave a global television audience of millions a close up of his Puma boot. It later emerged that Pelé had been asked to attend to his boot by Puma's representative in return for a $120,000 sponsorship deal.

That sum is peanuts compared to what the top players can earn today from boot deals. At the height of his powers David Beckham was paid a purported £7 million a season by Adidas to wear their Predator boots, while Nike allegedly give Cristiano Ronaldo £5 million to wear their brand.

Manufacturers, meanwhile, are on a never-ending quest to improve their product. Recent years have seen foam free midsoles, air cushioning, moulded blades instead of studs, synthetic microfibre leather and, in 2008, the first carbon fibre football boot, weighing under 200g.

But have the bootmakers become too big for their boots in their drive for perfection? Recent seasons have seen a spate of injuries to footballers' feet and ankles, prompting Craig Johnston to declare in 2009: "People say that the boots don't provide enough protection. In fact the opposite is true. The problem is that the boots are so well made there is no give at all in the materials, especially the cheaper synthetics... something has to give and in this day and age it is the ligaments and the metatarsals that are giving way – not the boots."

Telephone

On the afternoon of 14 February 1905 the telephone rang in the office of Jim Gill, the sports editor of the *North Eastern Daily Gazette*. Over the phone Gill, whose hard-hitting column in the newspaper appeared under the byline "Old Bird", was told some startling news, news that would stun British football. On the other end of the line were Councillors Alf Mattison and T. G. Poole, directors of the Middlesbrough Football Club, and it was their pleasure to inform Gill that they had signed the country's best striker – 24 year old Alf Common, a native of Wearside with a sharp eye for goal. As Gill wrote in the evening edition of the *Gazette*, the Sunderland inside right "should prove a valuable acquisition to the borough, who must win five out of their remaining ten engagements to stand any chance of escaping relegation."

But it was when Mattison and Poole revealed what they had paid for Common that Gill nearly dropped the receiver in amazement. One thousand pounds. Gill could barely believe it. No club had ever paid such a sum for a player and it was that fact that headlined Gill's article. "Football's first four-figure fee – Middlesbrough's signing of Alf Common", screamed the front page.

It took a few days for the news to filter south; when it did, the London press and the Football Association vied to see who could express the most outrage that Middlesbrough, who had only been admitted to the Football League six years earlier, were attempting to buy their way out of trouble.

"Seemingly every club has its price," roared the *Athletic News*, "but what a price!" The paper reminded its readers that the previous record transfer fee had been the £520 Sunderland had paid Sheffield United for Common (with Sheffield's reserve goalkeeper, Albert Lewis, thrown into the bargain) the previous year. "As a matter of commerce," mused the *Athletic News*, "10 young recruits at £100 apiece might have paid better, and as a matter of sport the Second Division would be more honourable than retention of place by purchase."

Middlesbrough didn't think so, particularly when Common scored the only goal of the game (a penalty) against Sheffield United a fortnight later in his first match for the club. It was Middlesbrough's first away win in two years, prompting Gill to write in the *Gazette*: "Weary had been the wait, but coming as it does at such a critical time in the history of the club the success of Saturday at Sheffield has given rise to unbounded satisfaction. Borough supporters' enthusiasm had been allowed to droop to a very low ebb, but a revival has now set in, and I can only hope that the victory of Saturday will hearten the players on to deeds that will thrill enthusiasts on Teesside to their heart's content."

Common continued to score for the rest of the season as Middlesbrough lost just two of their next seven League games, pulling themselves clear of the relegation zone and justifying the directors' purchase.

But the fallout continued down south. One paper wrote: "we are tempted to wonder whether Association football players will eventually rival thoroughbred yearling racehorses in the market," and the FA moved quickly to address the issue. On Monday 7 March, after a lengthy council meeting, the game's governing body announced that "after the 1st January, 1908, no club shall be entitled to pay or receive any transfer fee or other payment exceeding £350, upon or in respect of the transfer of any player." In addition the FA also capped footballers' wages so that the maximum a player could earn during his first season was £4 per week, during the second season £5 per week and "during the third and each subsequent season £6 per week, and the payment of bonuses dependant on the result of any match shall not be allowed."

Although it was possible for the top players to earn a few pounds more through endorsements, the maximum wage severely restricted their earning potential. The fact that the players were also in thrall to their clubs, who through the retain-and-transfer system controlled their career, meant that even someone like Alf Common was taking home a modest wage.

Common scored fifty eight goals in 168 appearances for Middlesbrough before moving to Arsenal in 1910. Way past his prime, Common, whose tooth was nearly as sweet as his right foot, struggled with his weight and was quickly moved on by the Gunners, joining Preston North End in 1912 for £250. He retired from football in 1914 and spent the rest of his life as a publican back in his native north-east.

When Common died in 1946 the life of the professional footballer had little improved; the maximum wage was now £12 (reduced to £10 in the summer) and clubs still controlled the players' destinies. Transfer fees on the other hand had gone through the roof. The FA's £350 limit had been short-lived, and in 1928 Arsenal set a new transfer record when they paid Bolton £10,890 for the services of David Jack.

Then, in 1947, a year after Alf Common's death, England

centre forward Tommy Lawton was sold by Chelsea to Notts County for a new record of £20,000. With wages still set at £12 Lawton found ways to supplement his income, one of which was to release his autobiography in 1948. He called it *Football Is My Business* and inside he complained that "for the majority of players there's little else to be made out of the game, other than a salary that an American baseball or ice-hockey player, or a world-famous boxer wouldn't even look at." He hoped he didn't sound bitter, Lawton told readers, but he couldn't help thinking it wasn't right that a player "who by his skill helps to draw a £25,000 gate... then receives at the most only £10 extra from this vast sum (as happens in a Wembley international match)."

"Your country needs you"

Finger pointing, moustache bristling, the secretary of state for war reminds all upstanding Britons of their duty. Lord Kitchener's 1914 recruitment poster is one of the iconic images of the twentieth century, a jingo-istic call-to-arms that cost three quarter of a million young men their lives. Some of them were footballers, mostly amateur but several professionals; among them Sandy Turnbull, the Manchester United forward; England and Leeds half back Evelyn Lintott; Welsh international goalkeeper Leigh Roose; and Donald Bell, a defender for Bradford Park Athletic who was awarded a posthumous Victoria Cross in 1916.

Yet despite the sacrifice of so many footballers, the First World War altered Britain's relationship with the game for decades to come. The common perception was that the sport – certainly in comparison to rugby union and cricket – had not "done its bit" in defeating the Kaiser and his Germany military machine.

In September 1914, a month after Britain had declared war on Germany, the Football Association wrote to the War Office offering to follow the example of rugby union and suspend all matches until the Hun was beaten. The FA was told there was no pressing need; after all, the war would be over by Christmas, wouldn't it?

But it wasn't, and the heavy losses suffered by the British Army in the early months of the war in France and then Belgium swung public opinion against football.

Young British men were being killed in their thousands, new recruits were needed and yet here were hundreds of fit and healthy men playing football. One Mr Pollock-Hill wrote to the *Daily Mail*, thundering that "the patriotic British public will view with disgust and shame" the continuation of the football league when the country was at war. He then ended his letter by warning the FA that they would suffer for their failure to act as "brightly and gloriously" as rugby. The rugby authorities gleefully capitalised on such sentiments, RFU president George Rowland accusing the FA of being "solely and entirely governed by commercial principles" and labelling footballers "shirkers and bullet-funkers".

Football fought back. On 27 November G. Wagstaffe Simmons, honorary secretary of the Hertfordshire Football Association, wrote to *The Times* explaining that of the country's 5,000 professional players 2,000 were serving in the armed forces, and most of those that weren't were being held to their club contracts. In addition, said Wagstaffe Simmons, more than 100,000 amateur football players had taken the King's Shilling and didn't warrant such widespread opprobrium.

William Joynson Hicks, member of parliament for

Brentford, thought it might be prudent to raise a football battalion in order to dissipate public condemnation. Colonel C. F. Grantham was appointed the battalion's commanding officer, but in March 1915 he felt compelled to write to all the professional clubs in England. In his letter he acknowledged that the formation of the battalion had eased criticism of football because the public now believed they were doing their bit but:

> ... this is not the case, as only 122 professionals have joined. I understand that there are forty League clubs and twenty in the Southern League with an average of some thirty players fit to join the Colours, namely, 1,800. These figures speak for themselves. I am also aware and have proof that in many cases directors and managers of clubs have not only given no assistance in getting these men to join but have done their best by their actions to prevent it. I am taking the opportunity of your meeting on Monday to ask you gentlemen if you and your clubs have done everything in your power to point out to the men what their duty is: Your King and Country calls upon every man who is capable of bearing arms to come forward and upon those that are unable to use their best endeavours to see that those that can do so.

Tom Watson, manager of Liverpool, wrote to *The Times* in defence of professional football, but all he did was bear out the colonel's complaint. The players, protested Watson, "are donating 12.5 pr cent of their salaries to the assistance of the needy and to the war funds." In addition eighteen footballs had been sent to the front, a military band played at home games and players were drilled twice a week by a retired army officer. But as to how many players had volunteered, Watson conceded just one, along with "two sons of directors".

The following month, April 1915, the Football League finally suspended professional football and dozens of players – now freed from their contracts – rushed to enlist. One of them was the Sunderland and England forward Charlie

Buchan, who joined the Grenadier Guards and was later awarded the Military Medal for his gallantry during the battle for Bourlon Wood in 1917.

When the war ended in November 1918 the cost to sport had been immense. One hundred and eleven rugby union internationals had been killed; the London Scottish club had lost a staggering forty five of the sixty players who had turned out for the last game of the 1913–14 season, and cricket had seen a number of its finest sons fall. Football, too, had suffered. As well as the likes of Turnbull and Lintott, Spurs had lost eleven former players and seven Heart of Midlothian players from the 1914 season were dead.

But what stuck most in the mind of many Britons was the tardy response of the Football Association in those opening months of the conflict. In February 1919 an anonymous headmaster wrote to *The Times* saying that rugby "has proved itself to be unequalled by any other game as a school of true manhood and leadership... It is all the greater pity that there should still be some great schools that follow the less inspiring and less severe discipline of Association football... Is it too much to hope that all schools will consider seriously the adoption of Rugby football as the winter game for all the youth of the nation?"

Scores of public and grammar schools in Britain abandoned football in favour of rugby, among them Winchester, Ampleforth and Radley. Schools' membership of the Rugby Football Union increased from twenty seven to 133 in the 1920s, and rugby once and for all became the sport of the British middle classes. It was a phenomenon that lasted until the 1990s.

And yet when we think of the First World War today we conjure up images of mud and barbed wire and gas, and a Christmas truce in 1914 when Germans and British soldiers clambered out of their trenches and walked out into No Man's Land, where they shook hands, swapped cigarettes and played the soldiers' favourite game – football.

List of odds

TO BEAT

GERMANY

2-1

£10 WINS

This next object will probably provoke a similar reaction to the one you feel when you take your seat at a game and find yourself next to the world's biggest football bore who thinks he knows it all. If only he didn't exist; but he does, and there's just no escaping him.

Rather like match-fixing, the cancer of the modern game (or so we're led to believe) is represented here by a bookmakers' odds. Why that? Well, we've chosen such an object to demonstrate that far from being a recent problem, match-fixing has been an unsightly pimple of the chin of football for the best part of 100 years.

Remember what Charles Alcock wrote in 1906, gently chiding those naysayers who fretted that the introduction of a competitive tournament such as the FA Cup would "lower the general standard of morality among those who compete"? He was wrong about that, but at least football's founding father was no longer alive when the game was rocked by its first match-fixing scandal.

Just nine years after Alcock's ingenuous words Liverpool and Manchester United joined forces to heap shame upon each other. The date was Good Friday 1915, the venue Old Trafford, and United were a little too close to the First Division's relegation zone for comfort. The Red Devils beat Liverpool 2-0, a victory that condemned Chelsea to the drop instead of them, but the *Manchester Daily Dispatch* found little to celebrate, commenting the next day: "The second half was crammed with lifeless football... Liverpool scarcely ever gave the impression that they would be likely to score."

A local bookmaker was even less impressed. He'd posted odds of 8-1 against United winning 2-0 but shortly before the game a flood of bets had been made on such a score line. The Football Association launched an investigation and discovered that the game had indeed been rigged. Meeting in a Manchester pub several players from both sides had agreed it would be a good idea if United won 2-0 with a goal in each half. In its report, the FA revealed that "a considerable sum of money changed hands by betting on the match, and that some of the players profited thereby."

Three United and four Liverpool players were banned for life, and the press – already on football's back for carrying on playing despite the war – had a field day with their moralising. They were at it again in 1964 – the players match-fixing and the press moralising – when a total of thirty three professional English footballers were prosecuted as part of a match-fixing ring. Then there was the curious case of Bruce Grobbelaar, the Liverpool goalkeeper who was secretly filmed by a British tabloid newspaper in 1994 discussing match-fixing with known members of a gambling syndicate. And as recently as January 2014 three non-league footballers in England were charged with conspiracy to defraud after an investigation into match-fixing.

But it's not just the English involved in the murkier end of the game. The German *Bundesliga* has had its share of strange results, in the 1960s and again in 2005, as have the French (Marseille were stripped of their 1992–93 league title after being found guilty of match-fixing), and more recently there have been cases in Croatia, South Africa, Brazil, Hungary, Turkey and China. And as for Italy… how long have you got? They go through match-fixing scandals the way Chelsea go through coaches, with the most recent investigation – launched in 2012 – focusing on suspicious results in thirty three matches involving twenty two clubs and fifty two active players.

FIFA is worried and wants Interpol to come to their aid. Betting on sport – legal or otherwise – now generates annually between €400 billion and €500 billion; of this colossal sum FIFA estimates that possibly as much as €15 billion are a result of fixed matches. Organised crime knows a lucrative market when it sees one.

The motivation for players getting involved today is the same as it was for those Liverpool and United players nearly a century ago – money. You're unlikely to find a big-time player getting caught up in match-fixing; with their wages they don't need to jeopardise everything for a few extra grand. According to FIFA it is the players lower down the pecking order who are most susceptible to becoming entrapped; their wages are poor, they have no sponsorship deals, and with an increasing number of smaller professional clubs struggling to survive in the tough new economic world, they are the ones in the sights of the criminal gangs.

But that's still not an excuse. Match-fixing is as wrong today as it was 100 years ago, and the punishments have to be swingeing. As the Football Association concluded in its investigation into the 1915 scandal: "It is almost incredible that players dependent on the game for their livelihood should have resorted to such base tactics. By their action they have sought to undermine the whole fabric of the game and discredit its honesty and fairness."

Pools coupon

It wasn't just the "Lambeth Walk" that the British working classes were doing in the 1930s. They were also "doing the pools", and doing them to such an extent that they became an institution. By 1938 an estimated one million men and women up and down

the country were sitting down each week trying to predict whether a league game would end in a home win, an away win, a score draw or a no-score draw. Their stakes totalled more than £40 million, a huge sum that warrants inclusion in our history of football because the pools helped popularise football among a large section of the population who hitherto had not had much interest in the game.

Writing in *The Road to Wigan Pier* in 1937, George Orwell said the lot of the average working-class Briton was pretty grim, and that while whole sections "have been plundered of all they really need [they] are being compensated, in part, by cheap luxuries... the movies, the radio, strong tea and the football pools have between them averted revolution."

The first football pools were Littlewoods, introduced in 1923 by John Moores, three years after the Football Association had persuaded the government to pass the Ready Money Football Betting Act. This act prohibited all forms of gambling on football. It wasn't well received and John Moores was the first to find a way round the act.

Moores claimed the pools were a test of skill not a game of chance and as a consequence they fell outside the remit of the Betting Act. Others followed Moores through the loophole, including Vernons in 1925 and Zetters in 1933.

The simplicity of the pools captured the imagination of the British public. Each competitor paid an entry fee to take part, and this was then pooled and distributed among the competitors who had been most accurate in predicting the scores on that given day.

The Football Association were furious, especially as they received no cut of the vast fortune being made from the pools, the coupons of which were either collected by designated agents or posted to the organising company. In an act of staggering pettiness, the FA hit back in February 1936 by announcing they would no longer release the weekend fixture list until forty eight hours before kick-off. This would make it impossible for the pools companies to print and distribute the coupons.

The FA's childishness caused uproar, the press siding with the public. The clubs did too – they recognised that the pools were good for business. Faced with a three-pronged enemy the FA backed down after a rancorous three week stand-off. More than twenty years later, however, the Football League came up with another solution to the problem of the pools: in the summer of 1959 they copyrighted the fixture list and agreed a deal with the four leading pools companies. In return for the right to print the fixture list the companies would grant the Football League 0.5 per cent of their gross stakes with the minimum amount payable set at £245,000 a season.

By the early 1960s it was estimated that 39 per cent of the British population were doing the pools. Not even the winter weather was allowed to interfere: in the bitterly cold winter of 1962–63, when a raft of games were abandoned due to the inclement weather, the Pools Panel was introduced: a team of experts – former England greats Tom Finney and Tommy Lawton were among those on the first panel – who sat down and predicted the scores of the thirty eight matches that had fallen victim of the weather. The results were announced live on television on 26 January, with the panel deciding upon seven draws, eight away wins and twenty three home wins.

Half a century later the pools have lost some of their lustre but none of their lucre as a Scottish man proved in late 2010 when he won a record payout of £3,001,511 by predicting eight 2-2 draws in the Scottish, English and Spanish leagues. "This is truly a historic moment in the history of the Football Pools in Britain," said Pools director Jon Sheehy.

Today it's possible to do the pools online and on French, Spanish and Australian leagues. Ninety years after John Moores handed out 4,000 coupons to Manchester United fans on their way to a match at Old Trafford, the pools are still allowing football fans to dream of hitting the jackpot.

White horse

OBJECT 26

"LED BY A LION–HEARTED INSPECTOR ON A SNOW–WHITE, PRANCING HORSE" (*Daily Express*, 30 April 1923)

"CUP RIOT PREVENTED BY POLICE RESOURCE, OFFICER ON A WHITE CHARGER HERO OF THE DAY" (*Daily Mirror*, 30 April 1923)

The newspaper headlines following the 1923 FA Cup Final left no doubt as to who stole the show. Man of the Match? Make that Horse of the Match – 13-year-old Billy, aided and abetted by his police rider, Constable (not Inspector) George Scorey. Between them the pair prevented a disaster at Wembley, saving countless lives and ensuring the inaugural Wembley final passed off without incident. Even if it was forty five minutes late kicking-off.

Strictly speaking, Billy is lucky to make it into this list, seeing he's flesh and blood, but then again he was a horse so forgive us if we bend the rules just this once. Plus he's long dead so he is an inanimate object after all.

Billy was very much alive on the afternoon of April 28 1923 when Wembley opened its doors for its first FA Cup Final. Stamford Bridge had hosted the showpiece event in the English football calendar since 1920 while the Football Association oversaw the construction of a new national stadium to replace the clapped out Crystal Palace. The first piece of turf was ceremonially cut by the Duke of York in January 1922, and then the building was left in the hands of Sir Owen Williams, the head engineer, and Maxwell Ayrton, the architect. Neither knew much about stadium design and neither bothered to consult Archibald Leitch, the country's premier football ground architect. The result was a stadium that lacked the intimacy and atmosphere of Leitch's many creations.

The 127,000-capacity Wembley stadium was finally finished on 24 April 1923, a mere four days before West Ham United and Bolton Wanderers arrived to contest the cup final. With them came... well, nobody is quite sure how many football fans descended on Wembley that afternoon.

On the morning of the match the *Daily Mirror* printed a route map so fans, particularly the thousands from Lancashire, would be able to get to the stadium in time to welcome King George V. They were there on time all right. As for how many exactly, estimates vary from 200,000 to 300,000, completely overwhelming the stewards and policemen on duty. They vaulted turnstiles, climbed fences and flooded the pitch so that by the time His Majesty arrived the turf was a sea of humanity.

Enter Billy, who was actually more grey than white, and PC Scorey, together one unit of a mounted police team which helped push back the crowd, gently, cautiously, like shepherds with a large flock of sheep. What finally restored order, claimed the official report, wasn't a white horse but the playing of the national anthem over the loudspeaker system. Thousands upon thousands of men in flat caps, many of them veterans of the Great War, moved off the pitch with military precision so the game could get underway.

Bolton won the cup by two goals to one, but the papers on the Monday were more concerned by the crowds. It was a miracle, they wrote, that no one had been killed. One thousand people had required medical attention but only twenty two were detained in hospital overnight. It had been a splendid example of English order and discipline. While the *Daily Mail*, a friend of the Establishment, blamed the fans for the disorder, the *Mirror* and the *Daily Herald* fingered the stewards and particularly the police. Their reporter, a veteran of many years, compared events at Wembley to those at the 1910 FA Cup semi-final between Barnsley and Everton at Leeds.

In that instance, he wrote, "mounted police had to clear the pitch, and I would say they had a hundred, and did their work quickly. On Saturday with a much bigger crowd under a couple of dozen mounted men were available, and they did not arrive until after the mischief was done."

So Billy in fact did nothing exceptional at Wembley, but that didn't prevent the press dubbing it the "White Horse Final"; after all, a celebrity – and a mute one at that – was one way to romanticise a shambles. Soon the press, with the connivance of the FA, turned the Wembley mob, unruly and agitated, if not violent, into a friendly, malleable mass, who meekly and cheerfully did as a policeman on a white horse told them.

It was important that the world saw football, particularly football in Britain, as popular but safe, a sport one could go to whatever one's age or sex. Football was the people's game, even if it was all controlled by a horse.

OBJECT
27

Viennese coffee house

In the 1920s Austrian football woke up and smelt the coffee. And as it savoured the taste, Austria created their *Wunderteam*, the most exciting and innovative side of the era. The Viennese coffee house represents their football because it was here that football evolved from being merely a physical pursuit into a cerebral one.

The British brought football to Austria in the late nineteenth century, but unlike South America, where the game was played by men involved in shipping and railways, it was bankers, merchants and diplomatic staff responsible for importing the game into central Europe. It quickly caught on, and in 1898 workers in a Viennese hat factory created a club called Wiener Arbeiter FK, now known as Rapid Vienna. In 1909 Hakoah Wien was formed, a Jewish club with the Star of David sewn into the players' shirts. It was these two clubs, and the Jewish coach Hugo Meisl, who would turn Austria into one of the world's finest teams in the 1920s.

Meisl liked to hang out in the coffee houses of Vienna, as did so many of the city's bourgeoisie. Legend has it that sacks of coffee beans were discarded by the soldiers of the Ottoman Turkish Army when they abandoned their siege of the Austrian capital in 1683. Two years later the first Viennese coffee house was opened and within 200 years they proliferated throughout the city. In discussing how football flourished in Austria in the early twentieth century, Alan Tomlinson writes in *German Football: History, Culture, Society* that: "The coffee house, the true drawing room of Viennese writers in the First Republic and plotting ground and venue for witty conversation and repartee, was a key site. Some of the many coffee houses that existed served as proper football coffee houses, a meeting place for officials, players and fans."

The coffee house to Austrians was what the public house was to the British in the 1920s, a place to discuss and dissect football. But whereas in pubs the talk among the working class (who now dominated British football) was blunt and basic, in Austria it was altogether more intellectual. Then in Austria, as now in Britain, football was trendy among artists, writers and actors. The difference was the Austrians actually knew what they were talking about.

In 1924 a two-tier professional league was formed with crowds of 40,000 plus not uncommon at matches. Football became tribal (albeit a very refined tribalism) and coffee houses were commandeered by rival sets of fans. Rapid Vienna became synonymous with the Café Holub, and Austria Vienna had the Café Parsifal as their base. The Ring Café, meanwhile, welcomed football fans of every hue and became the unofficial headquarters of the game in Austria.

At the heart of this HQ was Hugo Meisl. A friend of Herbert Chapman and Italy's great coach Vittorio Pozzo, Meisl took charge of the Austrian national side in 1913 but it wasn't until the late 1920s, as the country began to recover from the First World War, that his passing game bore fruit.

Meisl chose as the spearhead of his side a slightly built centre forward called Matthias Sindelar. The media dubbed him *Der Papierene* (The Paper Man), but what Sindelar lacked in bulk he made up for in touch and timing.

Like so many of their European rivals, Austria had declined the invitation to attend the inaugural World Cup in Uruguay; had they done so they might well have come back with the trophy. Instead, Meisl's side embarked in April 1931 on a 14-match unbeaten run, adopting a 2-3-5 formation and playing with such elegant grace that their style was summed up as a "Danubian Whirl". The mighty Scotland were thrashed 5-0, Germany succumbed 5-0, Switzerland were humiliated 8-1 and Hungary capitulated 8-2. Sindelar scored eight goals in those four matches, including hat-tricks against Germany and Hungary. Reflecting on the striker's prowess in his 1978 book *Die Erben der Tante Jolesch* (*The Heirs of Aunt Jolesch*), Friedrich Torberg, one of the foremost of the coffee house writers and a contemporary of Sindelar's, wrote that: "One could never really be sure which manner of play was to be expected. He had no system, to say nothing of a set pattern. He just had... genius."

Austria's winning run was brought to an end by England in front of 42,000 fans at Stamford Bridge. Austria had the finesse but the home side had the physique and in the end the muscular English side hung on for a 4-3 victory. By the time of the 1934 World Cup Meisl's side had peaked. They defeated France and Hungary en route to the semi-final but against Italy they lost by a solitary goal. Two years later the same opponents beat them in extra-time in the final of the Olympic Football Tournament in Berlin.

Meisl died of a heart attack in 1937, but by then the coffee house culture of Vienna was already disappearing. Austrian Jews were being hounded out of the country and in 1938 their fate became far grimmer when Austria was annexed into the German Third Reich.

Matthias Sindelar refused to play for Germany and instead bought a café. A few months later he was found dead inside his establishment. The authorities said suicide; Sindelar's friends said murder. The theatre critic Alfred Polgar thought it was the former, writing in Sindelar's obituary that for him "to live and play football in the downtrodden, broken, tormented city meant deceiving Vienna with a repulsive spectre of itself."

The *Radio Times*

Football without radio commentary: like Manchester United without Old Trafford or Germany without efficiency, it's almost unimaginable. But for the first sixty four years of football's official life there was no excitable chap getting worked up under his headset. That all changed on 22 January 1927, and to commemorate the historic moment we present a copy of the *Radio Times* from that week as object number 28.

In fact, the honour of hosting the

inaugural live outside broadcast commentary of a sports event belonged to rugby union. On 15 January 1927, a fortnight after the government took charge of the British Broadcasting Company, thereby turning it into a public corporation, Henry Blythe Thornhill Wakelam (better known as "Teddy") commentated from Twickenham as England beat Wales in the Five Nations Tournament.

Considering he'd had just two days to practise, Wakelam did a decent job, mindful of the fact that pinned to the inside of the rickety old commentary hut on top of an even more rickety piece of scaffold was a large sign on which was scrawled: "Do Not Swear".

So well had the experiment gone that the following week Wakelam was sent by the BBC to Highbury, the most convenient venue as Highbury was just up the road from the BBC's HQ at Alexandra Palace, for what would be the first ever live radio commentary on a football match.

To help listeners, that week's edition of the BBC listings magazine, the *Radio Times*, published a numbered grid of the Highbury pitch: there were eight squares in total, four in each half, with 1 and 2 in front of the North Bank and 7 and 8 in front of the Clock End. Squares 3, 4, 5 and 6 were in the middle of the pitch. It listed the event as: "2.5 Community singing and Arsenal v Sheffield United Association Football Match (relayed from Arsenal ground, Highbury)."

According to the BBC archives it was Wakelam's producer, Lance Sieveking, who thought up the numbered grid, the idea being "that the listener at home could follow the play from his armchair using the grid on his lap. Many believe this is the origin of the phrase 'Back to Square One'."

Squeezed next to Wakelam in the wooden commentary box "that largely resembled a garden shed" was Captain C. A. Lewis, already a well-known radio personality. His job, while Wakelam commentated, was to call out the number of the square so that listeners could track the progress of the ball. Complicated? To modern ears, yes, but by all accounts our ancestors judged the commentary marvellous.

Reviewing the event, the *Manchester Guardian* said the football commentary had been "more successful than that from Twickenham the previous week. In the Rugby match listeners only heard one commentator whereas on Saturday there were two, and with the aid of the plan of the ground issued by the BBC and their information it was possible to follow fairly closely the movements of the ball."

The paper went on to give an example from the commentary: "'Oh! pretty work, very pretty (section 5)... now up field (7)... a pretty (5,8) pass... come on Mercer... Now then Mercer; hello! Noble's got it (1,2)'... with the chart before one, it was fairly easy to visualise what was actually happening and the cheers and the groans of the spectators help considerably the imagination of the listeners."

The match ended one apiece with Arsenal's Charlie Buchan having the honour of scoring the first goal on radio. The *Spectator* predicted that "that type of broadcasting has come to stay."

Realising they were on to a winner, in the months that followed the BBC broadcast live the Grand National, the Derby, the Boat Race and the FA Cup Final between Arsenal and Cardiff City. Meanwhile, newspapers and sporting associations, who had been against live broadcasts initially for fear that they would draw people away, relaxed their opposition when they realised the radio wasn't a rival.

More than three quarters of a century after Wakelam's foray into the "garden shed" at Highbury, radio commentary is enjoying a boom period. In the 2011–12 season, the BBC broadcast 128 Premier League matches live, while since the start of the 2013–14 season Talksport are broadcasting all 380 Premier League matches each season in English, Mandarin and Spanish. As the Premier League grows in popularity in the USA, India, Indonesia and China radio is on the rise... and the commentators still refrain from swearing.

Mitropa Cup

OK, so object 29 is a little obscure, a football footnote that has been largely forgotten. Nonetheless, the Mitropa Cup deserves its place in our list because it demonstrates how, as early as the 1920s, the football authorities were looking to expand club football beyond national borders.

The man behind the Mitropa Cup was Hugo Meisl, the coach who created Austria's *Wunderteam* and who was also instrumental in establishing that country's first professional league in 1924. The league had proved a success and professional football in Austria was flourishing. So too in Italy where professionalism had been legalised in 1926 and moves were afoot to establish a two-tier league (Serie A and Serie B would debut in 1929).

In 1927 Meisl and representatives from the Czech, Yugoslav and Hungarian football federations met in Venice to discuss a European club competition. They all agreed that the concept was a cracking idea, one which would swell the clubs' coffers and raise standards in central Europe.

The men in suits called it the Mitropa Cup (*Mittel Europa* meaning central Europe) and decided that each round would be played over two legs, one home one away, so that gate receipts were fairly distributed and every club got the chance to experience another football culture. Plans were also drawn up to broadcast matches live on the wireless, a daring and glamorous innovation.

The meeting in Venice was held in July 1927, and the

opening round of matches in the Mitropa Cup were staged just the following month. Two teams each from Austria, Yugoslavia, Hungary and Czechoslovakia entered and the inaugural competition was won by Sparta Prague. By the start of the 1930s clubs from Italy, Romania and Switzerland had joined the Mitropa Cup.

But as the competition expanded so did its difficulties. Europe in the 1930s was a continent bubbling with rancour. Mussolini had seized power in Italy, Hitler in Germany and in Yugoslavia the king had been assassinated. Perhaps it was the Mitropa Cup that George Orwell had in mind when, in 1941, he made his famous comment: "Serious sport has nothing to do with fair play, it is bound up with hatred and jealousy, boastfulness, disregard of all the rules and sadistic pleasure in unnecessary violence. In other words it is war minus the shooting."

The 1932 semi-final between Slavia Prague and Juventus ended in a full-scale riot with hundreds of soldiers battling spectators. Both clubs were expelled from the competition. Five years later, when Admira Vienna hosted Genoa, demonstrations were staged against Fascist Italy. The Italian interior ministry retaliated by banning the Austrian side from travelling to Genoa to play the return leg.

In between the riots and political posturing there was plenty of good football on show, all enjoyed by 50,000 plus crowds. In the 1935 Mitropa Cup, thirty two games produced 153 goals and featured some of the great strikers of that or any other time: Austria's Matthias Sindelar, the Austro Czech Pepi Bican, and the gifted Italian goalscorer Giuseppe Meazza.

No club or country dominated the competition either, Bologna FC 1909's two victories in 1932 and 1934 the closest any side came to a stranglehold.

Újpest of Budapest won the title in 1939, but by then Europe was already falling apart. Austria had been annexed by Hitler the previous year and he was in the process of breaking up Czechoslovakia bit by bit when Újpest defeated

Ferencvárosi of Hungary in the final of the Mitropa Cup.

The 1940 competition was started but never finished, and though the Mitropa Cup returned some years after the war it – like Europe – was never the same again. An Iron Curtain now divided the continent.

Nonetheless, the Cup had left its footprints across the football fields of Europe. Now there were those further west in the continent who saw what the tournament had achieved and set out to carry on what Meisl had begun when he gave the continent its first club competition.

Brass farthing

"I don't care a brass farthing about the improvement of the game in France, Belgium, Austria or Germany."

The words of a deranged English defender who'd headed one too many heavy leather balls? Unfortunately, not. Rather, it was the declaration of one Charles Sutcliffe, a prominent official of the Football League throughout the 1920s. Never the most enlightened man, Sutcliffe objected to the admission of South American countries to FIFA because they were "midgets" and the idea of them staging a World Cup he dismissed as a "joke". Perhaps Sutcliffe's finest hour, as xenophobia goes, was in 1930 when he described the idea of non-British players plying their trade in the Football League as "repulsive to the clubs, offensive to British players and a terrible confession of weakness in the management of a club."

But Sutcliffe wasn't a one-off lunatic; his views were

shared by many of his colleagues who ran the British game in the 1920s, and their arrogant intransigence came to a head over the Olympic Football Tournament of 1928.

Four years of ruinous war had not only brought Europe to its knees economically, it had also shattered the goodwill and harmony between Britain and the rest of the footballing world that had been nurtured by Daniel Burley Woolfall between 1906 and 1914.

In 1919 the International Olympic Committee (IOC) had told Germany and the Austro-Hungarian Empire that they were no longer welcome in their organisation, and the following year the Home Nations pushed for FIFA to sever all associations with the defeated powers, including the prohibition of club matches with the countries concerned.

This was too much for Italy and Sweden, who accused the British football associations of too stringent a punishment, so in a fit of pique all four Home Nations resigned their FIFA membership. Their sulk lasted four years (by which time Ireland had become a republic and formed its own football association) and in 1924 the English, Welsh, Scottish and Northern Irish football associations slunk back to FIFA.

They did so at a time when membership was growing rapidly: Yugoslavia, Estonia, Latvia and Lithuania were just four of the new affiliates, all emerging from the rubble of war as new and ambitious nations. Egypt and Palestine also joined, as well as Brazil and Uruguay, but the proliferation of affiliates troubled the British.

Foremost among their concerns was the issue of professionalism. Britain shared the same view as the IOC when it came to paying international sportsmen, believing absolutely in amateurism. The four British nations had declined to participate in the 1924 Olympic Football Tournament (a competition won easily by Uruguay) because they viewed with suspicion any international tournament.

In 1926 Switzerland proposed a motion that amateur players should be reimbursed for lost earnings while representing their country. The motion was passed, to the fury of the British, and when in 1927 the FIFA pressurised the IOC into allowing broken-time payments at the 1928 Olympics, it got all too much for the Home Nations. They could see all too well where international football was headed – towards a professional World Cup. All four associations resigned from FIFA in 1928. After all, they didn't need Europe, Europe needed them, an attitude the *Daily Mirror* reflected in its famous 1930s headline: "FOG IN CHANNEL – CONTINENT CUT OFF."

Britain and FIFA went their separate ways for the next eighteen years, during which time the world first caught up and then overtook England and Scotland. Not that that was of any concern to Charles Sutcliffe. "The FIFA does not appeal to me," he said in 1928. "If central Europe or any other district wants to govern football let them confine their power and authority to themselves and we can look after our own affairs."

Shirt numbers

OBJECT 31

When football's first international match kicked off in November 1872, both sides had on shirts in team colours – dark blue for the Scots and white for the English. The shirts also had badges embroidered into the breast, Scotland sporting their Lion Rampant and England their Three Lions. What neither side had was a number – as on this shirt, object number 31.

Shirt numbers didn't appear until the start of the 1928 season, when Arsenal lost 3-2 at Sheffield Wednesday. The home side wore numbers 1 to 11 and the Gunners donned 12

to 22. According to the official Arsenal website: "The introduction of shirt numbers was largely down to the visionary
Herbert Chapman (manager of Arsenal at the time). His idea
was that it would be easier for players to know where they
were on the field in relation to their team mates... [but] the
Football League Management Committee refused to sanction
the wearing of numbered shirts for many years."

Arsenal tried again to introduce numbered shirts, wearing them at Highbury in December 1933 when they hosted
a friendly match against FC Vienna (comprised of the entire
Austrian national XI). Arsenal may have won 4-2 but the
Football League still weren't having the numbered shirt idea
and rejected the concept during their 1934 general meeting.

It was television that finally dragged the powers-that-be
into the twentieth century. The BBC had broadcast its first
football match in 1937 (coincidentally involving Arsenal) and
the following year the FA Cup Final between Preston North
End and Huddersfield Town was televised. What could be
of more assistance to viewers in the age of distant black and
white pictures than players wearing numbered shirts?

At the annual general meeting of the Football League
Management in June 1939 numbers were put to the vote and
those in favour triumphed 24 to 20 against. Shirt numbers
were first worn in league play during the 1939–40 season
with both sides wearing 1 to 11. Further, the FA insisted that
numbers were allocated to specific positions according to the
2-3-5 team formation. In other words the keeper wore 1, the
right back 2, the left back 3, the right half 4, the centre half 5,
the left half 6, the right winger 7, the inside right 8, the centre
forward 9, the inside left 10 and the left winger 11.

Unfortunately, by 1939 the 2-3-5 formation was antiquated,
rendered so by the introduction in the late 1920s of Herbert
Chapman's W-M system at Arsenal. As Jonathan Wilson
explained in his masterly book on football tactics *Inverting
the Pyramid: The History of Football Tactics*: "The full-backs
marked the wingers rather than the inside-forwards, the

wing-halves sat on the opposing inside-forwards rather than on wingers, the centre half, now a centre back, dealt with the centre forward, and both inside forwards dropped deeper: the 2-3-5 had become a 3-2-2-3; the W-M... meant that teams using the W-M lined up, in modern notation, 2,5,3; which is why 'centre half' is – confusingly – used as a synonym for 'centre back' in Britain."

There was further innovation at the 1954 World Cup: each player in his country's 22-man squad was allocated a number for the tournament's duration. Consequently, while 1 to 11 lined up in their specific positions, those wearing 12 to 22 wore shirts that were irrelevant to their position. Four years later, at the 1958 World Cup, a 17-year-old Pelé ended up with the number 10 shirt when FIFA randomly dished out the numbers after the Brazilian Federation forgot to send in their squad list on time. He wore the same number for the rest of his career.

After the numbers came names on the shirts, although not until the 1992 European Championships. The following season, players' names appeared for the first time on the back of their shirts in English football, and by a twist of fate Arsenal and Sheffield Wednesday were again the two teams involved as they had been sixty five years earlier when numbers were introduced. Arsenal and Wednesday contested the League Cup Final in April 1993, playing this time in numbers and names.

For the 1993–94 season the FA made names on shirts obligatory, as well as adopting the same system for squad numbering as was in use for World Cups. Other European football federations followed suit, so it was no surprise in 2003 when Porto goalkeeper Vitor Baia wore the 99 shirt in their victory over Celtic in the UEFA Cup Final.

One consequence of the naming of shirts was that the sale of replica shirts went off the charts. In the 1993–94 season sales of shirts in the Premier League increased by 640 per cent as more and more fans wore their heart on their backs.

In 2012, as the Premier League celebrated twenty years of its existence, they revealed that the most popular replica shirt was the number 10 worn by Wayne Rooney. The Manchester United striker was just ahead of Liverpool captain Steven Gerrard and Chelsea's Fernando Torres. A spokesman for the Premier League's replica products explained why wearing the name of a favourite player was so important: "Fans' identification with star players in this way has demonstrated both the player's performance and celebrity and has served to reinforce their identification with their club," he said, adding: "But first and foremost, it demonstrates allegiance to the underlying talent of the player."

That would all have been gibberish to Herbert Chapman, focus of our next object, who couldn't care less for stars or celebrities. When he lobbied for shirt numbers he'd just wanted to make life less complicated, not more costly, which is what replica shirts are to fans these days.

OBJECT
32

Bronze bust of Herbert Chapman

Numbers on shirts wasn't Herbert Chapman's only innovation. The man was a veritable revolutionary in the world of inter war football, an illiterate miner's son whose avant-garde ideas frightened the Football Association and transformed Arsenal FC forever. A bronze bust of Chapman – for many years on display in the marble halls at the old Highbury Stadium – is now housed in the Arsenal offices, while a life-size statue of the visionary manager was unveiled outside the Emirates Stadium in 2011.

Before Chapman took over at Highbury in the summer of 1925, Arsenal had never finished in the top five of the First Division. The Gunners, like all southern clubs, were there to be rolled over by the likes of Liverpool, Huddersfield and Sunderland. In May 1925, having just avoided relegation to the Second Division, Arsenal placed an advert in the newspaper for a new manager, stipulating that the candidate must "possess the highest qualifications for the post, both as to ability and personal character."

Chapman got the job on account of his previous managerial experience; his career had started at Northampton Town in 1907 and culminated in back-to-back First Division titles with Huddersfield in 1924 and 1925. So Chapman had the ability, and the personal character, though he wasn't without flaws. While in charge of Leeds United the club was accused of making illegal payments to players. When the club refused to cooperate with the FA they were kicked out of the League and Chapman was banned from the game for two years, returning to take over Huddersfield in 1921.

Installed as the new boss at Highbury, Chapman warned the Arsenal board it would take five years to turn them into a force in the First Division. In addition he needed two things: money to buy players and a promise from the board that they wouldn't interfere in his grand scheme. He got both.

The first player Chapman signed was an odd choice. Charlie Buchan was nearly 34, a decorated war hero and former England forward considered long past his best. Buchan was working in his sports shop in Sunderland when Chapman walked in and announced: "I've come to sign you."

Together the pair exploited the recent change in the offside law (the number of players needed between an attacking player and the goal to put them onside fell from three to two) by devising what Buchan called the W-M formation. This system converted the centre half into a third back, or stopper, and pulled the two inside forwards back into the midfield leaving the centre forward and two wingers up front.

It took another four seasons before the system was fine-tuned to Chapman's satisfaction. In the meantime he scoured the leagues for the players he thought would best fit the W-M formation: he signed the unknown Herbie Roberts from Oswestrey Town for £200 and paid Kettering Town £900 for Eddie Hapgood, both of whom were used in defence. Up front Chapman signed Alex James and Cliff Bastin, and gradually his team began to take shape.

Having lost in the 1927 FA Cup Final to Cardiff, Arsenal won the trophy in 1930, and the following year became the first southern club to be crowned First Division champions. As the *Daily Mail* commented, Chapman was "breaking down traditions... he was the first manager who set out methodically to organise the winning of matches."

Chapman's methods were met with suspicion by the FA, who pooh-poohed his suggestion of shirt numbers and thought he was faintly mad to propose playing under floodlights. Undeterred, Chapman continued to revolutionise the Gunners. This was a man born in 1878, the first generation of the working class to benefit from the 1870 Education Act that made schooling compulsory up until the age of 12. As a result, Chapman and his ilk were not only educated, they were ambitious and eager to prove themselves in a post-war world which no longer believed in the upper classes' right to rule.

Chapman therefore had no time for tradition; he was innovator, as he proved with a raft of advances at Highbury: a clock – three metres in diameter – was positioned in the North Bank in 1928 (in 1935 it was moved to the south terracing when the North Bank was redeveloped); white sleeves were added to the all red shirt (in the belief that the white helped players see each other in their peripheral vision) and the club badge was sewn onto the left-hand side of the shirt; the Gillespie Road tube station changed its name to Arsenal and every Friday Chapman discussed tactics for Saturday's match with his players.

Arsenal won their second League title in 1933 and were on course to retain their crown when, on 6 January 1934, Chapman died of pneumonia a few days before his fifty sixth birthday. Chapman was dead, but his team lived on, winning the league title in 1934, 1935 and 1938, and defeating Sheffield United to win the 1936 FA Cup. No other club would dominate English football the way Arsenal did in the 1930s until Bob Paisley's Liverpool, forty years later.

Many of Chapman's innovations remain today – Arsenal's red and white shirts, the tube station and the clock – but his W-M system has been long since discredited. Negative, defensive and uncreative was how its critics described it. Chapman agreed. Well, he was ahead of the time and could see perfectly well where football was headed, and where managers would be headed if they didn't get results on the pitch. "It is no longer necessary for a team to play well," he once said. "The measure of their skill is, in fact, judged by their position in the league table."

Jules Rimet Trophy

If Herbert Chapman was an innovator *par excellence* in English football, then his French counterpart was Jules Rimet, a man who had never played football but who believed the game could bring nations together and heal the wounds caused by the First World War. Football, he once said, allows men "to meet in confidence without hatred in their hearts and without an insult on their lips." Oh well, the road to hell, etc...

Nonetheless, Rimet's good intentions gave football its World Cup, and the trophy (our next object) awarded to the winners is in honour of the noble Monsieur Rimet. He was born in eastern France in 1873 and from an early age saw how sport could change men and nations for the better. Not for him the lofty ideals of his compatriot Baron Pierre de Coubertin, founder of the modern Olympics, whose views on sport were snobbish and sanctimonious.

Rimet himself was never much good at the game; his forte was administration (he was a lawyer by profession), and having established the Red Star sports club in Paris at the end of the nineteenth century, in 1904 he was involved in the creation of the Federation International de Football Association (FIFA).

After his experiences in the war – in which he fought in the French Army – Rimet became ever more determined to use sport as a force for good among nations with the establishment of a global tournament. The British thought he was mad and wanted nothing to do with his scheme. Rimet, who was elected president of FIFA in 1921, carried on in pursuit of his dream. According to Rimet's grandson, Yves, Jules was a "humanist and idealist, who believed that sport could unite the world. Unlike many others in his time, he realised that, to be truly democratic, to truly engage the masses, international sport must be professional."

Fortunately there were other enlightened souls in football who shared Rimet's vision, one of whom was FIFA secretary Henri Delaunay. Alarmed at how the amateur Olympics soccer tournament was the most prestigious event of its kind, he warned in 1926 that "many countries where professionalism is now recognised and organised cannot any longer be represented there by their best players." Thus at the 1929 FIFA Congress in Barcelona it was agreed to stage the first World Cup in Uruguay the following year.

Rimet commissioned a 50,000 franc trophy from the French sculptor Abel Lafleur, which the FIFA president carried in his luggage during the three-week voyage by sea to Montevideo. The trophy was 35 cm tall and weighed 3.8kg and depicted the winged Greek goddess Nike holding aloft an octagonal cup on a base of blue lapis lazuli. It was made of sterling silver and gold plated and called "The Goddess of Victory".

In 1946 Victory was renamed the "Jules Rimet trophy", a nod to the president of FIFA who had remained in his post during the Second World War. The trophy itself had spent the conflict in a shoebox under the bed of Ottorino Barassi, an Italian vice president of FIFA who took the Cup trophy from a Rome bank and hid it from Mussolini and Hitler.

Far from shattering his belief in the efficacy of sport, six years of war only strengthened Rimet's views of sport as a healer. His last act before stepping down as FIFA president was to present his eponymous trophy to Fritz Walter, the captain of the West Germany side that beat Hungary in the 1954 World Cup Final.

Rimet was gone but his trophy remained – for a time. On 20 March 1966 it was stolen from the Methodist Central Hall, Westminster, while on display, ahead of that year's World Cup in England. The FA received a ransom note demanding £15,000 for the trophy's return, but the handover went wrong and though the kidnapper was caught there was no Goddess. She eventually turned up a few days later when a young man called David Corbett was out walking his dog in a suburb of south London. "I put the lead on Pickles and he went over to the neighbour's car," recalled Corbett forty years later. "Pickles drew my attention to a package, tightly bound in newspaper, lying by the front wheel. I picked it up and tore some paper and saw a woman holding a dish over her head and disks with the words Germany, Uruguay, Brazil. I rushed inside to my wife... 'I've found the World Cup! I've found the World Cup!'"

Seventeen years later the Jules Rimet trophy was stolen again, this time from the headquarters of the Brazilian Soccer Federation, where it had resided since the 1970 World Cup. "Its true value is spiritual," said federation president Giulite

Coutinho in appealing for its return. "This was a piece of history for Brazil and the world."

Coutinho offered a reward of $1,000 for a trophy valued at $47,000 and which had been given by FIFA to Brazil after they won the World Cup for a third time in 1970. The president said the federation was "open to negotiations" if the thieves were after a ransom, adding: "It's not the value of the thing, this cup was a piece of glory for a nation that only thinks of soccer."

But the trophy was never returned, the Brazilian police concluding it had been melted down shortly after its theft. The crime would have appalled Jules Rimet, as would have the state of the modern game. As Yves Rimet said in 2006: "My grandfather would have been disappointed with the money-dominated business that football has become. That was not his vision."

His vision was to spread football throughout the world and in that he succeeded. During his thirty three years as president of FIFA membership grew from twenty to eighty five countries. In all of those countries the majority of people play the game for love not for money. That was what Rimet wanted.

OBJECT
34

Estadio Centenario, Montevideo, Uruguay

Coming up with the idea for a World Cup was easy; sorting out the logistics proved a little trickier. Jules Rimet and

FIFA managed it in the end, although the 1930 World Cup featured thirteen nations and only four from Europe, the game's heartland back then.

Still, the tournament was ultimately a success, won by the host nation with the final played in the magnificent Centenary Stadium in Montevideo. Although the stadium wasn't open for business until five days after the World Cup began, the *Centenario* was ready for Uruguay's opening game against Peru. Austere and imposing, the stadium was called a "temple of football" by Rimet.

And throughout the 17-day tournament Uruguayans flocked to their temple to watch their boys in action. Uruguay had dominated international football during the 1920s, winning the 1924 and 1928 Olympic gold medals, though that wasn't the reason they beat off competition from Italy, Holland, Sweden and Spain to stage the inaugural World Cup. The small South American country of under 3 million people had the honour bestowed on them by FIFA because their government wanted to use the World Cup as the showpiece for Uruguay's centenary celebrations, the huge party to mark 100 years of independence from Spain and Portugal.

To that end Uruguay offered to meet the travelling expenses of all competing countries and to build a stadium especially for the tournament. They could afford such largesse; the 1920s had been good to their exports of beef and wool. Little did they know that within weeks of their offer Wall Street would come crashing down, a cataclysmic event that ultimately forced Uruguay to withdraw from travelling to Italy in 1934 to defend their title.

Juan Scasso was the architect commissioned to build the Centenary Stadium, and he set to work straight away, importing the concrete from Germany as South America had yet to establish its own manufacturing plants. The concrete came from Germany but none of its footballers made the trip to Uruguay for the World Cup. Neither did any British side accept an invitation, nor the other European powerhouses such as Austria, Sweden or Hungary.

Romania sent a side, as did Yugoslavia, while Jules Rimet persuaded the French to attend and the Belgian vice-president of FIFA, Rudolf Seedrayers, sweet-talked his compatriots into making the three-week voyage across the Atlantic. At least the Uruguayans could count on the support of their fellow Americans: Bolivia, Argentina, Chile, Brazil, Mexico, Paraguay, Peru and the USA made up the thirteen entrants.

There was a clear gulf in quality, Argentina, Yugoslavia, Uruguay and the United States winning their pools with ease. The hosts and the USA didn't concede a goal in their two group matches. A different story in the semi, however, where the USA were slaughtered 6-1 by Argentina. Uruguay ran up a similar score line against Yugoslavia to set up a mouthwatering final on 30 July.

The Centenary Stadium was a fitting venue for such a momentous occasion: it was the continent's first concrete stadium, with what David Golblatt described as "four stands that fanned out like the multi-layered petals of an art-deco flower." In addition, on the north side of the stadium was the extraordinary *piece de resistance*, "a nine-storey tower rising 100 metres above the sunken pitch... an extraordinary statement of modernist optimism."

On the day of the final 98,000 fans crammed into the stadium. They were well-behaved, commented the *Daily Express*, although "that may have been due to the fact that 6,000 supporters of the visiting team were relieved of their revolvers by Uruguayan officials as they landed from steamboats which had brought them from Buenos Aires."

Uruguay scored first but Argentina replied with two goals to go into the break 2-1 up. The second half, however, belonged to the hosts and goals from Pedro Cea, Santos Iriarte and the one-armed Hector Castro secured the Goddess of Victory trophy for Uruguay.

In Buenos Aires there were riots, but in Montevideo

the mood was far different. The correspondent for the *Daily Express* depicted the scene in his match report: "The Uruguayans were having an orgy of rejoicing. Champagne ran like water, and those whose pockets did not run to such luxuries threw down all their money on the table and invited waiters to bring alcoholic beverages within the limit revealed... cabarets and restaurants were filled to overflowing. Money meant nothing. The watchword was 'celebrate', and throughout the night processions of fans marched through the city, singing, shouting, proclaiming their victory through great megaphones."

So the first World Cup ended with the host nation partying and FIFA delighted at what had unfolded. The tournament had captured the imagination of the footballing world and the stay-at-home nations in Europe regretted their absence. Or some of them did. England, the sport's founding father, still considered that they had nothing to gain from stooping so low as to play against the South Americans. In contrast, the World Cup had given Uruguay a sense of its identity. "The sky-blue shirt was proof of the existence of the nation," wrote Uruguayan novelist Eduardo Galeano in *Football in Sun and Shadow*. "Uruguay was not a mistake. Football pulled this little country out of the shadows of universal anonymity."

OBJECT 35

Knight Bachelor insignia

Sir Stanley Matthews, what a one-off. He could have featured in our history as far forward as object 53 – the sombrero George Best wore in 1965. As it is, he finds himself featured between the inaugural World Cup Stadium and the great Italy team of the 1930s.

The 1930s was the decade it all started for Matthews, the only footballer to be knighted while still playing the game. That was in 1965, when he was still plying his trade for Stoke City – a full thirty four years after his debut.

Stoke was the city where Stan was born in 1915, and where he died in 2000. He loved Stoke and Stoke loved Stan but it was with Blackpool that Matthews enjoyed his glory years. He joined the Tangerines for the start of the 1947–48 season. "You're 32," exclaimed Blackpool manager Joe Smith. "Do you think you can make it for another couple of years?"

Matthews helped turn Blackpool into the one of the great teams of the early post-war years. Three times in six years they reached the FA Cup although it was only on the last of those appearances – 1953 – that Blackpool finally triumphed. Stan Mortenson scored three of Blackpool's goals in the 4-3 win over Bolton but they still called it "the Matthews Final", such was the splendour of the 38-year-old's play.

And still Matthews kept going, beating Real Madrid's Alfredo Di Stéfano to the first ever European Footballer of the Year award in 1956 (to go with the inaugural Football Writers' Association Footballer of the Year accolade of six years earlier). So what was his secret? Good genes, of course, but Matthews was ahead of his time in so many ways; he avoided red meat, forsook the booze and the fags, and took care of his body. He even got his boots refashioned so they were light and soft, better able to caress the ball.

His England career spanned twenty three years; Matthews made his debut against Wales in 1934 and won the last of his fifty four caps in May 1957 against Denmark. He was 42 that day, playing in an England side that contained a 20-year-old left half called Duncan Edwards.

Matthews returned to Stoke in 1961 in his forty seventh year. The Potters paid Blackpool £3,500 for the privilege of getting Stan back, and gave him a weekly wage of £50 plus a £25 match fee, not a bad increase on the £1 a week he'd received when he joined Stoke aged 15. But that had been in

February 1930, before the advent of the World Cup, the first televised match and the first European Cup match. Matthews' magnificent career had spanned all these momentous footballing events, and on he kept going.

On 1 January 1965 he was knighted for services to football, and the following month Matthews, five days after his fiftieth birthday, played his final game in the football league, helping Stoke to a 3-1 victory against Fulham. Manchester United won the League title that season thanks in no small part to 19-year-old George Best. The passing of Matthews and the emergence of Best was symbolic, the moment footballers began the ascent to stardom and celebrity. When an adoring biography of Matthews was published in 1990 he was too embarrassed to read it.

The modern follower of football might think Matthews was lucky to have been born when he was. The "Wizard of the Dribble", as he was known, played the game in an era when players had more time on the ball. Football back then, as in life in general, was less hurried and frantic. There was space for a player of Matthews' talent to thrive. He used to do on a regular basis what Manchester United winger Ryan Giggs (like Matthews a man able to defy age) did to Arsenal in the 1999 FA Cup semi-final replay, dribbling half the length of the field before blasting the ball into the net. But how many times since has Giggs done that? Defenders nowadays close him down before he's gone more than a couple of yards.

Matthews would have doubtless adapted his game, as Giggs has done in the twenty first century. He was that good. And don't forget, defenders weren't carthorses in the 1930s and 1940s. They were big men who came hard, and few came harder than Johnny Carey, the Ireland full back who played over 300 matches for Manchester United. Contributing to a 1949 football training manual, Carey advised budding young full backs what to do if ever they found themselves on the same pitch as Matthews: "Against Stan it is imperative to get to the ball first; if not, then just to tackle him as often as you can and with as much help as you can get from your colleagues. By this you will gather that I consider Matthews a football genius. The impression I got when I first marked Stan, in 1938, was of an object appearing before me, shuddering, and was gone. He is the finest ball player I have ever seen; it is an honour to play with or against him."

Stick of chalk

OBJECT 36

Like so many of the most successful coaches, Vittorio Pozzo wasn't much good as a player. He could run fast but that was about it. Pozzo's greatest gift to football was his brain. Like Herbert Chapman and Hugo Meisl, Pozzo was ahead of the game in the 1920s and 1930s.

Pozzo was a pragmatist with barely a romantic bone in his body. Winning for him was as much about stopping the opposition from scoring as it was about his own side putting the ball in the back of the net. He was also a raging disciplinarian and, of all the objects that could have been chosen to represent him, nothing smacks of Pozzo's authoritarian streak more than a stick of chalk.

He taught languages as a young man in England so he could live in the birthplace of football and learn all there was about the game. Back in Italy he used blackboards to instil in his sides the concept of man to man marking. His methodology paid off: Italy won the World Cup in 1934 and 1938 playing organised, disciplined football. "Kind, but with a strong hand," was how Pozzo described himself. "If I let them make mistakes I'd lose my authority."

Pozzo was born in 1886 and studied business techniques

at Zurich's International School of Commerce in 1908. Able to speak several languages, he improved his English in Bradford in the years before the war, teaching French, Italian and German to students while studying Manchester United. He hung around training sessions, befriended the players and when he settled back in Italy in the 1920s much of his football strategy was based on what he had learned in England.

Pozzo became coach of Italy in 1929, seven years after Benito Mussolini had assumed control of the country. The extent to which Pozzo espoused Il Duce's fascist views is still debated in Italy today; his patriotism was never in doubt (he'd fought in the First World War) but while he happily instructed his players to give the fascist salute at the 1938 World Cup evidence has emerged in recent years suggesting Pozzo worked with Italy's anti-fascist resistance during the Second World War.

Whatever his political views, Pozzo cut an extraordinary figure in the 1930s. John Foot, in his book *Calcio: A History of Italian Football*, describes him as "short, tubby, with black glasses and a shock of bizarre white hair...a kind of dictator."

One of Pozzo's first acts was to strengthen the national side with South American players of Italian stock. Known as Oriundi, they began arriving in Europe in the 1920s and some of the finest players in Italy in the 1930s came from this caste. Enrique Guaita, born in Brazil to Italian parents, was one of three Oriundi players on the Italy side that won the 1934 World Cup.

Pozzo cared little for a man's heritage. What mattered more to him was that they conformed to his way of thinking and conducted themselves like professional players. Those that did were nurtured by Pozzo in a strict but paternalistic manner; those that failed to step into line soon fell out of favour.

Pozzo turned out technically efficient teams using a formation based loosely on the W-M system introduced by Herbert Chapman at Arsenal. It was more of a 2-3-2-3 (a W-W) and, combined with Pozzo's man-marking innovations, it allowed Italy to shut out more naturally gifted opponents.

In the 1934 World Cup semi-final, the great Austrian striker Matthias Sindelar was rendered virtually anonymous as Italy won by one goal to nil. Czechoslovakia were defeated 2-1 in the final in front of a delighted Rome crowd. There were subsequent accusations that Mussolini's Italy had benefited throughout the tournament from benevolent refereeing decisions, a claim directed at nearly every country that's won the World Cup on home soil. In truth, Italy won because they were solid, defensive and organised.

They proved as much when they went on to win the gold medal in the 1936 Olympics Football Final, and again when they beat Hungary 4-2 to win the 1938 World Cup in France. One Italian journalist, Mario Zappa, said of his national team in the 1930s that "the big secret of the Italian squad is its capacity to attack with the fewest amount of men possible, without ever distracting the half backs from their defensive work."

The one country that Italy couldn't beat was England. Their first fixture, in Rome in 1933, ended in a 1-1 draw, and the following year, with Italy having been crowned world champions, England won 3-2 at Highbury. The visitors "played like a platoon of gladiators" but it devastated Pozzo that his methods weren't good enough to conquer the English.

Worse was to come. In a 1948 friendly England hammered Italy 4-0 at Turin and Pozzo was forced to stand down after nineteen years at the helm. Under his stewardship Italy had won sixty of eighty eight matches, drawing sixteen and losing just twelve times. The Azzurri wouldn't win the World Cup again until 1982, but only Brazil in 1958 and 1962 have emulated their feat of winning back-to-back World Cups.

Pozzo's greatest accomplishment, argues John Foot, was that his coaching helped the Italy side "create a very strong identification between Italians and their national football team". It's a legacy still very much in evidence today.

Television set

Life wasn't much fun if one wasn't an Arsenal supporter in the inter war years. As we've already seen, the world's first football radio commentary, in January 1927, featured the Gunners, as did the first live broadcast of an FA Cup Final later that year. Then, a decade later, as television technology advanced, it was again Arsenal to whom the British Broadcasting Corporation turned.

With the BBC's Alexandra Palace headquarters three miles down the road from Highbury Stadium, it was just easier to turn to the Gunners rather than traipse to Tottenham or journey halfway across London to Chelsea. And anyway, Arsenal in the 1930s were the glamour club of English football thanks to the legacy left by Herbert Chapman.

He had become manager of the club in 1925, the same year John Logie Baird gave the first public demonstration of low definition television. In the years that followed, both Arsenal and television evolved, the former becoming the most successful club in the country and the latter developing as a result of the competition between Marconi-EMI's 405-line system and Baird's 240-line system.

From 1932 the BBC had conducted experimental transmissions from a studio in Broadcasting House, and by 29 August 1936 they felt confident enough to take a camera to Highbury and film Arsenal playing Everton. Highlights of the Gunners' 3-2 victory were shown on television but, according to the BBC, "transmissions reached only the 20,000 homes with a television within a 35-mile range of Alexandra Palace." The result was deemed a success, and in November 1936 the BBC opened the world's first regular service of high-definition television from Alexandra Palace. Sir John Reith, the founder of the BBC, was underwhelmed by the occasion, confiding to his diary that he "declined to be televised or take part" because he regarded television as "an awful snare".

Ten-inch television sets, which cost £100, were still very much a plaything of the wealthy a year later when the BBC returned to Highbury to broadcast the first match live on television. It was Arsenal against Arsenal reserves, so it's a moot point how many people would have watched the game even if they had had a telly. By now Marconi's 405-line system had been chosen by the BBC ahead of Baird's system, and in 1938 they broadcast live their first FA Cup Final at Wembley between Preston North End and Huddersfield Town. It wasn't a classic, and after twenty nine minutes of extra-time it was still a dreary 0-0. "If there's a goal scored now, I'll eat my hat," announced commentator Thomas Woodrooffe. Preston scored a few seconds later and a day or two afterwards Woodrooffe ate a cake baked as a hat.

Such quaintness seemed a lifetime away when football resumed after the war. Television had now overtaken radio as the world's preferred broadcast medium, aided by the development in the quality of the picture and the reduction in price of a set. When Stanley Matthews' Blackpool met Bolton in the 1953 FA Cup Final an estimated 20 per cent of the population owned a television.

Though the BBC was leading the way in coverage of European football, others on the continent grasped its potential, among them Gabriel Hanot (see object 44), the man responsible for the European Cup. Television and floodlights were a dream team, one that could accommodate Hanot's vision. The European Broadcast Union (EBU) had shown nine matches from the 1954 World Cup in Switzerland – and they hadn't been asked by FIFA for any rights fee. That would come later; in the meantime those nine matches had proved hugely popular with the public and boosted the sales of television sets across Europe.

It took another six years before the first European Cup Final was broadcast live across the continent, the BBC doing the honours from Hampden Park as Real Madrid put on a show for viewers with a 7-3 crushing of Eintracht Frankfurt. Kenneth Wolstenholme, best remembered for his description of England's defeat of West Germany in the 1966 World Cup Final, was the commentator, and the BBC paid just £8,000 for the privilege of acquiring the rights to what many consider still to be the greatest ever European Cup Final.

By the end of 1960s most homes in Europe had a television, and most European countries now had a football highlights show. The Germans were first in 1961 and the Italians had theirs up and running in 1967, also introducing the slow motion replay.

The BBC's highlights programme was called Match of the Day, and it launched at 6:30 p.m. on 22 August 1964. The first edition showed only one match, and guess who it involved?

Of course, who else, Arsenal against Liverpool.

OBJECT 38

Old sock

Our next object is a sock, circa 1945, though it is not just any old sock. Rather it is a rolled up sock that was once one of a pair owned by João Ramos do Nascimento. Note its threadbare appearance and simple design.

The significance of this sock in the history of football cannot be overstated. For without it a young boy from the village of Três Corações in south-east Brazil might not have grown up to be the greatest player the game had ever seen.

The boy was born Edson Arantes do Nascimento on 23 October 1940, the son of an injury-prone centre forward called João Ramos. When Edson was 4, he and his family moved to the city of Bauru, north-west of São Paulo, in the hope that his father would find work. But there was none, and with little money with which to put food on the table, buying a football was out of the question. Instead young Edson and his brother, Jair, stole their father's odd socks, "shaping it out as best we could into a sphere and then tying it with string... I got into trouble with my father because he could never find matching socks in the house."

Together the brothers played with their "ball" in Rubens Aruda Street, using tin cans as goalposts and the kerb as the touchline. Sometimes the ball hit the power line that ran overhead and the street was plunged into darkness. It also meant the end of the sock. "Every now and then we would come across a new sock or bit of clothing," remembered Edson. "Sometimes it must be said from an unattended clothes line."

With his ball Edson began to acquire the skills that would later mesmerise football: dribbling, juggling and becoming its master. "If you ever want to be a decent player, you have to learn to use each foot equally without stopping to think about it," he explained, adding: "Perhaps you are born with certain skills and talents, but quite frankly it seems impossible to me that one is actually born to be an ace football player... It is hard work, perseverance, learning, studying, sacrifice and most of all, love of what you are doing."

The slight discolouration on the sock is a result no doubt of being kicked around by young Edson and the rest of the "Shoeless Ones", the name of the street side they formed in the late 1940s. None among Zé Roberto, Vadinho, Ari, Cidão and Dino could afford any shoes, let alone a shirt or a ball, until Zé Porto came up with an idea of how the Shoeless Ones could make money. They stole peanuts from the Sorocabana store and sold them outside the cinema until they had enough cash to buy shoes, shirts and even a ball. "It wasn't an official one," recalled Edson. "It didn't even have a valve... but that didn't matter. It was a ball, and it wasn't made of socks."

Now the proud owner of a ball, Edson soon took possession of something else with which he had to familiarise himself – a nickname. His dad played up front for Vasco De São Lourenco and the goalkeeper was called Bile. In young Edson's mouth the name "Bilé" became "Pilé", and then "Pelé" because of his thick *Três Corações* accent. His friends from Bauru laughed and began calling Edson "Pelé". It stuck, and then spread, first throughout Bauru, then Brazil until finally the whole world knew the name Pelé. "Good to meet you," said Ronald Reagan when introduced to the Brazilian in the early 1980s. "I'm the president of the United States. You don't need to tell me who you are – I know you're Pelé. Everybody knows!"

Everybody knew the name because by the time Pelé retired in 1977 he had achieved what no other footballer had ever achieved: he'd won the World Cup three times, scoring twice when Brazil thrashed Sweden 5-2 in the 1958 final, and netting once in the 4-1 humbling of Italy twelve years later. They were just two goals from Pelé's first-class tally of 1,283, a record that will almost certainly never be beaten.

But it was more than just goals that gave Pelé his greatness. He had speed, strength and skill, but above all he had style – the Samba style that showed up the sterility of the European game and turned Brazil into a byword for brilliance. The ball was Pelé's dance partner and where he led it followed, just as one of his dad's old socks had once done on the backstreets of Bauru.

Round plastic disc

So much could stand for the great Matt Busby, but in the end we've chosen a small round disc as our object – a simple object for a man of simple tastes, yet a man all the same who modernised English football at a time when it was firmly stuck in the past.

"I wanted method," he declared early in his managerial career, and, as always with Busby, he was true to his word.

He arrived at United in 1945 having spent most of his playing career with the club's two greatest rivals – Manchester City and Liverpool. But United fans didn't care; theirs was a club deep in ruins – literally. Old Trafford had been destroyed by the German air force, and United's reputation had been badly damaged by twice being relegated to the Second Division during the 1930s. Plus the club was £15,000 in debt with the added humiliation of having to pay Manchester City £5,000 a season, plus 10 per cent of all United's "home" gate receipts, for the privilege of sharing Maine Road while Old Trafford was slowly repaired.

Who in their right mind would want to take on such a club? United director Louis Rocca (an Italian immigrant ice cream tycoon) knew just the man. Once before he had tried to bring Busby to United, in 1930 when the Scot was a 21-year-old right half. He'd failed that time but not the second, despite the demands of the inexperienced Busby.

He told Rocca and United chairman James Gibson that he'd manage the club but only if he was in complete control.

He'd appoint coaches and scouts, buy and sell players and select the starting XI. No one else. Rocca and Gibson agreed, and Busby took over from caretaker Walter Crickmer, who was only too happy to step aside and revert to being the club secretary. "He'll build up the team and put it where it belongs," predicted Crickmer. "At the top."

Within months Busby was working his magic. The club finished runners-up to Liverpool at the end of the 1946–47 season (the first one after the war) and to Arsenal the following season. That same year United won the FA Cup Final, beating Blackpool 4-2; this was a Blackpool side featuring Stanley Matthews and Stan Mortensen. But United by now had captain Johnny Carey as right back (moved from inside right by Busby) and a front line spearheaded by the prolific Stan Pearson.

In 1949 Carey and Busby contributed their thoughts on the game to a training manual called *Football is My Goal*. Carey, referring to "Mr Busby" throughout, praised the manager for giving them the confidence to express themselves: "We have a whole team of imaginative players," wrote Carey, "players who do not wait for openings but create them."

When it was Busby's turn to contribute he was modest in what he said, writing that he was glad United "gives huge pleasure to the spectators" in the way they played the game. Not for him the dull football that characterised the English game at the time with the "stopper" at its heart, what Busby called "this stay-at-home pivot". His football philosophy, he explained, was "to have my forwards attacking, and for the rest of the team never to desist from feeding the attack. It is goals that count; without them you cannot win."

Busby then let readers in on a couple of his managerial secrets. Much of his time was devoted to team tactics and to this end he had laid out a small-scale pitch in the Old Trafford gymnasium (by 1949 the stadium was operational again). "We use round discs for the players," he continued. "With these we work out moves and counter-moves and I indicate to my players what I consider the other side's strong points. I look upon these tactical talks as a ritual. So often a match can be won that way, behind the scenes, provided your players are completely with you and have the intelligence to create a game in their minds."

Without wishing to brag, Busby then gently warned United's opponents – particularly Arsenal, whom he considered their biggest rivals – that they would only improve in the seasons to come. United's youth programme was beginning to bear fruit and the current squad "includes six local boys, all of whom cost us nothing in transfer fees."

One of these six was Roger Byrne, just 20 at the time. Nine years later Byrne was the captain of the "Busby Babes", the strongest side in the land who had won the league championship in 1952, '56 and '57. But the silverware Busby craved most was the European Cup.

Beaten in the semi-finals in 1957 by Real Madrid, United's 1958 campaign took them to Yugoslavia in February to face Red Star Belgrade. United drew 3-3, a result that was good enough to take the Babes through to the semis because of their first leg advantage. But the United side that lost to AC Milan in the semis was no longer the Busby Babes; they had been destroyed three months earlier when the aircraft returning from Belgrade crashed in Munich.

Byrne and seven of the Babes, along with a number of United staff and football reporters, were killed. Busby survived, and ten years later he finally guided United to European Cup glory; their 4-1 defeat of Benfica was the first time an English club had lifted the trophy.

Busby stepped down a year later and spent the rest of his days following United as a supporter. In October 1993 he was at Old Trafford to watch a new up and coming United side take on Hungarian side Honvéd in what by then had become the Champions League. Sat next to him was Frank Taylor, a former reporter who, like Busby, had survived the Munich Air Disaster. "Alex Ferguson is doing a great job," Busby told

Taylor. "I think they can go all the way to win the European Cup... but I know in my heart that no one can ever forget what those young boys did as the first English team to challenge Europe's best. They were unforgettable."

Pile of dirty dishes

This next object wants handling with care, unless, that is, you want the dishes to go the way of the 1950 England team – broken and in bits. But let's start our story in 1930, the year of the inaugural World Cup, a tournament that England declined to attend. Nor did they deign to appear at the following two competitions, considering it pointless – everyone knew England were the best in the world.

Even after the war the prevailing attitude in England (and indeed Britain) was that there was nothing Johnny Foreigner could teach their boys about the game, particularly when they didn't play by the book. In his 1948 biography, *Football is my Business*, England centre forward Tommy Lawton complained that "these continentals never seem to play the way we do in this country. They are rougher and do not always adhere strictly to the rules. Sometimes they try to play without the ball, which makes it a bit awkward when you are trying to play the game as she was writ."

Damn their impertinence! And it was a similar message from Reginald Moore, editor of the 1949 training manual for schoolboys *Football is My Goal*, in which he wrote: "To a lover of the game even a map of the British Isles can stir the blood... so let us hope that our present contributors are addressing themselves to many young soccer stars of the future who will maintain Britain's reputation as the seedbed of a noble sport."

But delve inside the manual and one of those contributors, the Preston and England forward Tom Finney, had a warning for men like Moore. Three years serving overseas in the armed forces had opened Finney's eyes to the footballing pedigree of "other races". He added that "we have certainly started something by spreading our national game throughout the world and will have to keep wide awake if we are to continue to come out on top in international matches."

A year later and Finney was in the England side that lined up against the United States in the Brazilian city of Belo Horizonte. Finally the English – though not the Scots – had deemed the World Cup worthy of their presence. They arrived the self-styled "Kings of Football" with the bookies installing them as 3-1 tournament favourites. England had Finney, Alf Ramsey, Wilf Mannion and the two Stans – Mortensen and Matthews (though the latter was rested for the USA match), while the Americans had a postman, undertaker and dishwasher.

The dishwasher wasn't even American. He was Joe Gaetjens, the son of a Haitian mother and a Belgian father who worked part-time as a dishwasher while studying at Columbia University in New York. Gaetjens was one of three non-Americans in the team but he promised he would apply for citizenship as soon as his studies were over.

The Americans had warmed up for the World Cup by playing a touring English amateur side in New York. They lost 1-0. The USA's goalkeeper Frank Borghi had but one hope for the match: that he "could hold them to four or five goals".

The press box was packed with British reporters, all licking their lips at the impending carnage. One paper described the Americans as "no hopers". The sole American pressman was

Dent McSkimming of the *St. Louis Post Dispatch*, who had paid his own way to Brazil.

What unfolded at the Belo Horizonte on the afternoon of 29 June 1950 remains the biggest upset in international football. The USA, the 500-1 tournament outsiders, beat England one nil with Gaetjens getting the goal seven minutes before half-time. "I took the ball and shot it, and Joe, true to form, just found a way to make something happen," recalled Walter Bahr, a high school teacher. Gaetjens got enough of his head on the ball to surprise Bert Williams in the England goal.

England huffed and they puffed in the second half but they never broke down the American defence. "Bloody ridiculous!" exclaimed a stunned Wilf Mannion at the final whistle. "Can't we play them again tomorrow?" The British press were merciless in their analysis of the England team, Charlie Buchan writing in the *News Chronicle*: "I rated the Americans on a par with a third division team like Rochdale, yet by sheer guts and enthusiasm they humbled mighty England."

But England's next game was against Spain, and when they also lost that they were on the boat back to Britain. They might as well have been travelling on the good ship *Schadenfreude* such was the glee the rest of the world felt at England's humiliation. Sure, the English had brawn, but not much in the way of footballing brain.

The States also went out after a 5-2 thrashing from Chile; they arrived back in the States ignored and unsung, and football continued to be a backwater sport for the rest of the century.

In England the result was dismissed as a fluke. It wasn't even an American team, whined the press, seeing as how three of their players were immigrants. Wilf Mannion, now the shock had sunk in, took a more sober view, warning that "there is always something to learn about soccer and having taught the game to Continental countries we are now getting back something from them." But England would prove to be slow and reluctant learners.

As for Gaetjens, his goal put an end to his dishwashing career. He signed for French Second Division side Troyes, had a spell with Racing Club de Paris and then returned to his native Haiti to play for the national team. In July 1964 he was arrested by the military police of Haitian dictator François "Papa Doc" Duvalier on trumped up charges of political activism. If Gaetjens had applied for American citizenship perhaps he would have been safe. His body was never found.

Charles Buchan's Football Monthly

"Our object is to provide a publication that will be worthy of our National game and the grand sportsmen who play and watch it."

With these words Charles Buchan launched the world's first football magazine, the eponymous *Charles Buchan's Football Monthly*, in September 1951. Conceited on Charlie's part to put his name in the title? Well, why not? One of the great English players of the early twentieth century (remember we left Charlie scheming with Herbert Chapman to turn Arsenal into England's best side), he had subsequently carved out a career as the respected football correspondent of the *News Chronicle*.

As Charlie had shown with Chapman, he was a thinker,

an innovator, a man with an eye for a good opportunity. And what he couldn't fathom as the 1940s drew to a close, was why there was no "weekly bible of the game". Cricket boasted its own bible, the *Cricketer* (founded 1921), while rugby union had had since 1946 *Rugger*, both of which featured photos, cartoons, and news and views from around the world. But football had nothing.

Having established his own publishing company in London, Charlie launched the first issue of his *Football Monthly* in September 1951 with Stanley Matthews in colour on the front cover. Inside were full-page photos of Arsenal's Joe Mercer, Manchester United's Henry Cockburn and, in a sop to the Scots, Jimmy Mason of Third Lanark. There were team photos of Newcastle (FA Cup holders) and Spurs (League champions), while one of England's finest writers, J. B. Priestley, contributed an article titled "It were Nobbut a shilling thrawn away". In his editorial Buchan predicted that "new youngsters and new tactics will make this the best season."

The magazine was a roaring success, with 60,000 copies of the first issue sold. "It has caught on so well that it was obvious something of the kind was desperately needed," commented Buchan in 1955, adding: "It is a new field for me and I am getting as much pleasure from it as I did from my playing days. One is never too old to learn."

A year later one of Buchan's former Sunderland team-mates, Raich Carter, put his name to *Soccer Star*, a weekly magazine that never challenged the dominance or prestige of Buchan's *Football Monthly*.

By the end of the 1950s *Charles Buchan's Football Monthly's* circulation was 120,000, helped in part by the founder's insistence at keeping the price at one shilling and sixpence, the cost of the first issue. Buchan died in 1961 but the magazine – sixty four pages from 1962 onwards – continued to flourish, and England's winning the 1966 World Cup sent circulation soaring to a quarter of a million.

The boom soon turned to bust, hastened, ironically, by that World Cup success. Football was now glamorous and exciting, attracting a new sort of fan to the game who was as interested as much in the celebrity player as they were in the centre forward. *Charles Buchan's Football Monthly* failed to move with the times; in one of its 1967 issues it featured a full-page photo of Sir Joseph Richards, former president of the Football League, being knighted by the Queen the previous month. There was an article from Basil Easterbrook, then nearly 50, reflecting on the day Yeovil beat Sunderland in 1949. But frankly, who cared, when there was George Best, Denis Law and Bobby Moore?

In 1968 *Goal* magazine was launched to capitalise on this trend. It was weekly, it was punchier and it was unashamedly more glamorous. Its inaugural issue had George Best on the cover along with "Win £2000 Free" in big letters; its launch party at the London Savoy was attended by "a bevy of dolly birds". George must have loved it.

Within eighteen months *Goal* was outselling *Charles Buchan's Football Monthly*. Along came *Shoot* magazine in 1969, another weekly to eat into Charlie Buchan's sales, and with the presence of *World Soccer* magazine (launched in 1960) the market was becoming too big for them all.

In 1971 Charles Buchan's name was ditched from the title in an attempt to shake off the past, but still the magazine struggled to keep up. Finally, in June 1974, after a run of 274 issues, *Football Monthly* turned off its printing presses. An editorial in the last issue blamed the closure on "the tremendous increase in the last few months of paper, printing and distribution costs." In truth, the magazine had had its day. It was old, tired and unable to keep up with the young pretenders, but *Charles Buchan's Football Monthly* was the founding father of the glossy, colour football magazine, and for that millions of boys and girls have reasons to be grateful.

Hungarian Army major's insignia

Nicknames followed Ferenc Puskás throughout his magnificent footballing career. He was "the Galloping Major" in Hungary's "Magical Magyars" side who, after their 6–3 humiliation of England in 1953, were rechristened the "new Wembley Wizards".

The "major" moniker was a nod to his rank in the Hungarian Army, though he never served in the military. Instead Puskás played for their football team, Honvéd, originally called Kispest, which is where he'd been born in 1927.

Honvéd won five Hungarian League titles between 1949 and 1955, but it was at another club, MTK (also known as Voros Lobogo) where the foundations were laid that gave rise to the dominance of the Hungary national team. The coach of MTK was Márton Bukovi who, as Jonathan Wilson explains in *Inverting the Pyramid*, devised an innovative new system in the late 1940s: Bukovi "didn't have the right style of centre forward [so] rather than trying to force unsuitable players into the position he decided it was better simply to do away with him altogether... as the centre forward dropped deeper and deeper to become an auxiliary midfielder, the two wingers pushed on to create a fluid front four."

This system was soon taken up by Gusztáv Sebes, coach of the Hungary team, and with it they won the 1952 Olympic gold medal, beating Yugoslavia 2-0 with Nándor Hidegkuti the deep-lying centre forward and Puskás and Sándor Kocsis the inside forwards.

According to Hidegkuti, coach Sebes further refined

the Hungary formation by pulling the two wingers, Zoltán Czibor and László Budai, back towards the midfield "to pick up passes to be had from [József] Bozsik and myself, and this added the final touch to the tactical development."

The first to feel the full force of this innovation was England on 25 November 1953. The English were still smarting from their shock 1-0 defeat to the USA in the 1950 World Cup and here – against the reigning Olympic champions – was the perfect opportunity to remind the rest of the world about the strength of English football.

Instead the Three Lions were mauled. Badly. Hidegkuti put the visitors one up in the first minute and though England equalised through Jackie Sewell they were 4-1 down at the break. Wembley was stunned: the famous stadium had never before seen its boys beaten. But the carnage continued after the interval, and Hungary inflicted a record 6-3 defeat on England.

"Yesterday the inevitable happened," reported *The Times* the next morning. "England at last were beaten by the foreign invader." Not just beaten, humiliated. "Now it's back to school for England," declared one British paper, while another lauded the Hungarians, calling them "The Wembley Wizards".

Puskás was singled out for particular praise. *The Times* had never seen such a skilful player; why, he'd even had the audacity to completely bamboozle England captain Billy Wright. On one occasion, noted *The Times*, "Wright went past Puskás like a fire engine going to the wrong fire."

Six months later, in May 1954, England went to Hungary for the rematch. They departed in confidence and returned in ruins, hammered 7-1, a result that remains England's heaviest defeat in international football.

While the English lion slunk off to lick its wounds and absorb the lessons of its double disaster (one of the side was Alf Ramsey, who twelve years later coached England to World Cup glory), Hungary went to the World Cup in Switzerland in high expectation. But in a shock result they lost to West

Germany in the final and the reaction in Hungary was savage. Sebes was fired, goalkeeper Gyula Grosics was imprisoned and Puskás was dropped.

The "Magical Magyars" were no more, and in 1956, shortly after Soviet Union forces had crushed the Hungarian Uprising, Puskás defected to Spain while playing in the European Cup with Honvéd. He embarked upon a new chapter in his career, joining Real Madrid, where along with Alfredo Di Stéfano Puskás formed half of the deadliest strike partnership in football. The climax came in the 1960 European Cup Final against Eintracht Frankfurt when Puskás scored four times in Real's 7-3 victory. In total Puskás scored 512 goals for Real in 528 matches and in 1962 played for Spain in the World Cup.

But it's as a Hungarian that the Galloping Major will best be remembered, and in particular the damage he did to England on that magical night at Wembley. Watching in the crowd that evening was the injured England striker Tom Finney. He later admitted: "I came away wondering to myself what we had been doing all these years."

Substitute board

OBJECT 43

We're giving our forty third object just a brief run, a cameo appearance, the chance to stretch its legs. Well, it is a substitute board and we're not sure it could have lasted the full 100 objects.

It took football ninety years before substitutes were officially allowed to come off the bench, with West Germany's Horst Eckel the first during a 1953 friendly against Saarland. He replaced the injured debutant Richard Gottinger in the midfield after thirty eight minutes, a switch that worked well for Eckel. He went on to play in Germany's World Cup Final victory over Hungary the following season; poor old Gottinger never played for his country again.

The English Football Association sanctioned substitutes for injured players at the start of the 1965–66 season (Scotland a year later) and Keith Peacock, a Charlton midfielder, had the honour of being the first. He had to come on just eleven minutes into Charlton's game against Bolton on 21 August 1965 when goalkeeper Mike Rose got injured. John Hewie replaced Rose between the posts and Peacock slotted into the defence. "I remember quite clearly I was disappointed at not playing," he said later. "Before then a spare player had travelled, in case of illness, but not got changed."

Initially substitutions, for both the FA and FIFA, were only to be made for injuries. But as Peacock explained: "After a couple of seasons there were a number of dodgy substitutions." Appreciating that officials were finding it ever harder to differentiate between a genuine injury and a "dodgy" one, the rule was changed for the start of the 1967–68 season to permit tactical substitutions. The number of substitutions permitted was raised subsequently to two, and since 1999 teams have been allowed to make up to three changes from a maximum of seven substitutes. Arguments about the most effective substitute in the history of the game could rage forever, but in any such discussion Manchester United's Ole Gunnar Solskjær would figure large. "The best substitute ever," was how then United manager Alex Ferguson described the striker who scored twenty nine of his 126 United goals having begun the game on the bench.

None was as precious as the goal he scored in the ninety third minute of the 1999 Champions League Final against Bayern Munich. Solskjær had only been on for eleven minutes but the goal won United the title. "I'd rather start games but when I was sub I tried to see the positive side," explained

Solskjær, adding: "I'd be fresh when other players were tired and I'd sit on the bench and analyse teams."

Recently, a former professional American soccer player turned egghead has published a research paper on the effectiveness of substitutions. Bret Myers, professor of management & operations at Villanova University in Pennsylvania, formulated what he called his "Decision Rule", and as the *Sunday Times* explained in an article in March 2012: "His research showed that when a team are losing, making a first sub before the fifty eighth minute, second sub before the seventy third minute and third sub before the seventy ninth minute gives them more than twice the chance of improving the score in their favour than changes made later than these times."

According to Professor Myers, Jose Mourinho, when in charge of Inter during their treble-winning season of 2009–10, followed his Decision Rule 86 per cent of the time and as a consequence the game changed in his favour on 83 per cent of those occasions.

He's not known as "The Special One" for nothing.

L'Équipe newspaper

OBJECT 44

If emotions qualified for our list then this next object would be "outrage". The outrage felt by Frenchman Gabriel Hanot the day after Wolverhampton Wanderers beat Hungarian side Honvéd at Molineux in December 1954.

Hanot, a famous French international before World War One, was the editor of the daily sports newspaper *L'Équipe* at the time, hence the inclusion of that estimable organ as one of our objects.

Having beaten Dynamo Moscow 2-1 and Spartak Moscow 4-0 earlier in the season Wolves, the English champions, then defeated Honvéd 3-2. The English went wild. This had been more than just a football match, it had been about revenge and redemption and reminding the world that England still dominated football.

Never mind that England had twice underperformed in the World Cup, had lost 6-3 to Hungary at Wembley in 1953 and then suffered a shameful 7-1 thrashing to the same opponents six months later. The sun, so declared the national press, would never set on English football.

The *Daily Express* declared Wolves the "club champions of Europe", the same phrase coined by the *Daily Mail*, while *Charles Buchan's Football Monthly* magazine celebrated the victory with a double-page spread of photographs and an exclusive interview with Wolves' midfielder Peter Broadbent, in which he promised the result wouldn't go to his head.

Hanot couldn't believe what he was hearing. Since losing to the USA in the 1950 World Cup, England had suffered one humiliation after another, but here was John Bull still bragging about his superiority. "If the English are so sure about their hegemony in football," Hanot commented, once he'd calmed down, "then this is the time to create a European tournament."

It wasn't the first time that Hanot had conceived the idea of a cross-border competition. In 1934, inspired by central Europe's Mitropa Cup in the late 1920s, he'd mooted expanding the competition further west in the continent but received scant support.

Twenty years later, however, and Europe had undergone such dramatic social and technological changes that a European club competition held much more appeal. Floodlights, television and commercial air travel would make the staging of such a tournament possible.

Hanot aired his idea in *L'Équipe*, proposing that each national federation enter one club in a knockout competition over midweek home and away legs under floodlights. The televised final would be held in Paris.

One of the first to respond was Juan Touzon, the president of the Spanish Football Association, who sent Hanot a letter in January 1955, saying: "This project appeals to me enormously and to my friend Santiago Bernabéu, the president of Real Madrid. We are ready to receive, in his stadium which has room for over 100,000 spectators, all the top teams in Europe."

Not all federations replied, so Hanot posted invitations to eighteen of Europe's strongest clubs, among them Chelsea, Real Madrid, Honvéd and AC Milan. Representatives from the clubs met in Paris in April 1955 and everyone was agreed: the European Cup would kick off the following season.

Hanot had achieved all this without the help of FIFA or UEFA (Union of European Football Associations), which had come into being the previous year. But in June 1955 Hanot handed over his vision to the new organisation who christened it the European Champion Clubs' Cup. He was 65, too old to be running such a mammoth operation while also editing a daily paper.

One of the first setbacks UEFA had to overcome was the withdrawal of Chelsea, the reigning English League champions. The Blues pulled out at the insistence of Alan Hardaker, the secretary of the Football League. "Too many wogs and Dagoes", he purportedly said of the European Cup.

Britain's sole representative in the inaugural sixteen club competition was Scottish club Hibernian. They lost in the semi-final to Reims of France, who in turn went down in a thrilling final 4-3 to Real Madrid. Forty thousand fans witnessed the final at the Parc des Princes, overwhelming confirmation that Hanot's hunch had been right: Europe was ripe for a cross-border competition.

But still the Football League thought otherwise. The

following season they tried to dissuade Manchester United entering as English champions, writing to manager Matt Busby that their "participation was not in the best interests of the League." Busby gave the reactionaries in the Football League short shrift, replying that "prestige alone demanded that the Continental challenge should be met, not avoided."

In a competition featuring twenty two clubs United made it to the semi-finals before losing 5-3 on aggregate to reigning champions Real Madrid; a combined total of 185,000 fans watched the two matches.

Such was the success of the European Cup that other cross-border competitions followed: the Inter-Cities Fairs Cup (later the UEFA Cup; now the Europa League) for the runners-up of domestic leagues, and the Cup Winners Cup, featuring the winners of European domestic cup competitions.

But it was the European Cup that captivated the continent. Ten years after its inception the tournament had swelled to thirty clubs, including champions from Malta, Ireland and Luxembourg. Three years later, in 1968, an English club won the cup for the first time – Matt Busby's Manchester United. This time Gabriel Hanot had no problem with the English newspapers boasting they possessed the best club side in Europe.

Floodlights

OBJECT 45

You'll recall that in discussing Herbert Chapman we mentioned in passing his belief that floodlights could benefit football. He wasn't the first, but it was to be more than twenty years after the death of the Arsenal man-ager that football finally gave the floodlight the green light.

By a strange quirk of fate, football's first floodlit game was in the same year Chapman was born – 1878 – and it was just down the road from his home in Rotherham. On the evening of 14 October four Siemens arc lamps were hoisted up into the cold Sheffield night sky at Bramall Lane atop 30ft wooden towers. It was the proud boast of the match programme distributed to each of the 20,000 spectators that "the electric light to be used for the illumination of the ground will be equal to 8,000 standard candles."

The match itself was unremarkable, a team called the Reds beating the Blues by two goals to nil, but the effect of the arc lamps was truly astonishing. In describing the "new light" (gaslight was the traditional method of illuminating rooms) the *Sheffield & Rotherham Independent* wrote the next day that "everybody seemed highly pleased with the result of the experiment, the light being most brilliant and effective."

But the successful use of floodlights at Bramall Lane was an exception. Other experiments with artificial light at grounds around the country ended in power failure and, in addition, the cost of deploying four lamps was prohibitive. Like a team of gentlemen amateurs, floodlights were soon consigned to football's past.

Despite advances in electrical lighting, the Football Association was adamant there was no future in floodlighting, passing a resolution in 1930 expressly banning their use. Chapman felt differently. He installed some lights at Arsenal's training ground in the early '30s so they could practise in all weathers.

Still the FA refused to countenance the idea of floodlights, even after an infamous occasion at Stamford Bridge in December 1938. Chelsea were hosting Charlton Athletic when a blanket of smog descended, prompting the referee to abandon the match. "Unfortunately," wrote Charlton goalkeeper Sam Bartram in the 1949 book *Football is My Goal*, "I did not hear his whistle because the crowd were making too much noise; they couldn't see a thing either. I was standing there with my hands on my knees and peering through the yellow murk when a policeman informed me that the game had been stopped. I returned to the dressing room to find all the other players in the bath; the game had been over for ten minutes!"

In the end it was the inexorable march of progress that won the day for floodlit football. The early 1950s were vastly different to the 1930s, both socially and technologically. Quite apart from the power that electric lights could now generate, people had televisions, they could travel quite easily on passenger planes and there existed a new generation called "teenagers" who craved entertainment. As we saw with our last object, the man who understood best how football could profit from all three innovations was Gabriel Hanot.

He gave Europe its first meaningful club competition and in turn the European Cup gave floodlit football its stage. Soon midweek matches under floodlights were being played across Europe; people wondered why it hadn't been done before. There was a glamour to games under floodlights, as the man from *The Times* wrote in February 1956, the morning after Portsmouth and Newcastle had contested the first English League match under artificial light (Scotland followed suit two weeks later). "There is a dramatic, theatrical quality about it," said *The Times*. "The pace of the game seems accentuated, flowing patterns of approach play take on sharper, more colourful outlines."

In essence, floodlit football was sexy and, in tandem with television, it revolutionised football. Floodlights offered television the possibility of broadcasting matches at times other than Saturday afternoon. It could be an alternative to the cinema; it could be a real money-spinner. The Newcastle and Portsmouth players had recognised that from the start. Asked to play under lights they complained about the unsocial hours; after all, in effect they were working a night shift. They were paid an extra £3 each for the inconvenience.

Typewriter

As we near the half time whistle in our tour of football's 100 objects it's time to take stock of how, nearly a century on from the formation of the Football League, the newspapers' relationship with football has altered. Remember how one Fleet Street rag, the *Sun and Central Press*, covered the inaugural FA Cup Final (object number 3) in 1872 in three thrifty sentences? That had all changed by the early twentieth century with the burgeoning market in "Pinks" and "Green 'Uns", the Saturday night papers that carried the day's football results. The accompanying reports were more than three lines but nonetheless they were usually as dry as the ground on the opening day of the season.

That altered in the inter war years as the circulation war between newspapers such as the *Daily Mirror, Daily Express* and the *Daily News* grew more intense. Editors wanted reports that were punchier and more opinionated, and if they were written by former players so much the better.

The first great ex-player turned pressman was Charlie Buchan, the former England forward who was Herbert Chapman's first signing when he took over at Arsenal in 1925. Buchan retired three years later and as a farewell gift the Gunners' squad clubbed together and bought him a brief-case and writing set. Buchan had need of both in the next stage of his life – football correspondent for the *Daily News* (which became later the *News Chronicle*).

He brought to the job an empathy for the player hitherto absent in football reporters. "The number of goals I scored from my [press] seat was phenomenal," he remarked. "Chances look so easy from a position high up in the stand. They aren't so simple on the actual field." Buchan was instrumental in establishing the Football Writers' Association in 1947, which the following year instigated its Footballer of the Year Award, at the time the most prestigious award a player could win in the English game.

One of the players on whose Buchan's pen touched was the great Manchester City goalkeeper Frank Swift. He followed Buchan into journalism after his retirement from the game in 1949, joining a press pack that was at the height of its power in covering football.

The game had never been so popular (post-war aggregate English League attendances peaked at 41.27 million in the 1948–49 season) and with television still a luxury for most households in the 1950s newspapers were how fans kept up to speed with their favourite team. Advances in photography and communications – not to mention the portable typewriter – made life far easier for journalists in the 1950s.

Football correspondents – not just on the national papers but the influential regional titles, too – were respected for their analysis by the public and the players. It helped that journalists such as Swift and Buchan had played the game at the highest level, but even those reporters who hadn't still enjoyed strong relationships with the men about whom they wrote. The players trusted the reporters, valued their judgement, and were happy to sit down and chat. There was never the whiff of any scandal. Sport was solely for the back pages and, anyway, as the venerable Henry Rose of the *Daily Express* declared to all young trainees on the paper, "never write anything of which you might later be ashamed."

Rose was killed with the cream of the Busby Babes in the Munich Air Disaster of 1958. So was Frank Swift of the *News of the World*, Eric Thompson of the *Daily Mail* and the *Manchester Evening Chronicle*'s Alf Clarke, who had played for United's amateur side. In all, eight of Britain's finest football reporters were killed in the crash.

Writing in *Football Nation: Sixty Years of the Beautiful Game*, Andrew Ward and John Williams claim that the Munich Air Disaster was a "watershed" for football reporting. The reporters who replaced the dead men came from a younger, brasher generation, and their editors were increasingly demanding stories about what went on off the pitch as well as on it.

Yet while the relationship was starting to alter it didn't happen overnight. The 1960s was still a decade when footballers and reporters liked and respected each other. Jimmy Greaves, one of the most famous players of the 1960s and a man with a thirst, recalled that "there was a gentleman's agreement about what could and could not be written. The press have seen minor indiscretions on the part of players, but kept them to themselves."

Greaves added that some of his "closest friends" were reporters, among them Ian Wooldridge, Brian Glanville and Ken Jones. Hugh McIlvanney, on the other hand, was a confidante of George Best in his early years, who sometimes helped the Irishman prop up the bar of the Brown Bull pub after Manchester United matches.

But it was Best more than any other footballer who inadvertently ruptured irrevocably the cosy relationship between player and pressman. He was more than just a footballer, he was the "Fifth Beatle", a celebrity. And celebrity sold. By the 1970s Best was being hounded by the press, his every dalliance and misdemeanour splashed over the pages of the tabloids. The public lapped it up, and so the papers began turning their spotlight into every nook and cranny of the game.

Bill Shankly statue

The 8-foot statue of Bill Shankly that stands proudly as object number 47 shows the Scot with his arms raised in triumph and a Liverpool scarf wrapped round his neck. The pose, which was unveiled outside Anfield in December 1997, was based on a real life incident in 1973: as Liverpool were parading the League Championship trophy in front of the Kop, a young fan had thrown his scarf on to the pitch in the hope that "Shanks" might pick it up. A policeman got there first, and kicked the scarf off the grass. "Hey," shouted Shankly to the policeman. "It's only a scarf to you, but it's the boy's life." Shankly then gathered the scarf and looped it over his shoulders.

"Shanks was always about the people and this statue sums that up," said the then Liverpool manager Roy Evans in 1997, who had begun his coaching career under Shankly. "The legend and foundations were laid in stone by Shanks... there were other people who did their bit, but Shanks was the football man, the front man and he was fantastic at it."

Shankly arrived at Anfield in 1959 when the club was at a low ebb. Stuck in the Second Division, Liverpool felt like a club in decline. Even their famous Kop terracing lacked vitality, the writer Arthur Hopcraft describing it at the time as "hideously uncomfortable... the steps are as greasy as a school playground lavatory. The air is rancid with beer and onions and belching and worse." Attendances had fallen to 30,000 or fewer and fans wondered how they'd ever again challenge Manchester United.

There were striking similarities between Shankly's predicament and that of Matt Busby when he'd become manager of Manchester United in 1945. Both were Scots from humble backgrounds who had enjoyed solid, if unspectacular, playing careers. Shankly had won two FA Cups with Preston North End in the 1930s and was, according to teammate Tom Finney, "a larger than life character."

Shankly began his coaching career at Carlisle in 1949 and moved through a succession of lower league clubs before arriving at Anfield a decade later. In all that time, Shankly had been watching the success of the Busby Babes, learning from them and from the nascent European Cup. In an article to welcome him to the city, the *Liverpool Echo* wrote in 1959: "Shankly is a disciple of the game as it is played by the continentals. The man out of possession, he believes, is just as important as the man with the ball at his feet."

Shankly also believed in assembling a good backroom staff, a coterie of coaches to aid and assist in his ambitions. He was lucky to find two of the best in Bob Paisley and Joe Fagan, and together the three of them transformed Liverpool. Despite his reputation for being "larger than life", Shankly set very high standards; he pushed himself hard and he expected others to do likewise.

It took a couple of seasons for Shankly's system to work, but they returned to the First Division in 1962 and two years later were champions. In 1965 they won the FA Cup, and in 1966 they were League champions again. By now Liverpool were playing in all red (up until 1964 they wore white shorts) because, as striker Ian St. John later remarked, "Shankly thought the colour scheme would carry psychological impact – red for danger, red for power."

There were other innovations introduced by Shankly: the sweat-box, air travel to away games and, of course, the legendary "boot-room" where tactics were discussed and strategies formulated.

Liverpool won their third League title under Shankly in

1973, and in 1974 they were on course for the Double before being edged out of the title race by Leeds. They won the FA Cup, though, beating Newcastle 3-0. The heart of that team would be there three years later when Liverpool beat Borussia Mönchengladbach to win their first European Cup.

But not Shankly. He had stepped down in July 1974, worn out by fifteen years spent restoring Liverpool's reputation. Arguably Shankly was the first manager to resign due to the pressures of the job. Once football management had been little more than maintaining cordial relations with the board of directors and settling changing room disputes; but the arrival of money into the game in the 1960s shone a new spotlight on the manager's role that was bright, fierce and relentless.

In an interview about Shankly with the *Guardian* in 2009, former Liverpool striker John Toshack reflected on what it was like to play under him. "He inspired us in every way," said Toshack. "In his belief in Liverpool Football Club, the standards he set for himself and for the club, the intensity that he went about his job. His quote about football being more important than life or death, he really felt that way. He rammed it into us how important it was to be playing for Liverpool, how privileged we were to be playing for these people."

Cork

OBJECT
48

Why a cork for our forty eighth object? Well, that will all be explained in due course, but first cast your mind back to object 22, the telephone, and how it had been used by two Middlesbrough directors in 1905 to inform the local paper that the club had just bought Alf Common in the first

four-figure transfer deal. The Football League's response was to impose a maximum wage of £4 a week for the top English players, a sum that by 1947 had increased to a miserly £12. England striker Tommy Lawton still considered this a derisory amount, as did his peers when the Football League raised the ceiling to £17 ten years later (£14 in the summer), which was equivalent to what "an electrician on overtime could then expect" – and they didn't have the pressure of performing in front of thousands of fans every week. "Most of the first class clubs are making a great deal of money out of the game," complained England striker Wilf Mannion, "and at present the men who provide the entertainment and thrills are being left out in the cold."

In 1958, under pressure from the charismatic and aggressive new chairman of the Professional Footballers' Association (PFA) Jimmy Hill, the Football League raised the maximum wage still further from £17 to £20. But this wasn't enough for Hill: he wanted the wage cap scrapped altogether and in addition he sought an end to the "retain-and-transfer" system that for well over half a century had shackled players to the clubs in possession of their licence, denying them the chance to move to another club when their existing contract expired. Hill called this system "a slave contract" and he wasn't far wrong. On one infamous occasion the Barnsley goalkeeper Harry Hough had requested a transfer to a certain club, only to be told by chairman Joe Richards: "You go where I tell you."

After a lengthy and bitter dispute with the Football League, Hill was still no closer to seeing an end to the maximum wage so at the start of 1961 he called a strike for Saturday 21 January. The League responded by telling clubs to bring the matches forward to the Friday, a reaction that brought them widespread ridicule in the national papers.

The government stepped into arbitrate, and for five hours on 18 January the PFA and the Football League exchanged views at the Ministry of Labour. When they emerged, Hill had won a partial victory: the maximum wage was no more. Within hours of the announcement Fulham had hiked up the wages of star player Johnny Haynes from £20 to £100. On the issue of the transfer system, however, the Football League refused to negotiate.

What Hill needed was a *cause célèbre* – and he got it in the slight shape of Newcastle United inside forward George Eastham. The Blackpool-born Eastham had joined the Magpies in 1956, playing regularly for four seasons until he fell out with the club in 1959. There were several minor grievances, but essentially Eastham wanted a fresh start with Arsenal; Newcastle wouldn't give him one and, under the retain-and-transfer system, held him to his contract, with one director telling the player he'd rather see him shovelling coal for the rest of his life than run out at Highbury.

Eastham, acting under the advice of the PFA, went on strike at the start of the 1959–60 season, reflecting later that "our contract could bind us to a club for life. Most people called it the 'slavery contract'. We had virtually no rights at all. It was often the case that the guy on the terrace not only earned more than us – though there's nothing wrong with that – he had more freedom of movement than us. People in business or teaching were able to hand in their notice and move on. We weren't. That was wrong."

Eastham moved south, for a while making a living selling cork in Surrey. Although Newcastle finally agreed to sell him to Arsenal for £47,500 in October 1960, Eastham had decided to take the club to court on behalf of future players who might find themselves in a similar predicament.

With the PFA financing the costs of the case, the case of Eastham v. Newcastle United was heard at the High Court in 1963. Mr Justice Wilberforce found largely in favour of Eastham, praising the PFA for their "convincing" evidence and agreeing that the retain-and-transfer system was unreasonable. "The retention system is, in my judgement, more of a restraint than is necessary to prevent richer clubs from buying all the best players," said Wilberforce.

In the face of the judgement, the Football League drew up a new code of practice establishing a transfer tribunal at which the PFA would be represented at any dispute between a player and a club. The clubs' sway over players had been weakened by George Eastham's stance, but it would be another thirty two years before the balance of power shifted dramatically in favour of the players.

"I suppose you can say that I was the father of the modern transfer market," said Eastham (who won nineteen England caps while with Arsenal) in a 2008 interview. "The money players receive these days is great in a sense. They won't have to grovel after they stop playing like we had to do in my day."

OBJECT 49

Real Madrid shirt

There's a legend about the first words Alfredo Di Stéfano said to Amancio when the Spanish striker joined Real Madrid in 1962. Arriving from Deportivo de La Coruña in 1962, Amancio wanted to know why his Real shirt had no shield on the breast. "You've got to sweat in it first, sonny," snarled Di Stéfano.

Sweat in it Amancio did for the next fourteen years, becoming one of the stars of the Bernabéu – but still he remained in the shadow of the great Alfredo Di Stéfano. During his time at the club – 1953 to 1964 – the man they called "The Blond Arrow" helped Real to eight Spanish League titles and five consecutive European Cup crowns. The Spanish club won the competition every year from its inauguration in 1955–56 to 1959–60. Five consecutive European Cup titles! The three consecutive titles won first by Ajax and then Bayern Munich in the 1970s are the closest any club has come to emulating Real's feat.

At the heart of the domination was Di Stéfano. He scored in each of the five European Cup finals, including a hat-trick in the 7-3 annihilation of Eintracht Frankfurt in 1960.

"The greatness of Di Stéfano," reflected Miguel Muñoz, coach of Real in the 1950s, "was that, with him in your side, you had two players in every position."

En route to the 1957 triumph, Real overcame Manchester United in two hard-fought legs. These were the great Busby Babes, and even though they held the Spanish club to a 2-2 draw at Old Trafford they went down 3-1 in the Bernabéu. Di Stéfano scored the second, and watching from the United dugout was a young Bobby Charlton. "Wherever he is on the field he is in position to take the ball, you can see his influence on everything that is happening," Charlton recalled later. "I had never seen such a complete footballer. In later years I would know Pelé as an opponent and a friend and I learned about his greatness, but that first impact of Di Stéfano crossed all boundaries. It was as though he had set up his own command centre at the heart of the game. He was as strong as he was subtle. You just could not keep your eyes off him."

Though Madrid had been formed in 1902, it wasn't until 1920 that King Alfonso XIII granted them royal patronage, allowing them to add "Real" to their name. In the years following Spain's Civil War, as the country slowly began to heal its wounds, it was Barcelona who emerged as the dominant force in Spanish football. But as the Catalan club celebrated three League titles in the late 1940s, so Real began its rise.

Santiago Bernabéu had become president of Real in 1943, laying foundations for the future literally and metaphorically. He persuaded Spanish banks to loan the club money to build a new stadium – the Nuevo Estadio Chamartín (later renamed the Bernabéu) which could accommodate 125,000 spectators – and he used his influence with Franco to benefit the club in other ways. Money was never a problem for Bernabéu and soon Real was signing up world-class stars.

The biggest was Di Stéfano, who arrived at the club in 1953 after Bernabéu had pinched him from under the noses of Barcelona. The Argentine was soon the side's totem, gifted, indefatigable and always game for a fight.

He scored goals (307 during his time at Real) but Di Stéfano also never gave up. He knew the Madrid fans wouldn't accept that. "It wants the team to fight," he said of the supporters. "It wants it to win... but it wants it to win first and then to play."

Real swept all before them in those five glorious years of European triumph which culminated in the astonishing 7-3 thrashing of Eintracht Frankfurt. Real Madrid put Spanish football on the map, but their greatest achievement was what they did to the image of Spain as a whole: they polished her up, as if she were a battered old trophy, giving her a lustre after twenty years of political isolation. "Real Madrid is a style of sportsmanship," said the country's Foreign Minister Fernando Maria Castiella in the late 1950s. "It is the best embassy we have ever had."

Door bolt

If you or I were Italian, we would call this next object *catenaccio*, but as we're not we'll call it a "door bolt". This was the nickname given to the defensive system perfected to a stupefying degree by Inter Milan coach Helenio Herrera in the 1960s. Using it he guided Inter through the most successful era in their history, winning two European Cups and three Serie A titles. He also sent a generation of football fans to sleep. As John Foot noted in his entertaining *Calcio: A History of Italian Football*, *catenaccio* came to "symbolize all that is bad about football: defensive play, aggressive fouling, cynicism."

So let's get this over with as quickly as possible, for distasteful as it may be to the true football *aficionado*, *catenaccio* is evidently influential enough to warrant inclusion as one of 100 objects.

Despite being synonymous with the Italian game, *catenaccio* originated in Switzerland in the 1930s under Austrian coach Karl Rappan. A Swiss journalist dubbed it *verrou* (doorbolt in French), and the defensive sweeper who operated in front of the goalkeeper and behind the defenders was the *verrouilleur*. Rappan used the system with success in League football before employing it with similar effectiveness with the Swiss national team at the 1938 World Cup, beating Germany in the opening round.

Upon the resumption of European football after the Second World War the contagion of *catenaccio* had spread to Italy where two coaches – Giuseppe Viani at Salernitana and Nereo Rocco of Triestina – used it to great effect. Rocco proved such an adroit coach of *catenaccio* that he was hired by AC Milan on the back of it; their defeat of Benfica in the 1963 European Cup Final was a victory for negativity but it delighted Helenio Herrera, who saw the win as a validation of what he had been coaching for three seasons.

Nicknamed *Il Mago* (The Magician), Herrera came to Europe from Argentina and played club football in France throughout the 1930s. After cutting his coaching teeth in Spain (including Barcelona), Herrera took over at Inter in 1960 and set about honing *catenaccio*. The ideology was simple: play defensively, cautiously and look to score on the counter-attack. Then, one goal to the good, pull everyone back and defend the lead. John Foot describes how Herrera ordered one of his frontmen to drop back and mark their opponent's centre forward. This then "freed up one of the central defenders to act as sweeper. That was it. Put so simply, this doesn't appear to be a revolution, but it was. The extra man in defence seemed to make a difference, frustrating the opposition and bringing them further forward, and freeing space for rapid counter-attacking."

Herrera was one the most methodical coaches that the world had ever seen. Nothing was left to chance in preparing his side and discipline was paramount. Then there were his strange rituals, such as holding out a ball before the start of a match and having his players run up to it chanting "I must have it! I must have it". But there was clearly method in the madness and Inter beat Real Madrid 3-1 to win the 1964 European Cup. The following season they defended their title, beating Benfica by a goal to nil.

Dark tales emerged subsequently, alleging Herrera gave his players performance-enhancing drugs and used his influence to rig matches. They remain allegations. As for *catenaccio*, although its bastard offspring is still alive today, it's far less dangerous to football than the Frankenstein created by Herrera. What killed off the beast was Celtic's wondrous performance in the 1967 European Cup Final when they overran the Inter midfield by playing in an attractive, expansive style. "*catenaccio* didn't die with La Grande Inter," writes Jonathan Wilson, "but the myth of its invincibility did. Celtic had proved attacking football had a future."

The Kop

OBJECT 51

We've seen with object 49 how Bill Shankly transformed Liverpool Football Club, now it's time to discover how the Kop revolutionised football crowds in England, and consequently the rest of the world.

The Kop came about in 1906 when Liverpool, the reigning First Division champions, decided they needed a stadium that reflected their success. As part of the renovation of Anfield (of course, designed on the draft table of architect Archibald Leitch), a brick and cinder banking was built at the Walton Breck Road end of the ground. This terracing could hold 27,000 supporters and was opened to the Liverpool faithful for the game against Stoke City on 1 September 1906.

According to the *Liverpool Echo*, in an article to mark the terrace's centenary, it was their sports editor Ernest Edwards who came up with the idea of christening it something other than the Walton Breck Road end. His idea was "Spion Kop", explained the *Echo*, "the small hill in the South African province of Natal where a bloody battle had taken place in the Boer War on January 24th 1900."

The battle had been a disaster for the British, and for the many Liverpudlians who had lost their lives in the defeat to the Boers. Spion Kop was soon shortened to "The Kop" and for twenty years the mound remained untouched.

In the summer of 1928 the Kop got a roof, making it 425 feet wide and 80 feet high, the largest covered terrace in the country. "The roof helped turn the Kop into a cathedral of sound and just 50 seconds into the opening game with Bury the acoustics were tested as debutant Billy Millar headed home," said the *Liverpool Echo*.

A quarter of a century after the Kop was covered, Liverpool were relegated to the Second Division, where they remained until 1962. Shankly brought them back to the top flight and the Reds then embarked upon an era of unprecedented success.

It was an era, too, when the Kop was enjoying its heyday. "The sight of 27,000 fans packed in, swaying and chanting, became renowned throughout the world of football," recalled the *Liverpool Echo*. Shankly reckoned that the noise generated by the Kop was worth a goal to his side every game. It was, said Shankly, as if that end of Anfield could "suck the ball" into the opposition net.

By the mid-1960s Liverpool fans were frequently

regaling their team with choruses from Beatles' songs such as "She Loves You", and soon they had adopted Gerry and the Pacemakers' "You'll Never Walk Alone" as the official anthem of the Kop. One of the most boisterous nights of the '60s was in May 1965 when Inter Milan arrived at Anfield for the semi-final of the European Cup. Liverpool had won the FA Cup four days earlier and the Kop was in fine voice as the trophy was paraded round the ground before kick-off. "The Italians thought they had heard noise in the San Siro, I can tell you they had never experienced anything like the noise from the Anfield fans as the cup was carried round," recalled Liverpool's Tommy Smith. "When we heard the crowd I could understand how intimidating it was for the Italians." When Inter ran out they were greeted with a chorus of "Go back to Italy", sung to the tune of "Santa Lucia".

When the BBC *Panorama* team visited Anfield in the 1960s, reporter John Morgan stood in the crowd and explained how "an anthropologist studying the Kop would find it as rich and mystifying as any Polynesian culture, their rhythmic swaying is an organised ritual. They seem to know intuitively when to begin singing. Throughout the match, they invent new words to old Liverpool songs, with adulatory, cruel or bawdy comments, but their heroes are acclaimed in Roman style."

Kopites, as they were called, gathered in pubs on Saturday lunchtimes to agree on which songs would be sung that afternoon. Song sheets were then distributed on the Kop and the singing began. The Kop was a microcosm of the city of Liverpool, containing the good, the bad and the mad, like the fan who kept a tally of how many corner kicks the Reds won in a season.

Then there was the ritual accorded to every new player Liverpool signed. Kevin Keegan, a Liverpool legend in the 1970s, recalled his debut in 1971. "The self-appointed representative of the Kop came on the field to greet me," said Keegan. "This Kopite was a nice old fellow with no harm in him. He kissed me, then kissed the grass in front of the Kop and went back to join his mates in the crowd."

In the 1970s the wit of Kopites had a new outlet other than singing – on the banners and flags that Liverpool supporters began waving after the fashion on the continent. None surpassed the banner made in tribute to defender Joey Jones after Liverpool had beaten Borussia Mönchengladbach in the 1977 European Cup Final: "Joey ate the frogs' legs, made the Swiss roll and now he's munching Gladbach."

The Kop is long gone now, replaced with an all-seater grandstand, but football owes it a debt of gratitude. On the Kop the game made contact with popular culture for the first time and watching a match became more than just a pastime: it became a passion and an obsession.

World Cup Willie mascot

OBJECT
52

Our next object – and no sniggering at the back – is a Willie. Or to give it its full name "World Cup Willie". Described by the *Daily Mirror* in 1966 as "a lion with a Beatle haircut, a Union Jack jersey and an address somewhere in Yogi Bear's Jellystone Park," Willie was the official mascot for the 1966 World Cup finals held in England. It was the first time a mascot had graced the tournament and Willie's presence in England was strangely at odds with the conservatism that so characterised the English game in the 1950s. The FA and the Football League had shown a stunning disdain for many of the sport's key innovations: floodlights, the pools, television coverage and, above all, the new European club competitions. Even when England was awarded the hosting rights to the 1966 tournament there appeared a reluctance on the part of the FA to embrace the

World Cup to its bosom. There were no new stadiums built and no desire to use the tournament to showcase England and the English game – except for their World Cup Willie.

The FA hired Walter Tuckwell & Associates to design a mascot for the tournament and officials briefed commercial artists Reg Hoye and Richard Culley at the firm's London offices. As Culley later explained: "We were given the task of creating a mascot to exploit merchandising beyond the insignia of the Jules Rimet trophy which was initially all we had to work with." In less than five minutes the pair had rejected a bulldog for a lion, and in another five minutes Hoye had sketched World Cup Willie. In an era when British identity wasn't as divided as it is today, the fact that Willie was wearing the Union Jack Flag and not the English Cross of St George was irrelevant to Dennis Follows, the FA secretary, who approved the design.

It took a while for World Cup Willie to get off the ground. The conservative English public, not unlike the FA, was suspicious of innovation, and anyhow supporters didn't want mementos of a tournament few expected their boys to win. England had never progressed beyond the quarter-final stage in their four previous World Cup appearances and throughout the 1966 tournament their squad was more workmanlike than wondrous. As Brian Granville writes in *A History of the World Cup*: "Though England may not at any time have matched the technique and artistry of the Brazilian teams which have won the two previous competitions, though they may have struggled all the way to the semi-final putting effort above creativity, hard work above joy in playing, the team had its undoubted stars."

These included goalkeeper Gordon Banks, captain and left half Bobby Moore, inside forward Bobby Charlton, and midfielder Alan Ball. There was also Geoff Hurst, the young centre forward who replaced Jimmy Greaves from the quarter-finals onwards.

Coach of the side was Alf Ramsey, an awkward, insular man who often seemed at odds with the world. But he was a good coach and he steered England through the opening matches, albeit with a distinct lack of excitement. Goalless against Uruguay, England then defeated Mexico 2-0, France by the same score line and in a brutal quarter-final against Argentina the hosts had Hurst to thank for their 1-0 victory.

Charlton scored both goals in the 2-1 defeat of Portugal in the semi-final and suddenly England were through to the final for the first time – and against West Germany.

Meanwhile, sales of World Cup Willie merchandise were going through the roof, with everything from T-shirts to money boxes to soft toys hitting the shops. There was even a World Cup Willie pale ale sold in pubs. Even the poor quality of some of the merchandise didn't appear to affect its popularity. "Manufacturing techniques were much cruder back in the 1960s," explained Culley in an interview with licensemag. com in 2006. "Stamps and moulds weren't effective and the overall quality suffered. Shipping times were much longer which meant it was hard to judge supply and demand. As the merchandise grew in popularity some lines would sell out, which actually increased the premium of the brand."

But what best increased the premium of the brand was Geoff Hurst's hat-trick in the 4-2 defeat of West Germany in the final. Now everyone wanted a piece of World Cup Willie, so much so that in total over 10 million items of merchandise had been produced a few months after England's triumph. As Culley explained, "there was no style guide and Reg Hoye would draw Willie to order."

Soon the whole country was singing along to Lonnie Donegan's hit single "World Cup Willie" and Prime Minister Harold Wilson was boasting that "we only win the World Cup under Labour." Wilson was right about that but wrong in believing England's success in 1966 would transform the country's fortunes. Britain continued its slow decline as a major political and economic power in the years that followed, mirrored by the decline of the England football team. As David Goldblatt points out: "England have not stopped talking about 1966 since and, for all the dismay at the ever-lengthening gap since England won the World Cup, it allowed the nation to live more comfortably with its post-imperial decline. The empire, the right to the number one spot, had gone, but England was still good enough occasionally to occupy it."

Alas, the legacy left by World Cup Willie has been just as painful, though for different reasons. World Cup merchandising is now huge business (it was estimated that the 2006 tournament in Germany generated more than $2 billion in merchandise sales alone) and mascots have been inflicted on the world at every successive World Cup since 1966. In the 1974 event in Germany it was two little boys, "Tip and Tap", and for 2014 Brazil had Fuleco, a three-banded armadillo (not a real one). Perhaps the nadir was reached in 2002 when co-hosts Japan and South Korea came up with Ato, Kaz and Nik, collectively known as "The Spheriks".

They were computer-generated, a far cry from Reg Hoye's hand-drawn Willie, which still stands up to the test of time nearly half a century later.

Sombrero

"I spent a lot of money on booze, birds, and fast cars. The rest I just squandered."

Ah, wee Georgie Best always did have the gift of the gab. The line above was a gem, as was the one about how "in 1969 I gave up women and alcohol — it was the worst 20 minutes of my life."

The jokes just added to Best's charm, the

fallen idol with the feet of clay which once had been the feet of one of the greatest players to grace the game. Some of Best's fans claimed the Northern Irishman was the greatest ever, a description that Pelé endorsed. Pelé was most probably indulging Best's ego. He was a great player, arguably the best to come from the British Isles and possibly even Europe, but to compare Best to Pelé or Maradona is as fanciful as claiming the Argentine never scored with his hand.

But what Best did have that his rivals didn't was glamour, a commodity that carried his appeal beyond the terraces and into the world of celebrity where Best thrived. He was nicknamed the "Fifth Beatle", he rubbed shoulders with actors and he slept with a bevy of beauty queens. And to think it all began with a sombrero.

Before Best came along, footballers – particularly in Britain – had been tough and taciturn, men like Billy Wright, Jackie Milburn and Tom Finney, all pillars of their local community. Wright married a beauty, one of the pop-singing Beverley Sisters, but the marriage was happy and solid and Wright took a job as head of sport in a television company.

Best had exceptional talent and a beautiful face, but he also had the good fortune to be at his best in the '60s, a decade when football and culture became sexy. Writing in *Football Nation: Sixty Years of the Beautiful Game*, Andrew Williams and John Ward assert that the likes of George Best and Mike Summerbee were representative of an "emergence of a new type of footballer: much more self-sufficient, more stylish, a little bit more brash, a regular at boutiques and nightclubs... they also realised that there was no way back to the pre-Beatle days of deference and austerity." The fact that more and more houses had televisions only enhanced Best's appeal.

Manchester United scout Bob Bishop was the first to spot Best's potential when he was still just 15, sending a telegram to manager Matt Busby in which he said: "I think I've found you a genius." He had. Best might have been rejected by his local club in Belfast for being too skinny and small but Busby recognised brilliance and gave the teenager his debut against West Bromwich Albion in September 1963.

Best was soon a standout player for United, even in a side containing greats such as Bobby Charlton and Denis Law. Arguably his finest performance in a United shirt was in March 1966, in the European Cup quarter-final away game against Benfica. The Portuguese club were the dominant force in Europe at the time, unbeaten at home in the European Cup, but Best – still just 19 – destroyed them, scoring twice in the first twelve minutes as United ran riot in a 5-1 victory.

But perhaps that was the night Best's fame, unlike the ball he so majestically controlled, began to run away from him. The Portuguese media dubbed him "*El Beatle*" and he arrived back in England wearing a sombrero, sunglasses and a triumphant smile. Television, which had broadcast his astonishing performance against Benfica, now used him to advertise everything from sausages to trousers. He bought a white Jaguar sports car, grew his hair long and opened a boutique with Summerbee, and began to be seen in the company of beautiful women. As one teammate was heard to say: "He has to be a great footballer to get away with that haircut and that outfit."

For the moment football still took precedence. Having helped United win the English title in 1965 and again in '67, Best was on hand to score one of the goals in their 4-1 thrashing of Benfica in the final of the 1968 European Cup. It was the first time an English side had won the competition and Best was further rewarded when he named the 1968 European Footballer of the Year.

Best would never again scale such heights as he did in 1968. Women and alcohol began assuming as much importance as football. He slept with actresses, models and beauty queens. "I used to go missing a lot," he later reflected. "Miss Canada, Miss United Kingdom, Miss World."

In 1972 Best walked out on United, returning for a brief spell before quitting the club for good in January 1974. He was 27. For the rest of the decade Best flitted from club to club and from woman to woman. Drinking was the one constant in his life, but by the 1980s it was bringing him to his knees. "Drink is the only opponent I've been unable to beat," Best said later.

Implants in his stomach failed to curb his excesses, and in 1984 Best was jailed for three months for drink-driving and assault. He left prison promising to reform but he couldn't. He drank right up to the end, 25 November 2005, when Best died from illnesses linked to alcoholism in a London hospital. He was 59. The tributes poured in for the Irishman, some heartfelt, some fulsome, some downright foolish. None shed much light on the real George Best, which was what he would have wanted. He was a sensitive soul underneath all the glamour, with a gift for one-liners that warded off anyone getting too close. In one rare moment of public introspection, Best once said: "That thing about being an icon, the fifth Beatle, I just found it so freaky. I even found it difficult to watch myself playing on TV because I couldn't identify with the person on the screen. I couldn't get to grips with it. It was as if it was all happening to someone else."

Airplane boarding pass

OBJECT 54

Zaire was overjoyed. They had beaten Morocco 3–0 in their final qualifying match and reached the World Cup, only the third African nation to do so after Egypt in 1934 and Morocco in 1970. President Mobutu decreed that the squad should be handsomely rewarded, and rewarded they were, as the *Guardian* newspaper reported at the time: "Each player and reserve was awarded a house, a car and 15 days holiday anywhere in the world."

It's easy to be wise in hindsight but perhaps the players should have used their boarding passes, the object of this article, to fly as far away as possible from West Germany, host of the 1974 World Cup. For when Zaire did make it to the finals they were abject, embarrassing not just themselves but the whole of Africa at a time when the continent was struggling to break through onto the world stage.

Of course, Zaire weren't entirely to blame for what happened. Zaire captain Mantantu Kidumu hinted at what might unfold in West Germany in an interview he gave shortly before the tournament kicked off. Praising the influence of the coach, former Yugoslavia goalkeeper Blagoje Vidinic, since his arrival three years earlier, Kidumu said: "I think he was rather horrified by what he saw... [but] it was not really our fault: We had seen only our fellow Africans play, and we did not appreciate that the standards and styles were all that different elsewhere. Mr Vidinic, of course, had coached all over the world, so he knew from his experience what was good and what was bad."

Unfortunately Mr Vidinic was unable to get his knowledge through to the Zaire players, none of whom had ever played against European opposition. And though Zaire regained their African Nations title in March 1974, beating Zambia 2-0, what awaited them in West Germany was off their scale of understanding.

The squad, lacking money and facilities, resorted to training in Lake Kivu National Park before flying to West Germany shortly before the finals. There they ran into the patronising European press, who wanted to know not about the make-up of the Zaire side but whether – as all Africans surely did – they had a witchdoctor in the squad. "I'm the witchdoctor around here," replied a stone-faced Vidinic. "I touch them on one leg and say, 'You score with him'."

Zaire began their World Cup odyssey with a 2-0 defeat to Scotland and then came the side they thought they stood the best chance of beating in their pool – Yugoslavia. Wrong! Zaire were routed 9-0 – a World Cup record to match Hungary's similar score line against South Korea twenty years earlier – and recriminations swiftly followed. The press wanted to know why Vidinic had substituted goalkeeper Mwamba Kazadi after just twenty minutes with the score at 3-0. Was it because he was in cahoots with the Yugoslav team? The next day, in an interview with Dutch magazine *Vrij Nederland;* Vidinic explained that Mr Lockwa of the Zaire Ministry of Sport had ordered him to make the change because the replacement keeper, Dimi Tubilandu, was President Mobutu's choice.

A more respectable 3-0 defeat to Brazil killed off Zaire, and they returned to Kinshasa in disgrace. No one greeted them at the airport and Mobutu, who previously had changed the nickname of the squad from the Lions to the Leopards (because the president had a fondness for leopard-skin hats), publicly disowned them.

And yet Zaire (since renamed the Democratic Republic of the Congo) deserve recognition for being the first sub-Saharan African nation to appear in the World Cup. That they were says as much about their efforts to reach the tournament as it does about the lack of effort on the part of the rest of the world to incorporate Africa into what FIFA calls the "football family".

Between Egypt's appearance in the 1934 World Cup in Italy and Morocco's inclusion in Mexico thirty six years later no African team reached a final. Why? Because there was no African football confederation formed until 1957, and even then the Confédération Africaine de Football (CAF) struggled to make itself heard. Ghana, Morocco, Nigeria and Tunisia all attempted to qualify for the 1962 World Cup but none was successful. Eventually CAF began to assert itself, withdrawing all African participation from the 1966 qualification process in protest at the FIFA's decision to award the continent just one place at the tournament in England. FIFA fined nine African countries 5,000 Swiss francs each for their boycott but the protest had had its desired effect. "Football in Africa is increasing in leaps and bounds," said FIFA President Stanley Rous in an interview with the *Guardian* in November 1966. "Africans are beginning to take over from Europeans, and as they learn something of administration we shall hear much more from them."

Rous, an Englishman, was innately patronising to Africans, and it was only when he was replaced by João Havelange as FIFA president in 1974 that Africa began to be taken seriously. They were helped, too, by Tunisia's performance in the 1978 World Cup, the North Africans beating Mexico 3-1 to record the continent's first win in a final. "The world has laughed at Africa," said Tunisia coach Abdelmajid Chetali, "but now the mockery is over."

Two African nations, Algeria and Cameroon, qualified for the 1982 World Cup in Spain, and the same year FIFA introduced legislation obliging European clubs to release their African professionals for international tournaments.

With post colonial African countries also more relaxed from the 1980s onwards about their best players earning a living in Europe, suddenly the continent's best players were gaining valuable experience among the world's top stars. This was reflected in the performance of African nations in the World Cup, culminating in Cameroon reaching the quarterfinals of the 1990 tournament. It had been a long journey but Africa had finally arrived in international football.

NASA logo

OBJECT
55

In the four years between the 1966 and 1970 World Cups the world underwent great change. Man walked on the moon, Martin Luther King was assassinated, colour television

arrived and students from San Francisco to the Sorbonne were up in arms.

The 1966 tournament was quieter and quainter, what with its World Cup Willie, whereas 1970 was a colourful carnival played in the stifling heat of Mexico. The stars of the show were the Samba boys of Brazil: Pelé, Jairzinho and Tostão, players who made football look easy.

But the Beautiful Game Brazil portrayed was a long time in the making. "In 1966 we went to England with the Brazilian people expecting us to win the trophy for the third time, but the team was not strong enough and our preparation was poor. It made us all the more determined to succeed in Mexico," recalled Jairzinho in an interview with FIFA. "We trained for over three months in Rio prior to going to Mexico, two sessions per day. In the morning we would work on our fitness and stamina and in the afternoon we worked with the ball."

Football was slow in embracing the science of sport but not in Brazil, not with Claudio Coutinho as their fitness coach. Coutinho trained the squad at the National Aeronautics Space Administration's (NASA) Human Stress Laboratory in Florida, using the same aerobic fitness tests as astronauts preparing for space. Mexico was altitude, so why not? Leave no stone unturned, that was Coutinho's philosophy, and in tribute to his diligence the NASA insignia is object number 55.

Then three months before the World Cup began, the Brazilian Federation removed coach João Saldanha and replaced him with Zagalo, a member of the 1958 and 1962 World Cup-winning squads and a man more in tune with the tournament mindset. Now the last piece of the jigsaw was in place. "Zagalo changed the formation of the side. He wanted three attackers and luckily he included me," recalled Rivelino.

Once in Mexico the Brazilian squad soon won over the locals, dishing out flags, pennants and autographs. They were in a tough pool but they overcame the reigning champions

England, Czechoslovakia and Romania, scoring eight goals and conceding just three.

Peru were beaten 4-2 in the quarter-final, and Jairzinho netted twice to continue his record of a goal in every game. Uruguay were all snot and aggression in the semi-final and for the first forty five minutes their brutish approach upset the Brazilian rhythm. But then Pelé – "fiendishly inventive", in the words of one British sports writer – took control, and goals from Jarzinho and Rivelino saw Brazil home.

The final was the one the world wanted, a clash of styles, a clash of the Old World versus the New World, a clash between two nations who had both won the Jules Rimet trophy twice. This one was for keeps.

Italy had their *catenaccio* defence (in their five matches en route to the final they had conceded four goals, three of them in the 4-3 semi-final win over West Germany) but Brazil had their Samba boys. As the *Sunday Times* wrote, the final on 21 June 1970 was viewed "as a showdown for the soul of football. Brazil, with their flamboyant style of play, represented Latin flair and all that was good about the game. Italy, with their emphasis on negative thinking, were, despite the undoubted skills their players possessed, the epitome of Latin fear."

Flair won out over fear on the day, with Pelé too good for the Italians. He scored the first of Brazil's four goals with a header on eighteen minutes, and created the last four minutes from time, lazily rolling the ball into the path of Carlos Alberto with the split-second timing of a footballing genius. Alberto didn't need to check his stride, he just pulled back his right foot and struck with ball with such sweet, savage precision. 4-1 to Brazil, and the Jules Rimet trophy was theirs.

Red card

Those of you still on your toes will recall that object number 7 was a referee's whistle, a grudging acceptance by the sport's governing body that football wasn't quite the gentlemanly pastime it once had been. According to legend, Nottingham Forest secretary-treasurer Walter Roe Lymbery bought the first referee's whistle in 1872. Little could he have imagined that almost 100 years later referees would require further means of bringing players into line.

True, as far back as 1930 Peruvian Mario de Las Casas had been banished from the field for a foul in a World Cup match against Romania, but it wasn't until forty years later that our next object made its appearance. The red card, along with its yellow partner-in-crime, was the brainchild of English referee Ken Aston.

Aston's entire adult life was devoted to whistle-blowing. He began refereeing in 1935, when he was just 20, taking charge of a match at the school where he taught. In 1936 he qualified as a Football Association referee and a quarter of a century later was arguably the best in the business. At the 1962 World Cup Aston was responsible for keeping the peace between Chile and Italy, no easy task given the two nations were at each other's throats at the time. "I wasn't reffing a football match, I was acting as an umpire in military manoeuvres," he said later of a match in which two Italians were sent off. On one occasion, Aston even needed the help of armed police to break up a fight between players.

For the 1966 tournament, hosted by England, Aston was

in charge of the overall refereeing and like everyone else was appalled by the scenes during the quarter-final between England and Argentina. Antonio Rattin was expelled from the Wembley pitch for "violence of the tongue" (abusing the ref in modern vernacular) while England had the Charlton brothers – Bobby and Jack – booked by the West German official during one melee. Or at least that's what the newspapers reported the next day. The Charltons weren't sure, and nor was England coach Alf Ramsey, who asked FIFA for clarification.

Aston recognised the system was broken if a player could be booked without knowing it. But how best to fix it? A short while later Aston was in his car on his way home from work when it came to him: "As I drove down Kensington High Street, the traffic light turned red," he later recalled. "I thought, 'Yellow, take it easy; red, stop, you're off'."

FIFA embraced the idea, introducing yellow and red cards in time for the 1970 World Cup in Mexico. Clearly the innovation had some effect. At the first tournament since 1950 not a player was sent off, with five yellows the sum total of cards brandished by referees in Mexico. The first, incidentally, was given to Soviet Union defender Evgeny Lovchev in the opening match against the tournament hosts.

Aston was pleased. He'd always envisaged the cards as being a deterrent, not a stick with which the referee could dictate to the players. "The game should be a two-act play with 22 players on stage and the referee as director," was Aston's philosophy. "There is no script, no plot, you don't know the ending, but the idea is to provide enjoyment."

Four years later, in the 1974 World Cup, there was a red card. In fact there were four of them, the first flourished in the face of Chilean Carlos Caszely for his second bookable offence, a foul on Bertie Vogts of West Germany. If Caszely was hot-blooded he was also stout-hearted and eight years later became something of a hero in his native Chile. Having qualified for the 1982 World Cup finals in Spain, the Chilean squad was presented to General Augusto Pinochet for what the dictator presumed would be a standard photo opportunity. It turned into a PR disaster for Pinochet as Caszely, the team captain, refused to shake his hand, telling him: "Sorry, but I can't take the hand of a killer of hundreds of my young communist *compañeros*."

Yellow and red cards were introduced into English League football on 2 October 1976 and there were two on the very first day. Blackburn winger David Wagstaffe got the first with George Best not far behind. The former Manchester United winger, by now playing for Fulham, was dismissed by referee Lester Shapter against Southampton for "using foul and abusive language".

Silver-tongued with the ladies but sharp-tongued with the refs, that was our George...

FIFA HQ

In May 2007 world football's governing body FIFA officially opened its new headquarters in Zurich. It was hard to know what was more breathtaking: the cost to build the HQ (£99 million), or the words of FIFA President Sepp Blatter as he inaugurated the vast complex. The FIFA HQ was glass-fronted, explained Blatter to the assembled throng, to "allow light to shine through the building and create the transparency we all stand for".

One can say many things about Blatter, but his ability to keep a straight face when talking baloney is impressive.

But then that's because he learnt from the master, the man who changed FIFA and did much to change football in the last quarter of the twentieth century. João Havelange also, in the words of the BBC, "laid the foundations for the World Cup becoming one of the most lucrative sporting events in the world."

In short, Havelange is probably the most influential administrator in the history of football, certainly in the history of FIFA. But if there was one thing the Brazilian was not it was transparent; Havelange is the original "Teflon man", long before Bill Clinton appeared on the scene.

Havelange was born in 1916 in Rio de Janeiro and, having represented Brazil at water polo in the 1936 Olympics, he rose steadily through the ranks of Brazilian sports administration until in 1974 he challenged Britain's Sir Stanley Rous for the presidency of FIFA. Rous had had his day by now, a man born in Victorian England who had refereed the 1934 FA Cup Final and whose view of the world game had an undoubted European bias. Football needed a new leader, but did it need Havelange?

When Havelange put his name forward for the presidency he had the full support of the South American nations, all of whom believed it was time for one of their people to be in the position that since 1904 had been occupied by Europeans. Argentina in particular were convinced they had been cheated out of the 1966 World Cup by England. But Havelange needed more votes from among other FIFA delegates if he was to unseat the venerable Rous.

Havelange looked to Africa for those votes. He knew that the African nations took issue with Rous on two counts: his support for apartheid South Africa, and his reluctance to grant them automatic World Cup qualification.

In his devastating expose on the machinations of FIFA – *How They Stole The Game* – author David Yallop says Havelange promised the World Cup would be expanded from sixteen to twenty four nations, and that there would be money to build stadiums and train referees and develop youth pro-grammes. Nothing wrong with that.

Rather it was Havelenge's "shuttle diplomacy" that caught the eye. Asked by Yallop about his global campaigning prior to the 1974 FIFA elections, Havelange cheerfully admitted: "In one period of two and a half months, some ten weeks, I visited 86 countries. My air ticket weighed several kilos." Asked in an interview with *Playboy* magazine in 1986 how he paid for all this campaigning – estimated to have cost as much as $3 million – Havelange said it was from his own pocket. Yallop disagreed and alleged it "came from embezzled funds from the Brazilian sports federation".

Then there were the allegations of bribes offered to del-egates in return for their votes, as well as other more enter-prising largesse on the part of Havelange. In June 1973 Brazil played Tunisia in a friendly and Havelange allegedly waived a large chunk of Brazil's share of the gross gate receipts. No need to ask which way Tunisia would be voting.

The outcome at the 1974 election was inevitable. Rous lost, and Havelange declared in his triumphal victory speech that it was "a great day for South American football. This has been a great victory for South America." An odd declaration, one might say, for a man elected head of a global organisation.

Havelange's grip on power lasted for twenty four years, during which time football underwent many positive changes at his instigation. African football finally began to be taken seriously, so, too, the women's game, and a raft of youth tour-naments including the U-17 and U-20 World Championships. The World Cup was also increased from sixteen teams in 1974 to thirty two by the time of the 1998 tournament, although opinions diverge on whether this has been beneficial.

Havelange modernised football; but at what cost to its soul? Almost immediately after coming to power the Brazilian with the piercing blue eyes formed a powerful partnership with Horst Dassler, whose father had founded the Adidas sport company.

This partnership would lead to the rampant commercialisation of football, particularly the World Cup, as companies across the globe fought to have their name associated with the Beautiful Game. But by what means did they fight? According to a 2010 BBC *Panorama* programme, Havelange and son-in-law Ricardo Teixeira (head of Brazil's football federation) accepted "millions of dollars in bribes from Swiss marketing agency International Sport and Leisure to retain the company as FIFA's sole official marketer." In 2012, Swiss prosecutors confirmed that this had been the case, and that Havelange and Teixeira's prosecution was only halted by their repayment of a small proportion of the £27 million the pair were alleged to have received.

By the time the allegations broke Havelange had been twelve years in retirement. He denied all wrong-doing but felt compelled nonetheless to step down from his position on the International Olympic Committee "for health reasons". As luck would have it this avoided his having to answer the charges of corruption.

When Havelange came to power in 1974 FIFA's headquarters – like its image in general – was outdated with a staff of just twelve (that has since increased tenfold). Today it's the slickest, savviest sports organisation in the world as its new glass-fronted nerve centre reflects. But transparent it ain't, and Jose Havelange is responsible for that.

Ajax jersey

OBJECT
58

England gave football to Holland and for seventy years or so the Dutch were content to play in the same stolid style as the men across the Channel. The height of Dutch ambition, according to an early twentieth

century Dutch player quoted by Maarten van Bottenburg and Beverley Jackson in *Global Games*, was to play "on English grounds with all their English customs and English strategies". Fortunately for the Dutch they were saved from a lifetime of underachievement by the arrival of Rinus Michels in an Ajax shirt, which is our fifty eighth object.

Named FIFA's Coach of the Century in 1999, Michels died in 2005 and a lengthy obituary was carried in the British newspaper the *Independent*. They remarked that Michels had "raised the game to the level of great art" and that "until Michels wrought his revolution, Holland was on a par with neighbouring Luxembourg as a European footballing power, and the country's clubs were also-rans in Europe. Under his coaching, Ajax of Amsterdam became European champions in 1971, and the national side reached the World Cup Final in 1974."

Michels was born in Amsterdam in 1928 and was a mainstay of the Ajax side throughout the 1940s and 1950s before being hired as the club's coach in 1965. At the time Ajax were in trouble but, with the financial support of the Van der Meijden brothers and the coaching savvy of Michels, the club began their rise to the top of the European game.

Michels was a disciplinarian and this underpinned all his beliefs. Ajax avoided relegation in Michels' first season in charge and in his second they won the League. Now he began to develop his system of "Total Football", aided by a crop of young and talented players of whom Johan Cruyff was the most gifted, with Johan Neeskens and Ruud Krol not far behind. These would be the rapiers but the rock of the Ajax team was Velibor Vasovic, a tough Yugoslav defender.

Cruyff was up there with George Best as the greatest European player of the 1960s; the difference between the two was that Cruyff loved money too much to squander it all on women and wine. Cruyff was imperious in the late 1960s as

Ajax won four League titles and lost to AC Milan in the 1969 European Cup Final.

Michels now changed Ajax's formation from 4-2-4 to 4-3-3 but that in itself wasn't the key to Total Football. The essence of the system was Michels' belief that it wasn't the number on a player's back that determined his position on the field but where he was at any given moment. In other words, he chose fluidity over rigidity, telling his players to exploit the space all around them and think of themselves as all interchangeable. "Football is best when it's instinctive," remarked central defender Barry Hulshoff. "Total Football means that a player in attack can play in defence – only that he can do this, that is all. You make space, you come into space. And if the ball doesn't come, you leave this space and another player will come into it."

Total Football came of age in an era when revolution was all around – socially, politically and sexually – yet Michels was as far removed from a revolutionary as could be imagined. What inspired him was his heritage. As David Winners writes in *Brilliant Orange*, "the Dutch think innovatively, creatively and abstractedly about space in their football because for centuries they had to think innovatively about space in every other area of their lives."

Ajax finally won the European Cup in 1971 when they beat Panathinaikos 2-0 at Wembley. They retained the trophy the following season, and again in 1973, becoming the first side since Real Madrid in 1958 to win three consecutive titles. Michels by now had moved on to a fresh challenge, leading Barcelona to the Spanish title in 1974. That same year he guided Holland to the World Cup Final where Cruff and co. crumbled in the final against West Germany.

In the 1980s, after a spell coaching in the USA, Michels returned to Holland and led the national team to the European Championship title in 1988, the first time the Dutch had won a major football tournament. In that side was Marco van Basten, the only player of his generation who could stand in comparison with Johan Cruyff. "He knew how to motivate a group and how to take away the stress at the right moments with his sense of humor," Van Basten said of Michels on hearing of his death "He could also be unusually hard in his decisions, and at other moments show his warmth... Michels was the father of Dutch soccer."

Kettering Town football shirt

This next object speaks for itself. On 24 January 1976 Kettering Town of the Southern League ran out for their match against Bath City wearing shirts that bore the logo of a local firm called "Kettering Tyres". The age of the sponsored shirt had arrived in football, and predictably the powers-that-be went potty.

Former Wolverhampton Wanderers and Northern Ireland striker Derek Dougan had brokered the four-figure deal in his capacity as Kettering's chief executive. The reaction of the Football Association was to ban all sponsored shirts to which Dougan replied: "I find it inconceivable that petty-minded bureaucrats have only this to bother about."

Determined not to be beaten, the ingenious Dougan changed the name on the shirts to "Kettering T", claiming that that "T" stood not for "Tyres" but for "Town". The FA wasn't impressed and warned Dougan that he either comply with their order or cough up a £1000 fine.

The FA's intransigence didn't last long as Kettering, supported by Derby County and Bolton Wanderers, pressurised them to relax the rules on sponsored shirts. In the 1977–78 season the FA grudgingly lifted its ban, although it stipulated that any wording on shirts must be small so as not to breach the BBC's strict rules about advertising. Derby found a sponsor in SAAB, the car manufacturer, but the club never wore the sponsored shirts in League matches.

According to Ray Spiller, founder of the Association of Football Statisticians, "the first top division club to carry a sponsor's name was Liverpool FC who signed an agreement with Hitachi on 24 July 1979, stipulating shirts with logos worn only in non-televised league matches." North of the border, meanwhile, Hibernian became the first club to wear a sponsor's name on their shirts when they struck a deal with shirt-makers Bukta's name in the 1977–78 season.

Initially, the sight of players running around in sponsored shirts stuck in the craw of traditionalists. "Footballers are nothing but glorified sandwich board men," whined one paper. Yet for the companies involved it was good business. For the privilege of seeing Liverpool run out at Anfield with their name emblazoned on the chests of Kenny Dalglish, Alan Hansen et al, Hitachi paid the then reigning League champions a mere £150,000. But so effective did the companies regard the innovation that soon the cost of sponsoring shirts rose dramatically. In 1981 Japanese electronics manufacturer JVC signed a £500,000 deal with Arsenal, an astronomical amount at the time but dwarfed by the deals done following the advent of the Premier League.

For the start of the 2002–03 season Arsenal agreed a four-year shirt sponsorship deal with mobile phone company mm02 worth £10 million, while Chelsea announced in 2005 a £50 million five-year shirt deal with Samsung. But both deals were small fry compared to the agreement struck in

2014 between Manchester United and sports manufacturer Nike. The deal will earn the Red Devils an estimated £60 million a year over ten seasons and is on top – literally – of a £35 million a year short sponsorship deal United agreed with clothes company Chevrolet that begins at the start of the 2014–15 season.

But are the deals worth it? Yes, according to an article in the July 2006 edition of Financial Management. As a result of Samsung's deal with Chelsea in 2005, they said, sales of its mobile phones among supporters quadrupled between August 2005 and March 2006.

But spare a thought for poor old Kettering Town of the Conference Premier. Having given English football the sponsored shirt all those years ago they are now obliged to regularly go cap in hand to companies. As recently as 2011, the club posted a notice on its website saying they were "now looking for new shirt sponsors... your business can gain maximum exposure for a whole season with the Poppies. In fact your company's exposure would be national, as over 5000 registered doctors receive a Kettering Town shirt when they register as a Locum."

Hooligan calling card

CONGRATULATIONS YOU HAVE JUST BEEN WHACKED COURTESY OF D.L.F DERBY LUNATIC FRINGE

Hooliganism, the "English Disease" that emerged in the late 1960s and spread across Europe in the decades the followed. The "disease" that killed dozens and dragged the good name of football into the gutter.

171

The hooligans gave their "firms" pseudo-warrior names – Red Army, Zulus, Headhunters, The Suicide Squad, Bushwhackers, the Legion – and dished out calling cards to their victims. They were well-organised and well-groomed, going to games wearing Burberry or Stone Island, but no matter how the hooligans dressed there was one common denominator: they were scum who cared nothing for football.

There was nothing courageous or glamorous about hooliganism, despite the slew of books that glorified the "firms" and the "crews", books commissioned by middle-class publishers for middle-class readers who got their vicarious kicks from the thuggery. Pathetic.

Hooligans don't deserve any space in a book about the history of football, and their sharp decline – a result of better policing, banning orders and the introduction of CCTV in and around grounds – is a blessing. Home Office figures for the 2010–11 season revealed more than 37 million people attended international and domestic football matches involving clubs from England and Wales, with only 3,089 people arrested ("less than 0.01 per cent of all spectators or one arrest for every 12,249 spectators"). This figure is a record low since the government began logging football-related offences in 1984–85.

The English Disease hasn't been eradicated, but it's being effectively contained.

Plaster cast for broken arm

In a startling interview in 2008 João Havelange (you remember him) claimed that two previous World Cups had been fixed so the host

nation would win. The dirty duo were England in 1966 and West Germany eight years later. The claims of the former FIFA president were met with widespread hilarity. Not so much for what he'd said but for what he hadn't. World Cups... fixed? Hmm, let's talk about what went on in 1978...

We'll get to the plaster cast in a moment, but first a bit of background to the 1978 World Cup. That it was held in Argentina was scandalous enough; this was a country in the grip of a ruthless military junta, one that was murdering its people with terrifying impunity. Though Argentina had been awarded hosting rights before Havelange assumed the presidency of FIFA in 1974, the decision not to remove those rights in the wake of the 1976 military coup remains one of the most shameful chapters in the history of FIFA.

Despite the fact that there were regular protests in Buenos Aires's Plaza de Mayo by the mothers of the *desaparecidos* (the "disappeared"; approximately 30,000 Argentine citizens would "disappear" during the seven years of the military junta), and despite the fact that the incorruptible chairman of the World Cup organising committee was murdered in August 1976 (speculation remains to this day as to who ordered the killing), FIFA refused to move the World Cup from Argentina. This was Havelange's "baby", and he had already put in place several lucrative deals; he couldn't be seen to back out.

His obduracy delighted the military junta, for as David Yallop writes in *How They Stole The Game*, the Argentina generals "knew that a time when their international image was hideous, a World Cup competition could be their salvation, and if by some miracle Argentina should win the World Cup, then the military would be forgiven much by their people."

The miracle happened and Argentina did win the World Cup, though the highly respected coach Giovanni Trapattoni (then in charge of Italian club Juventus) said that if the tournament had been played anywhere else in the world "Argentina would not even have survived the first round."

Argentina opened their first-round campaign against Hungary, winning 2-1 in a dirty match that saw fouls from both sides. Curiously the referee saw fit only to send off two Hungarians. Next up was France, and again Argentina won by two goals to one, and again they were helped by the official. Brian Glanville, in *The Story of the World Cup*, described how "two abominable decisions by the referee" saw the hosts awarded a penalty that never was and the French denied one that clearly was.

Then came Italy, and an Israeli referee with a spine and a conscience: the great Abraham Klein. He officiated the match fairly and the Italians triumphed 1-0. Argentina still progressed to the second round in a group containing Poland, Peru and Brazil. A 0-0 draw with Brazil, and an inferior goal difference, left Argentina needing to beat Peru by six goals in their final match if they were to reach the semi-finals ahead of the Brazilians. Few gave them any chance; Peru had conceded just six goals in their previous five matches and their captain, Héctor Chumpitaz, dismissed talk of a possible fix. Peru's job, he said, was to "safeguard the decency of the competition".

Fat chance. Argentina duly won 6-0 and eight years later an Argentine journalist called Maria-Laura Avignolo revealed that the country's military junta had ordered the match to be fixed. According to Yallop the bribes came in a variety of guises, and included a gift of 35 tonnes of grain from Argentina to the valiant losers, and the unfreezing of a $50 million credit line to Peru. In addition, three players accepted bribes of $20,000 each to throw the game. More than twenty years later one of the three admitted the fact to Yallop but on the understanding that his identity was kept a secret. "If my identity became known there would certainly be reprisals," the former player said. "Not only against me, but also my family."

Through to the semi-final Argentina beat Poland 2-0 to set up a showdown with the Dutch. Even without Johan Cruyff – who'd made himself unavailable for the tournament – a gifted

Holland looked too strong for their hosts. But Argentina had the benefit of home advantage.

First they kept the Dutch waiting on the field, emerging five minutes later from the dressing room into a maelstrom of shredded paper thrown from the stands on to the pitch. Then, seconds before kick-off, Argentina complained about the lightweight plaster cast worn on the wrist of Rene Van de Kerkhof. The Dutch winger was nonplussed; he had worn the cast in every other match to protect his damaged wrist. The Argentines insisted and the referee caved in to their games-manship, ordering Van de Kerkhof to remove the cast or wear a lighter bandage. The Argentines had not only rattled the Dutch, they had discovered they had a weak-willed referee.

Fortunately Argentina won the final legitimately, thanks to the brilliance of Mario Kempes, who scored twice in their 3-1 victory, and at the opulent banquet to mark the end of the tournament Havelange was moved to proclaim that "the world has seen the true face of Argentina."

Perhaps Havelange was referring to the bomb attacks, abductions and beatings that occurred throughout the tournament.

Seat, Pittodrie Stadium, Aberdeen

Please, sit down in our next object and make yourself comfortable while we enlighten you as to how football grounds began the slow journey from the functional if not altogether cosy stadia of Archibald Leitch's era to the secure and spacious grounds of today.

In 1971 the whole of Scotland had been stunned when sixty six were killed at Ibrox Park during the January Old Firm encounter. With Celtic leading 1-0 and just minutes remaining, many among the 80,000 crowd decided to head for the exit. As they did so, Rangers equalised, and the roar caused the departing fans to rush back to see what had happened. A tragic bottleneck occurred at Staircase 13, resulting in scores of dead and injured. An inquiry was subsequently launched, and in 1975 the Safety of Sports Grounds Act was introduced.

The first club in Britain to react to the Act was Aberdeen. There they believed that going to a football match was a form of entertainment no different from going to the cinema or the theatre, yet football fans were treated in a vastly inferior way to cinema-goers. So in June 1978 Aberdeen, having appointed Alex Ferguson as their manager in the same month, embarked on an ambitious £1.5 million redevelopment programme of their Pittodrie ground under Chairman Dick Donald. They converted the open south terrace into a seated area, explains Andrew Ward and John Williams in *Football Nation*, and then "took care to add toilets and washrooms of hotel standard, and the design included bright colours and plenty of room for people to circulate."

Pittodrie was now Britain's first all-seater and all-covered stadium, and although capacity was slashed as a result from 45,000 to 25,000 the renovation was declared a success. With a new ground and a new manager Aberdeen enjoyed the most successful spell in their history, winning three League titles, four Scottish FA Cups and the Cup Winners Cup in the next eight years.

In England, meanwhile, Jimmy Hill, no longer chairman of the Professional Footballers' Association but chairman and managing director of First Division Coventry City, thought to emulate Aberdeen's example. Attendances at Coventry's Highfield Road ground had fallen by 20 per cent between 1976 and 1981, in line with the general decline as the scourge of hooliganism scared an increasing number of supporters away from the game.

"It's harder to be a hooligan when you're sitting down," said Hill in announcing his decision to turn Highfield Road into an all-seater stadium for the start of the 1981–82 season. Unfortunately for Hill, Leeds United's notorious hooligan element proved him wrong in only Coventry's second home game in the new stadium. On 12 September 1981 Leeds' supporters ripped out 100 of the new seats, ransacked a bar and vandalised a toilet block; at least Hill was able to claim the violence had more to do with the fact Leeds had lost 4-0 rather than any inherent distaste for all-seater stadiums.

Ultimately, what caused Hill's all-seater experiment at Highfield Road to fail was the opposition of Coventry fans, who considered it just another one of Jimmy's "gimmicks". By 1982 gates had fallen to the lowest level for twenty years, and the club canvassed supporters' opinions with a questionnaire. More than 25 per cent called for a return of terracing with one claiming that "the introduction of nice facilities... does absolutely nothing to attract the average working-class supporter and he is the one who should matter most."

In 1983 Jimmy Hill resigned as chairman, and in 1984 a section of Highfield Road was transformed back into terracing. Within the space of a few short years the supporters would come to see the sense of Hill's foresight – but only after a tragedy of unimaginable horror.

Ballot box

OBJECT 63

It says much for how football is run these days that a ballot box is almost as important as the football. These are how the crucial decisions are made; decisions such as who administers the sport and who gets to host the World Cup.

It was João Havelange who treated the ballot box as his personal friend, starting from the moment it carried him to the presidency of FIFA in 1974. Over the next quarter of a century the ballot box did Havelange's bidding, as it has done Sepp Blatter's, the man who learned much from studying the methods of his Brazilian mentor.

"A FIFA congress is a curious affair to attend," wrote David Yallop in *How They Stole The Game*. "A large gathering, virtually all middle-aged or very elderly fat men, most of them eating and drinking throughout the proceedings, sitting in judgement on the whys and wherefores of the world's most popular sport."

Curious, and often incomprehensible thanks to the votes cast into the ballot box. One of the most glaring examples was the allocation of the 1986 World Cup to Mexico, a bidding competition that led the head of the USA delegation, the veteran statesman Henry Kissinger, to remark: "It makes me feel nostalgic for the Middle East."

Originally the 1986 World Cup had been awarded to Colombia but in early 1983 it was clear the country was too beset by violence and drugs to be a viable venue, so it resigned its mandate. Four others candidates bid to replace Colombia: the USA, Canada, Brazil and Mexico. Brazil was quickly discounted on the grounds of inadequate infrastructure, and so in May 1983 the remaining three candidates arrived in Stockholm to present their bids.

Mexico went first, and then it was Kissinger's turn. According to Yallop, he lived up to his reputation, giving a slick presentation on the good job the USA would do in hosting the tournament and how the World Cup would do wonders for the development of football in the States, hitherto impervious to the Beautiful Game. Suddenly an aide approached Kissinger and, cupping his hand to the statesman's ear, whispered that "the Mexicans down below were apparently very busy organising a victory celebration."

As Kissinger later discovered, Havelange and the executive

committee had already voted in Mexico at a breakfast meeting that morning, despite the fact the country had a deficit of $80 billion and was an economic "basket case". FIFA was just paying lip service to the North Americans. Kissinger left Stockholm in a blind rage and football in the USA was set back years.

When Havelange stepped aside as president in 1998, the man widely tipped to replace him was UEFA President Lennart Johansson, a popular reformist who, like many, had grown increasingly exasperated with how FIFA was run. Shortly before the election, the Swede told Yallop in bullish tones that he was sure he would poll 100 votes. Mind you, Blatter – Havelange's preferred choice – was equally confident of receiving more than 100 of the 191 votes on offer.

Where the two men differed was on how they wished the vote to be held. "Johansson's supporters argued for an open ballot. Blatter's supporters wanted, and obtained, a secret ballot," explained Yallop, adding: "The figures stunned many, but delighted even more. Blatter 111, Johansson 80."

Four years later Farah Ado, vice-president of the Confederation of African Football (CAF) and president of the Somali Football Association, claimed he was offered $100,000 to vote for Blatter. Though Ado said he turned down the money "eighteen African voters accepted bribes to vote for Blatter."

Blatter blithely brushed off the allegations, as he would do eight years later when there were fresh claims of ballot box rigging. This time FIFA were voting to see which countries would host the 2018 and 2022 World Cups. Qatar was desperate to become the first Arab state to stage a World Cup, indifferent to the fact its temperature, football infrastructure, population and attitude towards alcohol all militated against them hosting the world's premier football tournament. Qatar spent a reputed £70 million in preparing its bid (ten times what Holland and Belgium could afford for theirs) and offered generous financial incentives – legal nonetheless – to several nations. "For Qatar to win the right to host World Cup 2022 it required the traditional level of greed on these occasions," wrote Yallop. "What was also required was a collective madness to grip the majority of those voting."

There was madness aplenty as Qatar was awarded the 2022 World Cup and Russia the 2018 tournament, just twenty four hours after leaked cables revealed that US diplomats considered Russia to be a "Mafia state". As Blatter paused theatrically on stage before announcing the winner of the 2018 bid, a lone voice from the auditorium cried out: "Why the wait? How long does it take to count a bag of roubles?"

European Cup

OBJECT
64

We've seen how Real Madrid, Inter and Ajax came to dominate the European Cup at various times from the 1950s to the early 1970s, and now it's only proper that we turn our attention to the era of English hegemony.

The Cup was donated by Gabriel Hanot's *L'Équipe* newspaper to Real Madrid when they won the inaugural European Cup in 1956. Twelve years later the Spanish club were allowed to keep the trophy in honour of their six titles. The second trophy, which UEFA commissioned from a Swiss silversmith at a cost of 10,000 Swiss francs, was first lifted by Celtic captain Billy McNeill when they beat Inter 2-1 in the 1967 final.

The following year an Englishman got his hands on the cup for the first time, when Bobby Charlton led Manchester United to victory over Benfica. But it wasn't for nearly another decade until the English really cut a swath through Europe.

It began with Bob Paisley's Liverpool and the philosophy he'd inherited from Bill Shankly (see object 47). Paisley grew into a better tactician than his mentor following his elevation from the Boot Room to the manager's dugout in 1974. Past defeats in European competitions, most notably a 4-2 aggregate loss to Red Star Belgrade in November 1973, shaped the destiny of the club in the decade or more to follow.

Paisley analysed the reason why Liverpool – the reigning League champions – couldn't achieve similar success in the European Cup. The reason was simple, as he later explained: "The top Europeans showed us how to break out of defence effectively. The pace of their movement was dictated by their first pass. We had to learn to be patient like that and think about the next two or three moves when we had the ball."

This was a first – an Englishman admitting he had something to learn from continental Europe! Free from the narrow-mindedness that had hamstrung so many of his predecessors in English football, Paisley set about creating a team to conquer Europe. Within four years he accomplished his goal, allying a patient passing game with the more natural English traits of raw naked aggression. "We treated every match like a war," admitted Paisley.

Four days after losing the 1977 FA Cup Final to Manchester United, Liverpool beat Borussia Mönchengladbach 3-1 in Rome and later that night in the Italian capital players and fans celebrated together.

Twelve months later, in front of 92,000 fans at Wembley, Liverpool retained the European Cup by beating Brugge 1-0 with a team that contained two new faces from the side of a year earlier. Kenny Dalglish had replaced Kevin Keegan up front, while a young Scot called Alan Hansen partnered the veteran Emlyn Hughes in central defence.

Dalglish scored the only goal of the game midway through the second half as Liverpool became the first British side to win the European Cup twice. Their hopes of making it three titles in a row were ended the following season by their greatest domestic rivals of recent years – Nottingham Forest, whose passing game was strikingly similar to their own.

Under the stewardship of Brian Clough and his brilliant assistant Peter Taylor, Forest pipped Liverpool to the First Division title in 1978 having won promotion from the Second Division the previous year. In doing so, Clough became the first manager since the great Herbert Chapman to win the First Division title with two clubs. But Clough's success with Derby County in 1972 had ended with his departure from the club the following year; with Forest Clough went in another direction, leading them to the 1979 European Cup crown with a 1-0 defeat of Malmo.

In 1980, Forest lifted the Cup again, this time defeating Hamburg thanks to an early goal from John Robertson, but the following season Liverpool reclaimed English bragging rights in Europe by winning their third crown with a 1-0 defeat of Real Madrid, so joining Bayern, Ajax and Real Madrid themselves as the only side to win the competition three times. Bob Paisley became the first manager to achieve a hat-trick of European Cup titles.

Aston Villa made it six consecutive English victories in 1982, Bayern this time the victims, and though the winning streak was broken by Hamburg in 1983, back came Liverpool the following season for their fourth European Cup success in eight seasons.

Then came the calamity at Heysel during the 1985 European Cup Final, when rampaging Liverpool fans were held largely responsible for the deaths of thirty nine mostly Juventus supporters. It was the nadir of English hooliganism, a night that led Prime Minister Margaret Thatcher to declare that "those responsible have brought shame and disgrace to their country and to football."

Liverpool's reputation, and all the club had achieved in the past decade, was shattered. It would be another six years before they were allowed back into European competition.

World Cup Golden Ball

If it had been possible to persuade God to lend us his hand then, believe us, we'd have that on display for object 65. Alas, no hand was available, so we'll have to make do with the World Cup Golden Ball, the trophy awarded to the outstanding player in the tournament. In 1986 that was Diego Maradona, unquestionably. Wow, the wee Argentine was good. Indeed, one could argue that no player has so single-handedly decided the destiny of the World Cup the way Maradona did in Mexico all those years ago. "He is the World Cup," said Argentine coach Carlos Bilardo. "This is his World Championship."

Greats of the game lined up to praise the 25-year-old; Stanley Matthews described him as "the best one-footed player since Puskás" and the great Franz Beckenbauer admitted "there were moments when he reached the level of Pelé."

That greatness had already been glimpsed in the 1982 World Cup when Maradona, just 21, scored twice in Argentina's defeat of Hungary. But, and there always a "but" with Maradona, in the quarter-final defeat to Brazil he was sent off for a wild challenge on Claudio Gentile.

And therein lies the essence of Maradona: the beauty and the cheat.

In the 1986 World Cup he was four years stronger and more experienced than he had been in Spain. He coasted through the group stages and then exploded into action in

Argentina's quarter-final against England, fisting the ball into the net as he and Peter Shilton rose for a cross.

The officials never saw it but Shilton did, and so too his defenders. As one Italian reporter wrote, England were "in a state of shock, like a man who has just had his wallet stolen." Sensing this stupor, Maradona moved in for the kill, running at the England defence from wide out on the right and just inside his own half. On he advanced, stepping out of one, two, three, four, five England tackles before casually sliding the ball past Shilton to make it 2-0. It was a moment of brilliance, voted the "Goal of the Century" in a 2002 poll conducted by FIFA.

And the first goal? Maradona brushed that off after the game by telling reporters it was "a little bit of Maradona's head, a little bit of the hand of God."

The Goal of the Century and then the Quote of the Century; small wonder that the media attention now focused on Maradona's every move. On one occasion "a media pack of 250 chased him so madly that Maradona had to retreat behind a battered chain-link fence to answer questions without fear of getting crushed."

In the semi-final Maradona, assisted by Argentina, beat Belgium 2-0. The two goals he scored were wondrous. In describing the second the respected football writer Brian Glanville called it "extraordinary... a solo of sublime inspiration... there was so little space, around the edge of the box, as he swerved, dashed and dummied by four bemused defenders in turn, finally to shoot past Pfaff."

In the final Argentina defeated West Germany, Maradona creating the winning goal in their 3-2 victory. The Golden Ball was his and so were the accolades. Writing in the *Chicago Tribune*, veteran American sportswriter Phil Hersh described Maradona as "the expressionist painter [who] has made this World Cup his personal tour de force, exactly what was needed in a sport that had become a connect-the-dots picture."

As for the Hand of God, Hersh didn't much care. After

all, "what difference did it make that TV replays showed the handiwork was not only extra-terrestrial?... The Divine Mister M has proved that certain athletes need not be bound by earthly conventions."

They demurred in England. The *Sunday Times* accused him of blaspheming his God-given talent and hoped his act of cheating would "haunt Maradona for the rest of his days".

It hasn't. Maradona isn't the sort of man to dwell on past misdemeanours. Well, there have been so many of them. When he did last mention the incident there was little sign of contrition, explaining on Argentine television in 2005 that the "goal" was just "something that just came out of me. It was a bit of mischief."

From the "Hand of God" to a "bit of mischief". Here endeth today's lesson.

Cigar

Cigar anyone? And then perhaps we can talk about my 10 per cent cut for presenting this object. Welcome to the world of the football agent, a world that is murkier than a room full of cigar smoke and, so one might suggest, a lot unhealthier. At least it is for the game of football, if not the bank balance of the modern agent.

Agents have actually been around for longer than one might think, if not in Britain then certainly elsewhere. In the same decade that Arsenal's new manager Herbert Chapman walked into Charlie Buchan's sports shop in Sunderland and declared he wished to sign him (see object 32), agents were thriving in South America.

The 1920s was the period when Italian football began importing players from Argentina and Brazil to play in their leagues, and agents were dispatched across the Atlantic to lure the likes of Raimondo Orsi from Independiente to Juventus with the promise of "8,000 lire, a signing-on fee of 100,000 lire and a Fiat 509". What cut the agents received isn't known, but it's unlikely they headed west solely for their love of the game.

Agents began crawling out from... sorry, began appearing in British football in the 1960s, following the abolition of the maximum wage in 1961 and the relaxing of the draconian transfer system. Writing in the 1967 edition of the *Football League Review*, editor Harry Brown bemoaned "a new trend for leading professional players to use agents."

For the most part these agents were content to remain out of the spotlight, seeing themselves as discreet facilitators and in terms of respectability every bit as upstanding as a theatrical or literary agent. Football, after all, was a new form of showbiz by the 1970s.

Then came Eric Hall; the image of the football agent would never be the same again. Hall, who once cheerfully admitted he was "a sort of low grade" had been a music promoter before becoming an agent to the Beautiful Game in the mid-1980s. His philosophy was simple: "I have no morals when it comes to dealing with my clients. I would deal with the devil to get the best deal for them."

The philosophy worked, aided by the introduction of the Premier League in 1992 and the money that began pouring into the game as a consequence. By 1995 Hall had over thirty five top-flight players on his books; he also had a column in a national newspaper and rarely did a week pass when he wasn't seen on television with his trademark fat cigar and his trademark word – "monster". Everything was "monster" to Hall. As he told the *Guardian* newspaper in a 1995 interview: "I'm monster funny."

The *Guardian* wasn't impressed, describing Hall as "a

cocky cockney... the most flamboyant of the vilified breed of football agents."

But Hall was very good at what he did. He worked hard and he did what footballers wanted him to do – make them money. Part of his success, Hall once explained, was that he didn't understand football and saw it purely as a business. "That is the way it is. It is about deals. It is like any other business. Players need representation. Same as in show business."

Others disagreed. Bobby Gould, who managed Wimbledon in the 1980s when many of the side were represented by Hall, said: "In show business you have individuals with talent. Football is different. You have stars, but you need the stability of a team. Agents undermine that stability. The Football Association should have stamped on them years ago."

The Football Association started to license agents in the mid-1990s, and by the end of the decade there were ninety one official agents operating in Britain. Many were reputable and some had played the game themselves, such as former Manchester United defender Kevin Moran. "When I was a player, the greatest difficulty was that you never knew what you were worth," he replied, when asked why he'd become an agent.

Eric Hall's agency went into liquidation in 2001 and without his hi-viz presence agents once more slipped from the public eye. But they were still there, licensed but more powerful than ever. In 2006 Luton Town manager Mike Newell claimed football was rife with bungs and "back-handers" and pointed the finger of blame at agents, describing them as "the scourge of the game".

Five years later, in 2011, it was the turn of Alex Ferguson to lament what agents had done for the game. The previous October, Ferguson had clashed with Wayne Rooney's "advisor" (the word some agents prefer) Paul Stretford when the Manchester United striker handed in a transfer request. Rooney remained at Old Trafford – albeit with a new and improved contract – but Ferguson alleged the player had been talked into the transfer request. Then he said: "You have to deal with agents of this world today, which is difficult. There is no problem with players, but some agents are difficult."

In an interview with Irish broadcaster RTE, Ferguson said: "When I get annoyed is when managers phone me and say such-and-such player – and I'm talking about players who couldn't lace my reserve team players' boots – is asking for £1 million a year. That's when it becomes disappointing... the way some agents work a miracle by getting these terms for players who are not stars."

Asked how he enjoyed dealing with agents, Ferguson replied: "I don't deal with them directly but [the chief executive] David Gill has to, and it's a hard job. They have an imagination that is beyond belief."

By the way, in case you're wondering what happened to Eric Hall, his agency went up in smoke years ago. Not literally, you understand; he was always monster careful where he stubbed out his cigars.

Opera programme

OBJECT

67

Turandot

Giacomo Puccini

After agents I think we should take the book a little more highbrow, and brows don't get much higher than Luciano Pavarotti, particularly when he was belting out "Nessun Dorma", an aria from Puccini's opera *Turandot*, the programme of which is our next object.

The man credited with coming up with the idea of using "Nessun Dorma" as the BBC's theme for the 1990 World Cup was Philip Bernie, then the assistant editor of the corporation's World Cup coverage. "In 1989 I was cutting various montages for the World Cup draw and around that time I heard "Nessun Dorma" played on *Desert Island Discs*," explained Bernie, who by the time he spoke to the *Independent* one Sunday in 2010 was the BBC's Head of Sport. "It was surprising to hear that kind of theme tune instead of the jingly-jangly tunes they had around *Match of the Day* and other programmes. It is a very powerful but a quite slow-tempo theme and at that time themes were generally fast and high-tempo."

As Bernie explained, the theme tune "just took off" and Pavarotti shot up to Number two in the charts, in as much as the tenor could shoot anywhere. But why was it that "Nessun Dorma" captured so completely the imagination of the British public, from middle-aged and middle-class housewives to young men in their twenties who'd hitherto thought Opera played for Juventus?

After all, the 1990 World Cup was a shocking affair, setting a new record for the fewest goals per match in a tournament (2.21). There were few matches of any quality and apart from Cameroon's run to the quarter-finals and Paul Gascoigne's semi-final tears, there was little romance or human drama. As for the denouement, the cynical borefest between Argentina and Germany that was decided by Andreas Brehme's eighty-fifth minute penalty, the less said about that the better.

Simon Barnes of *The Times* addressed the perplexing "Pavarotti" question in the wake of the tenor's death from cancer in September 2007. "The song," wrote Barnes, "changed the way we looked at football, understood football, related to football. Many other things followed, but the song was the prime mover of the revolution."

The 1980s was football's decade of shame, a roll call of cataclysmic events from Heysel to Valley Parade to Hillsborough that resulted in the deaths of nearly 200 people. Then there was hooliganism, the sight of hundreds of thugs running amok at football matches week after week. Many clubs responded by erecting fences at grounds so that supporters were caged like animals in a zoo.

"Football stank," continued Barnes. "The game was something to do with the dregs; no politician boasted about the club he supported as a boy." As the author Nick Hornby (see object 72) was later to say: "back in the '80s if you mixed in polite society you kept quiet about the fact you liked football."

And then came Italy and Puccini and Pavarotti and "at a stroke, football was shown as something cosmopolitan and sophisticated... it was a validation. Pavarotti's lung-busting anthem of conquest sent out the message: it's all right to like football. It really is acceptable to allow football to lift your heart and set free your mind. Football is opera." And weren't Gascoigne's tears in the semi-final proof of this fact?

Television and football saw they were on to a winner, and within two years the Champions League was launched with an anthem composed by Tony Britten and inspired by Georg Friedrich Handel's *Zadok the Priest*. At the 1994 World Cup in the USA Pavarotti performed "Nessum Dorma" on the eve of the final between Italy and Brazil.

British football, meanwhile, was undergoing a cultural revolution every bit as big as the lungs on Pavarotti. Turner Prize-shortlisted painter Mark Wallinger was among the contributors to an exhibition called "Offside: Contemporary Artists and Football" at Manchester City Art Galleries, and minimalist composer Michael Nyman released an album called *a.e.t.* (after extra time) inspired by his love of football.

Writing about "Falling in Love with Football" in the *Observer* in 1995, Emma Lindsey explained how in June 1990 she "went to bed a football virgin and awoke with a smile on my face to the thrills of Italia '90. An ad-man's dream, my then boyfriend bought me the Pavarotti album so I could learn the words to "Nessun Dorma". Suddenly sharing a mul-tipack of beers while watching a prime-time game seemed like a good idea not a punishment. Aroused, women around the country sang the tune in the bath and got a feel for what this football lark was all about."

Football had cracked the British middle classes, all thanks to an opera set in China that was composed by an Italian and sung by an Italian.

A brush

A brush for our next object. It was either that or Gazza himself, but these days that's a high risk enterprise. The plight of Paul Gascoigne, unquestionably England's most talented player of his generation, is a tragic tale, and his many admirers pray the future gives him some measure of contentment.

After a troubled childhood, Gascoigne made his debut for Newcastle in 1985 at the age of just 17. At first glance the podgy teenager with the toothy grin didn't seem to have much about him, but Gascoigne had a genius for the game that none of his peers possessed. Physically strong, perfectly balanced and blessed with a razor-sharp footballing brain, Gascoigne was also the finest dribbler the English game had seen for years.

He also had a nose for trouble, a habit of keeping bad company, and early on in his career with Newcastle he and his best friend, Jimmy "Five Bellies" Gardner, fell afoul of the law.

But his football was sublime. Named the First Division's Young Player of the Year for the 1987–88 season, Gascoigne was a target for Alex Ferguson's Manchester United, but in the end he moved south to London and Tottenham Hotspur for a then British record transfer fee of £2 million.

Gascoigne now entered what for him would be one of the most – possibly the only – settled periods of his life. In Spurs' manager Terry Venables and England coach Bobby Robson he had two men he respected and who he came to regard as almost surrogate fathers.

Both men tolerated Gascoigne's man-child streak, his

hyperactivity, his childish pranks and his need to be noticed. Not that they couldn't get infuriated. Robson described Gascoigne as "daft as a brush" in one memorable interview early on in the midfielder's international career. Gascoigne's response was to appear at training the next morning with a brush wedged into his sock.

Though Gascoigne made his England debut in 1988, it was two years later that he finally showed the world how rare was his talent. The venue was Italy, the tournament the 1990 World Cup, and in a competition short on goals and verve, England's Paul Gascoigne's illuminated every match he played. Not just with his talent but with his temperament, too. In England's semi-final defeat to West Germany he wept when he was show a yellow card. England wept with him. No one knew why. That was the effect Gascoigne had on the nation.

He returned home a hero. He was "Gazza", he was public property, he was the darling of the media, and he was utterly unequipped emotionally to deal with it all.

To list Gascoigne's every misdemeanour, his every mistake and his every mindless act would take too long; there have been that many of them. There were still moments of brilliance that only a player of Gascoigne's quality could have conjured up; a thunderous free kick against Arsenal in the semi-final of the 1991 FA Cup and a superb individual goal against Scotland in the 1996 European Championships to name but a couple.

But by the end of the decade Gascoigne's 57-cap England career was over and he was the object of scorn among the press. One hateful article in the *Daily Mirror* labelled him "the most pampered immature yob ever... whose only true gift is to slap decent people in the teeth."

Arguably Gascoigne's greatest misfortune was to have been at the height of his powers just as football entered a new dawn: one of money, celebrity and an unprecedented media coverage thanks to the new-found interest of the middle class- es. In truth the tabloids saw Gascoigne as a cash cow and milked him for all he was worth, indifferent to the effect it had on his immature personality.

Ironically it was another man who had been serially maligned by the tabloid press who had the perception to predict a grisly future for Gascoigne post-football. "What I'm concerned about," said Graham Taylor when he was manager of England in 1991, "is that when Gazza dies, Paul Gascoigne will still be alive."

Taylor's prescient words have been proved painfully accurate in recent years as Gascoigne, having ended his playing days as player-coach of Boston United, lurched from one crisis to another, most of them fuelled by large amounts of alcohol and many ending in a court appearance.

In an interview in December 2013, Gascoigne admitted he had endured a troubled year with a spell in rehab and an arrest for assaulting a train guard but he vowed to stay sober in 2014. Many millions – those who care for Gascoigne and not Gazza – will hope he sticks to his pledge. "I look upon myself as two people," he said in his 2004 autobiography. "Paul Gascoigne is the sensible, kind, generous one, if a bit boring. Gazza has been daft as a brush."

Taylor Report

OBJECT

69

HOME OFFICE

THE HILLSBOROUGH STADIUM DISASTER

15 APRIL 1989

INQUIRY BY THE RT HON LORD JUSTICE TAYLOR

FINAL REPORT

Presented to Parliament by the Secretary of State for the Home Department by Command of Her Majesty January 1990

When Lord Justice Taylor published his comprehensive and compassionate report on the Hillsborough Disaster in January 1990, he expressed his deep regret that his was the ninth report on British football stadium safety in the twentieth century. From Ibrox in 1902 to Bolton in 1946 to the Valley Parade Fire at Bradford

in 1985, football had a scandalous record when it came to safeguarding its supporters.

Hillsborough marked the turning point. So horrific had the events been of that April day in 1989, when ninety six Liverpool supporters went to watch their team play Nottingham Forest in an FA Cup semi-final and never returned home, that Lord Justice Taylor determined there must never be another tragedy.

Yes, he said in his report, hooligans had made the policing of football crowds a challenge for the authorities but nonetheless "the ordinary law-abiding football supporter travelling away is caught up in a police operation reminiscent of a column of prisoners of war being marched and detained under guard."

He also savaged the facilities on offer to fans, describing them as "lamentable. Apart from the discomfort of standing on a terrace exposed to the elements, the ordinary provisions to be expected at a place of entertainment are sometimes not merely basic but squalid. At some grounds the lavatories are primitive in design, poorly maintained and inadequate in number. This not only denies the spectator an essential facility he is entitled to expect. It directly lowers standards of conduct."

The Taylor Report contained seventy six recommendations in total, the most important of which was the necessity for all First and Second Division clubs (and the Scottish Premier League) to make their stadiums all-seater within four years, and for those from the third and fourth tier to do likewise by 1999 (this was later amended to allow clubs to retain some standing terracing provided it met the required safety standards). The government threw their weight behind the Report, agreeing to shelve its idea for a national identity card scheme and reduce the amount of betting duty levied on the football pools by 2.5 per cent, provided the money was used to modernise stadiums.

As a result of the Taylor Report, twenty four of the 102 clubs in the English football league moved grounds between 1990 and 2007. Football said goodbye to some famous names from the past – Roker Park, Maine Road and the Baseball Ground to name but three – but few fans mourned as they took their seat in spanking new stadiums that provided good views, comfy seats, decent food and somewhere to answer the call of nature.

"Taylor ushered in seating and provoked the first major stadium modernisation programme in 30 years," said John Williams, a senior lecturer in the sociology of football at Leicester University.

There were complaints from some fans that all-seater stadiums lacked the atmosphere of terraces such as the Liverpool Kop and the Arsenal North Bank; a Premier League survey of fans in 1996–97 revealed that 60 per cent missed standing at matches.

Tough, said the clubs, who ran promotions to encourage families, women and supporters from ethnic minorities. In 2011 a spokesman for the Premier League announced that "we now have women making up 23 per cent of crowds, 11 per cent from black and minority ethnic groups and 13 per cent of Premier League season ticket holders were under 16 last season."

In concluding his report in 1990, Lord Justice Taylor expressed the hope that he had "made it clear that the years of patching up grounds, of having periodic disasters and narrowly avoiding many others by muddling through on a wing and a prayer must be over. A totally new approach across the whole field of football requires higher standards both in bricks and mortar and in human relationships."

This has been accomplished with stunning success, and as a result British football is safer and more popular than ever before.

Women's World Cup trophy

Tucked in between the Taylor Report and the Premier League Blueprint is the Women's World Cup, a trophy first contested in 1991. That might give the impression that women's football is a relatively recent phenomenon, but don't be fooled. Women were playing football before they were voting, or at least they were trying to. The challenge they faced – are still facing – was how to break down their opponents. Not the ones on the field but those off it, men who believed that the football field is no place for the "fairer sex".

It's still going on in the twenty first century. Witness the comments of a couple of Sky Sports presenters in 2011 about the performance of assistant referee Sian Massey. We haven't enough time for a detailed description but the gist of their comments was: "she's a bird, what does she know about football?" Cheer up, Massey (one of just three top-level female officials in English football at the time of the incident); if you thought that was bad you should hear what the sisterhood endured 100 years earlier.

The first all-female football team is believed to have originated in Glasgow in 1881. They weren't well received. The *Glasgow Herald* reported that a crowd of several hundred turned up, nearly all men, and "laughed, cheered and occasionally hooted, the most shocking imprecations and vulgarities being audible in all quarters." The match ended in chaos when some of the "rougher element" invaded the pitch and subjected several of the players to what today would be classified as sexual assault.

Similar scenes unfolded in Manchester and Liverpool in the following years, as the chauvinistic Victorian male gave unwitting impetus to the Suffragette Movement. A decade after the scenes in Glasgow, a women's exhibition game was organised in the British capital between a North London XI and a South London XI. Ten thousand spectators paid a shilling to watch, and the press was out in force. They weren't impressed. "It must be clear to everybody that girls are totally unfitted for the rough work of the football field," wrote the correspondent for the *Sketch*. The chap from the *Pall Mall Gazette* formed the opinion that the players were all "misguided females" and it was left to the female reporter of the *Manchester Guardian* to come to the defence of her sex. Obliged to wear long billowing knickerbockers to below their knees to protect their modesty, the women were restricted in their movements. No surprise, therefore, wrote the female reporter, that "only two of the girls were able to kick with any freedom and not many ran well."

Women's football in Britain fell into abeyance and only re-emerged during the First World War. With the men away at the front women took over their roles: driving buses, delivering milk, and playing football. Prime Minister David Lloyd George, who always had an eye for the ladies, encouraged the women to stage matches to raise money for wounded soldiers. In December 1920, 53,000 people paid to watch a Dick Kerr Ladies XI take on St Helens Ladies at Goodison Park, home of Everton.

The Football Association were aghast. It was bad enough that South Americans were now playing their sport, but the thought of women donning a pair of boots was just too much. On 5 December 1921, the FA issued a statement which began: "Complaints having been made as to football being played by women, the Council feel impelled to express their strong opinion that the game of football is quite unsuitable for females and ought not to be encouraged... The Council requests the clubs belonging to the Association refuse the use of their grounds for such matches."

Women's football in Britain collapsed. Within the space of twenty years the number of clubs fell from 150 to seventeen, and they didn't begin to climb again until the social revolution of the 1960s had swept away some of the sport's sexist dinosaurs.

But still the inaugural women's World Cup wasn't staged until 1991, sixty one years after its male counterpart, and of all places it was hosted in the People's Republic of China, a country which two years earlier had slaughtered many hundreds of its citizens in a bloody repression of democracy. Not the first – nor the last – FIFA decision that's left the world baffled.

The USA won the inaugural competition, repeating the achievement in the 1999 tournament (by which time the number of entrants had risen from twelve to sixteen). The United States were the sport's powerhouse, boasting 7 million registered players in 2000, none more famous than Brandi Chastain.

Chastain had scored the winning penalty for the USA in the 1999 World Cup Final, a feat she celebrated by whipping off her shirt and revealing her bra. Millions of Victorian men must have turned in their grave.

Suddenly women's football found itself on the front cover of the iconic magazine *Sports Illustrated*. But it was sex, not soccer, selling. In the decade that followed the USA's 1999 World Cup win, two attempts were made to launch a professional soccer league in the country. Both collapsed. But the demand for the World Cup kept growing. At the 2011 tournament in Germany nearly 850,000 spectators watched the thirty two matches as Japan won the title for the first time, while a crowd of 70,584 watched Team GB beat Brazil at Wembley in the 2012 Olympics, a record attendance for a women's match in Britain.

Not a knickerbocker in sight, not a sports bra in sight, just plenty of good football.

Blueprint

"Blueprint" is a boring word. It conjures up images of boardrooms and business jargon and reams of small print. So we'll be as brief as we can in discussing this object but without detracting from its monumental significance. Because the Premier League Blueprint is a big one as far as our history of football goes.

When the Football League was formed in 1888–89 its income for the year was £5; by the turn of the twentieth century it was £17,000; by the end of the 1980s the League was ailing for reasons previously outlined.

Graham Kelly had been secretary of the Football League throughout much of that decade before, in 1988, he was appointed chief executive of the Football Association. According to Andrew Ward and John Williams (writing in *Football Nation*), Kelly foresaw trouble ahead not long into his tenure, in the shape of a "power struggle developing between the government, the Football League management committee, the chairmen of the top League clubs, the Football Associations, the Professional Footballers' Associations [and] the television companies."

Kelly spoke to all the relevant parties (his discussions taking on far greater significance following the 1989 Hillsborough Disaster) and the outcome was the publication in June 1991 of the FA's "Blueprint for the Future of Football" in which it called for the establishment of "a Premier League within the administration of the Football Association".

The Football League was horrified by the idea but the top clubs had glimpsed the promised land, one free from the "corporatist organisation of the League", and on 29 June 1991 fifteen clubs resigned from the First Division. The League went to court claiming the FA's actions were illegal, but on 31 July Mr Justice Rose ruled that "the FA did have the constitutional power to set up its own Premier League."

On 27 May 1992 the FA Premier League was officially formed and none of the twenty two clubs in the new League spent much time worrying about their confrères in the lower divisions. Kelly soon realised that their goodwill didn't extend to the national team either. As Ward and Williams wrote in *Football Nation*: "The core Blueprint idea that all the income and commercial properties of the FA and the FA Premier League should be centralised (as a means of supporting the England team and the wider game) was soon ditched by the FA Premier League clubs. They refused to pool their sponsorship with the FA."

They also baulked at the idea of having an FA director on the Premier League board, the final proof for Kelly that his organisation had been cast aside in the race to rake in the millions. The players soon scented the opportunity to improve their lot by threatening to strike if they didn't have more of a voice – and a cut. The Players Football Association won a 50 per cent increase in their share of the television money, which would be a fair whack after the announcement of a lucrative deal between the FA Premier League and Rupert Murdoch's BSkyB (see object 73).

The inaugural Premier League season was launched in August 1992. Apart from one or two superficial changes (half-time was increased from ten to fifteen minutes and referees wore green not black) there was little that appeared different. But there was: there was a new glamour. In the wake of the Taylor Report stadiums were being modernised and this, allied to the decline of hooliganism and the improved image of football thanks to Pavarotti, transformed the top-flight of English football. Crowds rose from 9.9 million in 1991–92 (the old First Division) to 13.47 million by 2002–03.

In April 1996 the *Guardian* wrote how "English football reshaped itself into the Premier League, launched with the boost of a £250 million five-year contract from Rupert Murdoch's Sky operation." As a result a "working-class game has become a textbook example of rampant free market capitalism and is currently enjoying a boom which, like all booms, appears irreversible."

The *Guardian*, true to its socialist leanings, wondered whether the Premier League hadn't created a false market for itself. The League's chief executive Rick Parry rubbished the idea, saying there was no such as thing as a false market. "It's a market, that's all," he said. By 2005 the market was still booming, with the Premier League the richest in the world in turnover.

The one word of caution was sounded by Graham Kelly, the man who had driven the idea of a Premier League in the early days. "The last time this happened, when the money shot up in the boom of the late seventies, I believe the game tended to lose contact with its community base," he explained to the *Guardian* in 1996. "A lot of hard work has gone into re-establishing that. Football must always remember to keep in touch with reality, although that might be quite difficult when you look at the money involved... Football has got to recognise that there may indeed be a time when television isn't falling over itself to get its hands on the game. We won't be in the land of milk and honey for ever."

Fever Pitch

OBJECT
72

Next up is Nick Hornby's *Fever Pitch*, a warm, moving, honest account of one young man's unhealthy obsession with Arsenal Football Club. It was published in 1992 and became a literary phenomenon. As far as the middle classes were concerned

FEVER PITCH
A Fan's Life

***Fever Pitch* continued what Pavarotti had begun in 1990, demonstrating that there was more to football than bad haircuts, hooliganism and half-time cups of Bovril.**

Reflecting in 2005 on the stunning success of *Fever Pitch*, Hornby told the *Guardian* that he had been contemplating writing a football book for a number of years but "you have to remember that the public perception of football for most of the eighties was summed up by a *Sunday Times* article which claimed that it was 'a slum sport for slum people'. I had friends – lawyers, teachers – who would look incredulous when I said I was a football fan. It was like saying you followed wrestling."

Publishers' eyes lit up like a striker presented with an open goal after *Fever Pitch* topped the bestseller lists, and a year later Hornby was editing *My Favourite Year*, a collection of new football writing and featuring such luminaries of the literary world as Roddy Doyle, winner of that year's Booker Prize for *Paddy Clarke Ha Ha Ha*.

The release of *My Favourite Year* – and the news that the paperback edition of *Fever Pitch* had sold 100,000 copies in its first month – was proof to the *Observer* "of the emergence of a new class of football fan – cultured, discerning and widely-read. In it, the middle classes declare unashamedly that their game is not cricket or rugger, but football... and that they are not rampaging oiks." The *Observer* quoted Hornby to the effect that "people are beginning to see that culture and football can co-exist in one body," and by 1994 the game was even more entrenched among the British middle classes.

In January of that year, BBC2 began airing the first series of the cult show *Fantasy Football League*. The two presenters of FFL were the blokeish Brummie Frank Skinner and David Baddiel, a former public school boy with a double first from Cambridge. Working-class he most definitely wasn't. In October of that year England was named the host of the 1996 European Championships (a tournament for which

Skinner and Baddiel created the memorable song "Football's Coming Home") and the *Independent* wrote that there was "a new wave of optimism" sweeping English football: "A game once weighed down by shame proudly launched its coming-out party yesterday, one which may mark its final rehabilitation after the horrors of the 1980s," wrote the *Independent*'s football correspondent, Glenn Moore. There were myriad reasons, he added, why football had dragged itself out of the gutter, many of which sprang from the shock of the tragedy of Hillsborough in 1989. But the consequence was "that football has become socially acceptable, trendy even. The new mood was characterised by the publication, and subsequent success, of Nick Hornby's *Fever Pitch*, the story of a middle-class Arsenal fan. The news stands are full of football magazines, club shirts have become fashion accessories and crowds have risen for eight successive seasons."

In the spring of 2012, to mark the twentieth anniversary of *Fever Pitch*, the BBC published an article on its website in which it discussed the book's impact, and whether it had taken the game away from the real supporter and into the arms of middle-class dilettantes. "For those who support that argument," ran the article, "one man's name often appears on the list of reasons the game has moved beyond its traditional working-class roots. That man is Nick Hornby."

Noting that *Fever Pitch* has been translated into twenty six languages, sold millions of copies and been made into a major film, the BBC asked the author to defend himself against the allegation that his book had been bad for the working classes who now found themselves priced out of their sport.

The reality, said Hornby, is a "bit more complicated", adding: "My feeling is football changed in the 1960s, not when *Fever Pitch* was published – when England won the World Cup and George Best was like a pop star."

That was true to the extent that a minority of middle-class football fans began going to games, but for the majority football was still "kev-ball", a game on a par with wrestling, as

Hornby had told the *Guardian* in 2005.

According to John Williams, an expert on football at Leicester University, football was irrevocably changed by the Hillsborough Disaster and the subsequent Taylor Report. Football was in a deep trough in 1989 and much was being done to haul it out by the time *Fever Pitch* was published. But Hornby's book enlisted the help of the middle classes.

"Now publicly claiming to be a middle-class football fan was no longer a social faux pas," Williams told the BBC. "New, more affluent older supporters were drawn in."

And nearly all of them had read *Fever Pitch*.

Satellite dish

OBJECT
73

What Nick Hornby wouldn't have given for our next object in the 1970s – a satellite dish, which would have allowed him to watch his beloved Arsenal on those days when he couldn't make the long away trips as a kid.

Since the late 1960s, television rights in Britain had been fought over by the BBC and ITV, to the chagrin of the leading clubs of the day who believed they deserved more. The "Big Five" as they were known – Arsenal, Spurs, Liverpool, Everton and Manchester United – were unhappy with the existing arrangements, as Liverpool chairman John Smith told *The Times* in October 1985: "The big clubs are very, very impatient for many reasons. We are suffering financial hardship because there is no television agreement, we are not in Europe (following the five-year ban on English clubs entering

European competitions as a result of the Heysel disaster), gates are declining and altogether the state of our national game is in disarray."

The English game had yet to hit rock bottom – that would happen at Hillsborough in 1989 – but by 1988 there were changes afoot in how television covered the game. British Satellite Broadcasting, the country's first satellite channel, offered a four-season package worth £35.8 million, which was recommended to the clubs by the Football League Management. This prompted ITV to make an offer of £44 million with 75 per cent of that figure going to the First Division. The deal, which expired in 1992, was accepted although the Big Five still believed they were being undersold.

Then, as we have already seen, came the perfect storm of the Taylor Report, Italia '90 and the Premier League. Football was in the big time, and the Big Five were about to realise their dreams. The ITV deal, agreed four years earlier, ran out three months before the launch of the inaugural Premier League season in August 1992. ITV bid for the rights and with their 8 million-strong audience were confident of success. But Rupert Murdoch's satellite channel (now renamed BSkyB) made up for in money what it lacked in audience (approximately 2 million viewers). As Andrew Ward and John Williams write in *The Football Nations*: "BSkyB recognised that there were sufficient affluent working-class and middle-class consumers to produce the necessary profit. Many people had been captivated by England's success at the 1990 World Cup finals."

BSkyB bid £304 million for five seasons of coverage – a staggering sum in comparison to what had gone before – and secured the rights. In return for their money BSkyB would broadcast sixty live matches a season on Sundays and Mondays and the BBC would continue to show highlights on Saturday evening's *Match of the Day*.

"I think it is wrong that only 2 million [satellite] dish owners get access to such major sporting events," said Sebastian Coe, then-Conservative MP and former Olympic gold medallist.

Fears that such an unprecedented number of live matches would result in diminished attendances proved wrong; the reverse, in fact, and season by season audiences grew as a football fever gripped Britain.

In the summer of 1996 – mindful of the fact their contract expired the following year – BSkyB extended their contract for a further four years with a bid of £640 million. The *Independent* was as staggered as the rest of the country by the money tabled, and in a report titled "Football's Big Question: How to Spend the Lolly", Glenn Moore wrote that the "vast bulk of that [sum] goes to the Premiership. Leaving aside earnings from FA Cup and European games the Premiership clubs will get £185,750,000 between them next season. Some of this (about £10 million) will go to the Professional Footballers' Association to be used for various schemes which provide for the welfare of players young and old and the excellent Football in the Community programme."

And still the money continued to rise as BSkyB tightened its grip on Premier League coverage. In 2001 they bid £1.1 billion for sixty six live matches; in 2007 the figure had soared to £1.7 billion – a tidy sum, but peanuts to the deal brokered by BSkyB and BT in June 2012. Together they paid a total of £3.018 billion to the Premier League for the seasons 2013/14 to 2015/16, with Sky acquiring the rights to broadcast 116 matches per year and BT thirty eight. Every individual televised match will now cost the broadcasters £6.6 million, an increase of £1.9 million from the previous deal.

The deal means that those clubs lucky enough to be in the Premier League will receive approximately £14 million more per year, although Richard Scudamore, Premier League chief executive, warned clubs to think about where best to invest the riches. "We are entering a new era with financial fair play [see object 90]," he said. "I'm hoping it will get invested in things other than playing talent. It should also be able to achieve sustainability."

Flying pigs, Mr. Scudamore, flying pigs.

As the *Guardian* commented wryly, the eye-watering deal "is good news for club owners, players, their agents and luxury car dealerships and, on the evidence of previous deals, is likely to lead to another sharp rise in transfer fees".

Turnip

There might be a bad a smell from this object, so accept our apologies, but what would you expect from a 20-year-old turnip? The turnip in question first appeared on the back page of the *Sun* following England's 1992 defeat to Sweden. Under the headline "TURNIPS 1 SWEDES 2", the paper had superimposed manager Graham Taylor's head onto the inoffensive root vegetable. The "turnip incident" opened a new front in the way the press covered football: now it was no longer about criticising a manager's tactics or a player's performance; now it was personal and insulting, looking to ridicule and degrade. It was the late twentieth century equivalent of putting a man in the stocks and pelting him with fruit and veg.

As we saw with object 46, the typewriter, once upon a time the press and the playing staff were the best of pals, and even a player of Jimmy Greaves' refuelling habits could rely on the Fourth Estate to practise discretion.

So when did it all start to change? In his 2006 book *The Heart of the Game* Greaves dates the shift to the early 1980s, saying that the "working relationship between players and the media that in truth had become less and less convivial throughout the seventies took on all the attributes of a 'them and us' situation... not, it has to be said, those who reported on football but the 'newshound' type of journalists, who were assigned to cover big matches in the hope of finding a story that would titillate readers."

To a large degree Greaves was right. In 1969 Rupert Murdoch launched the *Sun* to challenge the *Daily Mirror*, *Daily Mail* and *Daily Express*. In 1978 another tabloid appeared, the *Daily Star*, and that was followed in the 1980s by the *Sunday Sport* and the short-lived *Today*.

Competition to "get the story" became fierce, cut-throat even, and football was seen as a good source of stories, second only to sex in selling papers. Footballers became caught up in this circulation war by accepting money to "write" columns for one of the papers; instantly they became "the enemy" of rival newspapers.

While the "newshounds" referred to by Greaves dug around for titillating tittle-tattle, some of the football correspondents became increasingly hostile in reporting the game, constantly reminded by their editors that controversy sells better than consensus. There was also the major misconception, harboured by an unfathomably large percentage of the English press and public, that the country was still a top-flight footballing nation, and not the second tier side that it's been for the best part of forty years.

So first the press went for Ron Greenwood in the early 1980s before turning their bile on his successor, Bobby Robson, after the 1988 European Championships. Robson resigned after the 1990 World Cup, sad to be leaving the post but not the press. "I was just a victim of the tabloid newspaper war," he said. "I had watched the cancer spread over the eight years I had been in the job."

Robson's departure let in Graham Taylor, who had achieved great things with unfashionable Watford in the 1980s. An intelligent and thoughtful man, Taylor was guilty of naivety in some of his dealings with the media. He agreed to take part in a television documentary about life as the England manager, and was portrayed as a gibbering idiot.

The tabloids held back while Taylor's England produced results (they were unbeaten in his first year in charge) but the moment they faltered they attacked. The "Turnips" headline appeared during the 1992 European Championships, a tournament in which England were poor. The following year England lost 2-0 to the USA in a friendly and the press pack descended on the house of Taylor's elderly parents, bursting into the kitchen and demanding to know "what you think of your son now?"

Taylor eventually resigned in November 1993 and the *Sun* celebrated by reprinting the vegetable picture on the front page under the headline: "TURNIP TAYLOR TURNS UP HIS TOES."

Taking the lead from the tabloids, sections of the public continued to pour scorn on Taylor long after he'd returned to managing League clubs. In an interview in 1997 he revealed that he was still wary of entering pubs, restaurants and other public places because "there's a small percentage of people who won't let go, always someone who thinks they can abuse you. It's worse when drink is involved. I won't put myself, or my wife, Rita, in that situation."

England have got through six more managers since Taylor, including Glenn Hoddle (described by one paper as a "deranged megalomaniac") and Steve McLaren ("the wally with the brolly"). In that time the Three Lions haven't had a sniff of an international trophy. The latest man to try his luck as England manager is Roy Hodgson who, a day after his appointment, was mocked by the *Sun* for his speech impediment. Since then the press has backed off but who knows what might happen if the Three Lions get a mauling in the Amazon during the 2014 World Cup.

Brown envelope

The year 1993 saw the closing of one chapter in English football and the opening of another. In February the great Bobby Moore died, the man who'd led England to their World Cup triumph twenty seven years earlier. "Moore was my friend," remarked Pelé. "The finest, the most honourable defender that I ever played against."

The new chapter opened four months after Moore's death, in the High Court of London, and nearly twenty years on no one's sure how much further it's got to run before we can close it.

The chapter's called "Bung" and has a cast of characters that includes some of the biggest names in British football and some exotic-sounding foreign types. Oh, and the chapter also features obscene amounts of cash, motorway service stations and brown paper bags.

It was 10 June 1993 and the High Court of London was hosting the latest proceedings in the battle between Terry Venables and Alan Sugar for control of Tottenham Hotspur. In an affidavit read out to the court, Sugar, the Spurs chairman, described how during dealings for the £2.1 million transfer of Nottingham Forest striker Teddy Sheringham to Spurs in 1992, "I was told by Mr Venables that Mr Clough "likes a bung". I told him I thought this was outrageous and that I would not run my company like this. I was told the usual thing was to meet him (Mr Clough) in a motorway cafe and he would be handed a bag full of money. I told Mr Venables I didn't want to hear about this and didn't want him to mention it to me again."

According to the *Daily Mail*, "the naming of Clough brought gasps – and a few chuckles – from the public gallery of Court 35, packed with Spurs fans loyal to Venables." Clough laughed off the allegation, asking reporters: "A bung? Isn't that something you get from a plumber to stop up the bath?" Others weren't laughing, however, and a five-year inquiry was launched to investigate if bungs and backhanders really were part of the English game. In the end Clough escaped punishment – not because he was cleared but because the FA decided to drop the misconduct charge, citing Clough's poor health.

Brushed under the carpet, said others, including Rick Parry, the then chief executive of the Premier League who headed the inquiry. In an interview with the *Daily Telegraph* in 2004, shortly after Clough's death, Parry said: "On the balance of evidence, we felt he was guilty of taking bungs. The evidence was pretty strong. I was very surprised when the FA took no action against him."

Others didn't escape, however, in the wake of Alan Sugar's high court allegation. In February 1995 George Graham was sacked as Arsenal manager, having admitted to accepting an illegal payment of £425,000 from Norwegian agent Rene Hauge during the transfer of John Jensen three years earlier.

By the end of the 1990s the FA was saying the "bung culture" chapter was closed and it was time to move into the bright uplands of the twenty first century. For a while all appeared well. Then, in January 2006, Luton Town manager Mike Newell claimed the game was more corrupt than ever. "If George Graham is the only one guilty of taking a bung in the last 10 years, I would be absolutely amazed," he said, before warning: "If the governing bodies don't eradicate some of the things happening, it will kill the game."

The FA set up an inquiry two months later to examine the claims. Lord Stevens, former Commissioner of the Metropolitan Police, was in charge. Having investigated corruption in cricket he was well versed in shining a light into the nooks and crannies of top-class sport. He began by investigating thirty nine transfer deals, and when he issued his final report in June 2007 Stevens expressed concern over the propriety of seventeen transfers involving fifteen agents, five Premier League players and two managers.

There were denials all round, and Barry Silkman, one of the agents whose practises were criticised by Lord Stevens, said: "People inside football, people that really matter – the top chairman, the chief executives and managers – they're laughing at it. They're actually laughing because they don't understand what the problem is."

Silkman's right: people at the top end of English football don't get what all the fuss is about. After all, who'll miss a couple of hundred thousand here and there in a game awash with millions?

Gun

OBJECT 76

Thank God this object, a revolver, has just a fleeting association with football. Long may that continue. though it will always be too late for Andrés Escobar, the Colombian defender who was gunned down in July 1994.

The exact details of how the 27-year-old Escobar came to be murdered have never fully emerged, nor has the exact nature of the link between the assassin and the organised drug gangs that had ruled Colombia for years. According to an article in the respected magazine *World Soccer*: "Colombian soccer in the 1980s and 1990s was inextricably linked to society... when the millions made out of the illegal drugs trade funded the sport, putting soccer domestically and at international level on an all-time high."

At the centre of this tangled web of narcotics and violence was Pablo Escobar, the ruthless boss of Colombia's drug trade who bore no relation to his footballing namesake. Escobar or *El Patrón* as he was known in Colombia was a curious figure, a man who thought nothing of murdering his enemies and anyone even vaguely linked to them, but who spent millions on improving facilities in his local community. Pablo Escobar was also mad on football and bought Atlético Nacional, a club in the city of Medellín, through which he allegedly laundered some of his profits from the drug trade.

World Soccer magazine claimed that Escobar "ensured that the club kept its best players and was able to pay them high enough wages to prevent them being enticed by rich clubs in Latin America, Mexico and Europe." Players were paid to play privately in front of Escobar and his drug boss associates, with huge wads of cash being bet on the outcome of the games.

The authorities finally caught up with Escobar in December 1993 and he was killed during a shootout in Medellín. The *patrón* was dead but those in his pay were still alive and still expecting Colombia to do well at the 1994 World Cup in the United States, their first appearance at the tournament in twenty eight years. Colombia had qualified in style, thrashing Argentina 5-0 en route, and raising hope that they might be the South American side to shine at this World Cup. "There were reports that soccer gambling syndicates had bet large amounts of money on Colombia's progression to the second round and players were receiving death threats from back home," said *World Soccer*.

How much the toxic influence of the drug cartels had seeped into the national squad remains a matter of conjecture. But certainly their 3-1 drubbing at the hands of a powerful Romanian side in their opening match did little for Colombia's standing.

Their second match against the hosts in Los Angeles now assumed a great significance: lose and Colombia would be going home in disgrace. Escobar was a defender, a player well respected in his homeland and known as the "Gentleman", which made it all the more distressing when he scored an own goal on thirty four minutes.

Trying to cut out a cross from the USA's John Harkes, Escobar diverted the ball past Óscar Córdoba and into his own net for the game's opening goal. The USA went on to win 2-1 and Colombia were knocked out of the World Cup. Escobar was obviously downhearted but in his column for the Bogota newspaper *El Tiempo* he signed off saying: "See you soon, because life doesn't end here."

Ten days after his own goal Escobar was in the El Indio nightclub in the Colombian city of Medellín with his girl-friend. According to witness statements he got into an argu-ment with some men about his mistake and to avoid trouble he walked out of the club. The men followed and one of them shot Escobar six times in the club's car park, witnesses saying he shouted "thanks for the own goal" as he opened fire.

In a subsequent documentary broadcast on ESPN it was claimed the man convicted of the killing, Humberto Castro Muñoz, was a bodyguard for one of the powerful Colombian cartels. Apparently he and his accomplices had "bet heavily on the team and were upset at having lost". With grim irony, the documentary also speculated that had Pablo Escobar been alive then so would have his namesake because the drug lord's love of football would have prevented anyone targeting the players.

"It's years and years that have gone by since, but you always think about it. I do," remarked John Harkes in 2010, the player whose cross Escobar put into his own goal. "Sometimes the sport transcends everything politically, culturally."

Tin of sardines

A tin of sardines may appear at first glance to be an unusual object to find in our history of football. Fish, other than minnows, have rarely had much to do with the game. But if the sardines are unusual then so is the man they denote. He was a maverick, a rebel, an *enfant terrible* – he was Eric Cantona.

To Manchester United fans he remains "King Eric", the magisterial man from Marseille who reigned supreme at Old Trafford for five glorious years following his arrival from Leeds United in November 1992 at a cost of £1.2 million. Inspired by his genius in 1993 United clinched their first League title for twenty six years. The following year they won the Double. In 1996 they did the Double again and in 1997 they won their fourth League title in five years.

The only season during Cantona's rule when United failed to win the title was 1994–95, and there was a reason for that. Sent off for stamping four minutes into the second half at Selhurst Park, Cantona was making his way towards the dressing room when he was confronted by Matthew Simmons. "You French bastard!", the Crystal Palace supporter allegedly screamed. "Fuck off back to France, you mother fucker!" Looking on the from the press box, the football correspondent of the *Independent* described Cantona's response: "He heard something and turned, then, sensationally, he moved towards a fan who was on his feet and appeared to be gesturing at him and took off, in kick-boxing fashion, landing his feet into the chest of the man. Cantona staggered back, recovered his balance and then landed at least two punches on the fan."

Cantona's act cost him dear. United fined him £20,000 and suspended him for the rest of the season. The FA extended the ban until 30 September 1995 and added a further £10,000 to the fine. He was even hauled before the beak and sentenced to two weeks in prison for common assault. Cantona appealed, won, and had his punishment reduced to 120 hours of community service. At the press conference that followed, the Frenchman was asked by the throng of reporters how he felt.

Eyeing his subjects with barely concealed disdain, Cantona sipped from a glass of water. Then he said: "When the seagulls follow the trawler it is because they think sardines will be thrown into the sea. Thank you very much."

Cantona rose and walked out, leaving behind a press pack in uproar. They ridiculed his metaphor – one paper calling it "gobbledegook"; was it because they realised they themselves were the seagulls?

There had been calls for Cantona to be kicked out of football forever following his kung fu kick. He did, after all, have previous. Fined by Auxerre for striking a teammate, suspended by Marseille for throwing his shirt at a referee and dumped from the France team for calling manager Henri Michel "a bag of shit". Even Alex Ferguson had struggled at times to keep Cantona under control, watching in disbelief in March 1994 as the Frenchman got himself sent off twice in four days.

Comparisons were drawn with George Best, United's most notorious bad boy, but the parallels were weak. Best's indiscipline was off the field, Cantona's on it. He wasn't a drinker, a gambler, a womaniser; he was a man of the arts who once said of Maradona: "In the course of time it will be said that Maradona was to football what Rimbaud was to poetry and Mozart to music."

Cantona's ban expired on 30 September. The following day he was back for United, scoring a penalty in the 2-2 draw with Liverpool. By the end of the season his nineteen goals had helped United do the Double and in the FA Cup Final it was Cantona's volley that beat Liverpool 1-0.

Ferguson made him captain for the 1996–97 season, an astute act of faith by the Scot that revealed another side to the Frenchman. Handed responsibility for the first time in his life, Cantona took a paternal pride in watching the rise of young United stars such as David Beckham, Paul Scholes and the Neville brothers.

United retained the League title in May 1997 and then a week later Cantona retired a fortnight before he turned 31. "I have played professional football for 13 years," he said in a statement delivered by club chairman Martin Edwards, "which is a long time. I now wish to do other things."

Those other things were acting, a career in which Cantona has established a reputation on both stage and screen. But while he abdicated his football throne more than fifteen years ago his reign continues to be remembered. In April 2012 when the Premier League unveiled its nominations in a series of categories to celebrate its twentieth anniversary, Cantona was shortlisted in five categories, more than any other player or manager.

The day after Cantona's kung fu kick the French sports newspaper *L'Équipe* accused him of shaming French football. "At 28," the paper thundered, "Eric Cantona is exactly as he was at 18 and as he will be at 38 – violent, rebellious, heroic and shipwrecked."

They were wrong on two counts. He's mellowed in middle age and he most certainly is not shipwrecked. But he remains rebellious and heroic, and our tin of sardines is a fitting tribute to the most charismatic footballer the English Premier League has ever seen.

Cone of chips

Is there anything more quintessentially English than our next object – a portion of chips? Sprinkle on the salt, add a drop or two of vinegar, perhaps a dab of brown sauce for the brave-hearted and, bingo, a snack to gladden the heart of every red-blooded Englishman.

But not a Frenchman. And when Arsène Wenger arrived at Arsenal in October 1996 he couldn't believe his eyes at what the players were eating. In his first major interview he lectured the *London Evening Standard* on the nation's culinary tastes: "In England you eat too much sugar and meat and not enough vegetables. I lived for two years in Japan and it was the best diet I ever had. The whole way of life there is linked to health... their diet is basically boiled vegetables, fish and rice. No fat, no sugar."

So what did that mean the Arsenal players could expect in the canteen? asked the *Standard*. "No chips," replied Wenger, also adding that "steak" and "jam roly poly and custard" would no longer be appearing on the menu. "As a coach you can influence the diet of your players," explained Wenger. "You can point out what is wrong. Some are wrong because they are not strong enough to fight temptation and some are wrong because they do not know."

It was a bullish move from the new Arsenal manager, the club's first to be born abroad, and the man appointed to restore the club's reputation after the scandal of George Graham (see object 75) and the mediocrity of Bruce Rioch. Not everyone was impressed. "Arsène Who?" asked the *Evening Standard*, overlooking the fact Wenger had guided Monaco to the French League title and two Cup triumphs during his time in charge. There was also success with Grampus 8 in Japan, not that that cut much ice with Alex Ferguson. "What does he know about English football, coming from Japan?" sneered the Manchester United manager shortly after Wenger's arrival at Highbury.

The Arsenal squad that Wenger inherited was similarly sceptical about the bespectacled Frenchman with a Master's degree from the University of Strasbourg and a distinctively unimpressive playing CV. Lee Dixon thought he looked "like a geography teacher", Tony Adams doubted the quality of his English and Ray Parlour "did impressions of Inspector Clouseau". Ian Wright grumbled about having to eat broccoli.

Several of the players vowed to continue with the club's drinking culture, despite the fact two of their number – Adams and Paul Merson – had admitted to being addicted to alcohol.

Wenger had other ideas. Beer went the way of the chips, the Frenchman stating: "When we are together as a group we do not drink alcohol. Even on the team bus on the way back from games it is not allowed." Leading by example, Wenger shunned the English tradition of having a post-match beer with the opposition manager.

There were other changes. He overhauled the club's training facilities, introduced new training methods, encouraged the players to stretch and cool down, brought in an osteopath and signed a young Frenchman from Inter Milan called Patrick Vieira. But one aspect of Arsenal that Wenger left well alone was the defence. Adams, Dixon, Nigel Winterburn and Martin Keown may not have appealed to the Frenchman's aesthetic nature but he was astute enough to recognise they formed the foundations on which to build a side to challenge the dominance of Manchester United.

In the 1995–96 season Arsenal had finished fifth in the League, nineteen points behind champions United. At the end of Wenger's first season in charge Arsenal had moved up to third, eight points shy of United.

By the start of the 1997–98 season Wenger's French revolution was taking shape at Arsenal. Showing a deft *savoir-faire* in the transfer market, Wenger bought Dutch Marc Overmars from Ajax for £5.5 million, a teenage striker called Nicolas Anelka from Paris Saint-Germain for a mere half a million (he would be sold to Real Madrid two years later for £23 million) and, most significantly of all, paid Monaco £2.5 million for Emmanuel Petit, pairing him in midfield with Patrick Vieira.

Suddenly the club that for years had thrived on the tag of "boring, boring Arsenal" began to play with a verve that astounded opponents. Manchester United were beaten home and away as the Gunners won the League title and then doubled up in the FA Cup, defeating Newcastle 2-0 in the final. Wenger, lauded as the first overseas manager to win the Premier League, declared that "names come and go. People remember those who bring results."

In 2002 Wenger did it again, steering Arsenal to another League and Cup double with a side spearheaded by Thierry Henry, a signing which proved even more inspired than Patrick Vieira. Wenger was asked if his next objective was not only to win the League but to go the season unbeaten. "It's not impossible. I know it will be difficult, but if we keep the right attitude it's possible," he said.

Arsenal proved it was possible two seasons later, winning the title with a record that read: Played thirty eight, won twenty six, drawn twelve, lost zero. Not since Preston North End in 1888–89 had a side gone unbeaten in a season of top-flight English League football.

The record of Wenger since then has diminished. No trophies since they beat Manchester United in the 2005 FA Cup Final. Wenger's Arsenal have struggled to keep up with the financial clout of Chelsea and the two Manchester clubs.

But Wenger has given more to Arsenal than trophies. He transformed not just the way the club played, but the way they were seen. Once the most English of clubs Arsenal under

Wenger became the most unashamedly internationalist side in the Premier League. As Jason Cowley wrote in the *Observer* in May 2006, days after the club had played their last game at Highbury ahead of their move to the Emirates: "Arsène Wenger has effected a glorious revolution here in England, showing us not only how the game can and should be played – 'yes, even sometimes art' – but how young men of different races, religions and nationalities can work together harmoniously to create a moral example and vision of the cosmopolitan good life."

And all without chips.

Scales of justice

OBJECT 79

From a portion of chips to the scales of justice... you have to admit our history of football is eclectic if nothing else! To explain why the scales make our list we need to go back a few years, or in the context of this book, to object 48.

That was a cork, representative of George Eastham who, in 1959, had fallen out with Newcastle United over his proposed transfer to Arsenal. The case ultimately went to the High Court, and in 1963 Eastham won a partial victory when the judge ruled that the "retain-and-transfer" system was indeed restrictive.

So much for the High Court. In the subsequent years the player was still subservient to his club; even the European Community (now the European Union) struggled to make football abide by the rules that governed the rest of everyday life. Throughout the 1960s and 1970s, as David McArdle explained in his book *From Boot Money to Bosman: Football,*

Society and the Law, the EC had reminded UEFA of its obligation to the 1957 Treaty of Rome concerning workers' rights, but to no avail:

> UEFA had traditionally regarded itself as immune from external legal regulation and entitled to run its fiefdom in whatever way it saw.
> At various times, UEFA has been accused of acting in restraint of trade, placing unlawful restrictions on individuals' freedom of movement, engaging in racial discrimination and encouraging concerted practices. But the two practices that caused the most concern within the Community were the use of 'quotas' to control the numbers of foreign players at each club and the transfer fee system.

In 1978 the EC wrung a promise from UEFA to do away with the quota systems and make it easier for players to move from one club to another; but by the early '80s UEFA was still prevaricating and the EC was forced to threaten legal action.

In the end, however, it wasn't UEFA that went to the courts, but a little known Belgian midfielder called Marc Bosman. In 1988 Bosman, then 23, moved from Standard Liège to RFC Liège in a two-year deal that would earn him around £2000 per month.

When his contract came up for renewal in 1990 Bosman was offered an extension but with vastly reduced wages – just £500 a month, the minimum wage as imposed by the Belgian FA. Bosman thought he was worth more than that and rejected the offer, preferring to go on the transfer list.

In May 1990 the French Second Division side Dunkirk offered to take Bosman on a one-year deal worth 1.2 million francs with an option to sign him permanently at the start of the 1990–91 season for 4.8 million francs. But RC Liégeois backed out of the deal, the transfer collapsed and Bosman was without a club. Three times in the next three years Bosman went to court, with the financial aid of his union; once to sue RC Liégeois; once to sue the Belgian FA's transfer system; and once to sue UEFA for breaching the 1957 Treaty of Rome which said European citizens were entitled to freedom of movement.

Bosman was no longer making headlines on the pitch but off it his battle for justice was moving up the legal chain until it arrived at the European Court of Justice in Luxembourg in 1995. On 15 December the Court ruled that it was illegal for European clubs to prevent players from moving on a free transfer at the expiration of their contracts; it also scrapped the restrictions on the number of EU players at any one club.

"The law of the jungle has been abolished!" proclaimed a jubilant Bosman when the verdict – which came to be known as the "Bosman Ruling" – was announced. Writing in the *Independent*, former Millwall player Eamon Dunphy also hailed the ruling, citing his own suffering in the 1960s from unscrupulous clubs, and saying: "Professional football in England is cancerous with corruption, not because of players' greed, but because of the injustice of the transfer system... As a result of Bosman's hard-won crusade for justice, the transfer market – the trade in talent that is the wellspring of all football corruption – will finally be capped. Yes, football will never be quite the same again and good men everywhere should raise a glass to that."

Others were more circumspect. The *Guardian* predicted it would "make the rich clubs richer and hit smaller clubs who stay in business by developing and selling their players", and the FA chief executive Graham Kelly warned it "could sound a death knell of the transfer system".

Suddenly, after more than a century of oppression at the hands of their clubs, players were in control and "transfers were sealed by higher wages rather than higher transfer fees."

In 1992 the average Premier League player earned 3.7 times more than someone in a Division Two side; by 2010 it was 30 times more. When in May 2012 Deloitte's published their annual review of football finance, it was revealed that in the 2010–11 season total wages in the Premier League rose by £201 million (14 per cent up on the previous year) to almost

£1.6 billion. This left the ratio of wages to revenue at 70 per cent, an increase from 68 per cent the previous season. For the Premier League's first season, 1991–92, it was just 44 per cent. In 2011 the *Sun* newspaper went in search of Jean-Marc Bosman to find out what had become of the man who changed the face of football. They found the 46-year-old living in a small flat in Liège, a recovering alcoholic surviving on £625 a month. "I'm happy for footballers earning a lot of money," he told the paper. "I'm not jealous. I gave my career so European players wouldn't work like slaves... I just want to be recognised. People know there's a 'Bosman ruling' but they don't realise there's a guy who has given everything, who became an alcoholic."

Steel helmet

A steel helmet, in a history of football... surely some mistake? Yes, a big one as it happens, and one that achieved that rarest of things – a tabloid apology. It was during the 1996 European Championships as England prepared to face Germany in the semi-final that the *Daily Mirror* rolled back the years to 1944, declaring in its now infamous front page headline: "ACHTUNG SURRENDER – FOR YOU FRITZ, ZE EURO 96 IS OVER", under which was a mocked-up photo of England players Paul Gascoigne and Stuart Pearce wearing vintage British Army helmets from World War Two.

There was more inside for those still hankering for the days when Vera Lyn sang about white cliffs and eggs were rationed. On pages two and three the paper declared: "There is a strange smell in Berlin and it's not just their funny sausages, it's the smell of fear." On page six the newspaper's editor, Piers Morgan, wrote an editorial that took its inspiration – if one can call if that – from Neville Chamberlain's solemn speech to the British people on 3 September 1939 informing them they were at war with Germany: "I am writing to you from the Editor's office at Canary Wharf, London," intoned Morgan. "Last night the *Daily Mirror*'s ambassador in Berlin handed the German government a final note stating that, unless we heard from them by 11 o'clock, a state of soccer war would exist between us."

It wasn't a long war, as it happened; it didn't even last till Christmas. Germany beat England on penalties and the hopes the country had that football was coming home crumbled like the nerve of an England penalty taker.

It wasn't just the *Mirror* that had indulged in an orgy of jingoistic gibberish. The *Sun* and the *Daily Star* were also called to account by the Press Complaints Commission (PCC) several weeks later. Several hundred complaints had been received over the tabloids' coverage and Morgan issued an apology. The *Sun* was less contrite, defending its coverage by saying they'd simply been trying to "bolster national pride". The PCC suggested the *Sun* might like to re-examine its rules on "discrimination".

Tabloid coverage of England v. Germany matches had been deteriorating steadily for several years ("BASH THE BOSCH" was a 1990 offering) although ironically in 1966 there had been no mindless martial rhetoric. Newspapermen then were a different breed, and many had first-hand experience of war. Such men tend not to treat it with crass glibness.

Tabloids learned their lessons from the 1996 furore. As the PCC pointed out they had made a serious error of judgement in tastelessly drawing comparisons, however "humorously", between a football match and a world war – particularly as the war in question was half a century earlier. Since then there's been no repeat, not even when England thrashed Germany 5-1 in 2001, although the *News of the World* couldn't resist the benign "DON'T MENTION THE SCORE".

Nine years later England and Germany met in the last sixteen stage of the 2010 World Cup, the first time the two nations had met in an international tournament since the 1996 encounter. The PCC held its breath and probably cleared its schedule, but only the *Daily Star* donned its khaki, proclaiming: "NOW FOR THE HUN". But does the *Star* count as a paper?

Had the rest of the English tabloids laid down their pens? Was the war really over, and if so why? Had Fleet Street's finest capitulated to the Press Complaints Commission? Hardly. They'd just accepted that the world has moved on and left World War Two where it belongs – in the past. And anyway, what's the point of getting worked up about an England v. Germany match? What was it Gary Lineker said in 1990, after the Germans had knocked England out of the World Cup? "Football is a simple game; twenty two men chase a ball for ninety minutes and at the end, the Germans win."

Loaf of bread

Why a loaf of bread for our next object? Because if Jürgen Klinsmann had carried on working in the family bakery business instead of becoming one of the top strikers of the 1990s, the "dive" might never have become the blight on the world of football that it is today.

Young Jürgen had every intention of working in the Klinsmann bakers' shop in the early 1980s, earning a diploma in bread-making in 1982 from Stuttgart's Berufschule Hoppenlau college. But instead he turned professional with the city's football team, the start of a glittering 14-year career that included a World Cup winners' medal in 1990, a European Championship medal in 1996 as well two UEFA Cup titles and forty seven goals in 108 matches for Germany. Add to this his urbane and intelligent charm, his affable personality and open-mindedness, and Klinsmann should be remembered as one of the greats of the modern game. Which is he, as much as for his talent for diving.

What made Klinsmann's pantomime theatrics all the more incomprehensible was that they were so unnecessary. He was quick, skilful, agile and more than capable of beating a man with a shimmy and speed. So why did he do it?

Klinsmann himself maintains that his reputation was undeserved, not that it seemed to bother him during his season with Spurs in 1994–95 when, to celebrate the twenty one goals he scored, he swallow-dived to the turf in an act of self-deprecation (or was it atonement?) for what he had started.

Because before Klinsmann came along few footballers dived, at least not with his shameless enthusiasm. They might have taken the odd tumble, milked a rash tackle for a moment, but they didn't do what the West German did in the 1990 World Cup Final against Argentina as he tried to get past Pedro Monzón. As the *Observer* later recalled, the Argentine had committed himself to the tackle but before there was even what one could call proper contact "Klinsmann was soaring above him [and] arcing through the air he broke into three jarring, electric rolls." Monzón was sent off – the first player to be dismissed in a World Cup final – and West Germany went on to win 1-0.

Two years later and Klinsmann was at it again, in the final of the 1992 European Championships, but this time not even what the *Daily Mail* called the "worst excesses of feigning hurt, spoiling gamesmanship and sheer bad manners" could prevent a Danish victory. During the 1994 World Cup ITV commentator Alan Parry was moved to note that in a match against Spain Klinsmann had gone down "as if a sniper in row E had caught him".

He was just as bad in club football, whether for Stuttgart, Inter or Monaco, for whom he performed some spectacular playacting during the French side's 1994 Champions League semi-final against AC Milan. Two months after that match the *Guardian* published a piece by Andrew Anthony in which he said: "I hate Jürgen Klinsmann because where others stoop low, he dives even lower." He went on to say that others hate Klinsmann because they hear his name and "think of sinister East German triple agents in Len Deighton cold war thrillers".

Ten years later, long after Klinsmann's retirement from the game, Anthony sat down to meet his *bête noire* and discovered what many others had: that the German's off-field persona couldn't have been more different to his "cunning, cynical, histrionic" demeanour on it. Klinsmann was erudite and engaging and also "mystified" that anyone could think he was a diver.

The legacy of Klinsmann's charades is now all around us, even in Britain, despite a John Bull attitude among certain pundits and ex-players who maintain that only Johnny Foreigners go down unmolested. It took a Frenchman, Arsenal manager Arsène Wenger, to tell the English even their boys were in the habit of diving. "Yes, foreign players have brought this into the English game," he said in 2012. "But I must say the English players learn quickly!"

Players now dive at World Cups, European Championships and in every domestic league. From South America to South Korea to Southampton footballers dive and writhe, not caring if their deceit gets a fellow professional dismissed or results in a fraudulent penalty. From time to time managers, pundits and clubs (particularly in Britain) wring their hands and say something must be done, but when UEFA tried to take a stand in August 2009 the reaction was instructive. Arsenal's Croatian striker Eduardo was banned for two matches for "deceiving the referee" by diving for a penalty during the Gunners' Champions League defeat of Celtic. Arsenal were furious and submitted a 19-page response as part of their appeal, contending that it was impossible for UEFA or anybody to read any intention to deceive into Eduardo's fall. It was Wenger, ironically, bearing in mind his views on diving, who accused UEFA of having opened a "very dangerous door" by relying on video evidence which would mean "every single decision made by a referee, seen by a referee, can be challenged from now on."

UEFA didn't like the sound of that, and a fortnight later rescinded Eduardo's ban. "SPINELESS!" screamed the *Daily Mirror*, who also accused European football's governing body of lacking the balls "to sort out other cheats, which would have upset powerful men and endangered their five-star lifestyle."

Champions League logo

A change in the format of the European Cup was first proposed by Silvio Berlusconi at the tail end of the 1980s. Unable, however, to think how best to represent one of Berlusconi's Bunga Bunga parties, as one of our objects we've plumped instead to keep it clean and go with the logo of the Champions League.

Berlusconi had become president of AC Milan in 1986 at a time when the club were penniless, but within two years they had won the Italian League title. Berlusconi had made his fortune by building an Italian commercial TV empire and he now turned his attention to Europe and in particular how to increase the profitability of a pan-European competition. As the *Observer* remarked: "Berlusconi, president of Milan and militant capitalist... envisages an elite league of clubs strategically based in the great metropolitan centres which would be televised for sale throughout the world."

Berlusconi was impressed with events in England (see object 73) and the huge deal agreed between another media mogul, Rupert Murdoch, and the Premier League in May 1992. UEFA – as they had done with Gabriel Hugot's vision of a pan-European competition nearly forty years earlier – took up the running.

They changed the name from the European Cup to the UEFA Champions League, commissioned a classical anthem, designed a star-ball logo and, most importantly of all, changed the format: from the 1992–93 season onwards the Champions League would begin with a group stage, the best-placed teams progressing to the traditional knockout format. UEFA's next step was to centrally control all branding, television and sponsorship rights and for this they turned to Jürgen Lenz, who had done something similar with the International Olympic Committee in the 1980s. Soon the money was pouring in as the new format "delivered the drip-drip-drip of constant exposure over the entire football season." Sponsors fell over themselves to get a piece of the "clutter-free environment, the immense hospitality packages and licences for the one of the over 8,000 branded products associated with the tournament."

Traditionalists were horrified at what they regarded as a prostitution of a famous old tournament, particularly the new format that made it virtually impossible for clubs from smaller nations to pull off a giant-killing as they had in the old knockout European Cup. Fondly recalling how tiny Bangor of Wales had beaten the Italian Cup holders Napoli in 1962, Peter Corrigan of the *Independent* wrote: "It is all very sad, of course, and an affront to our traditional idea of what cup football should be – an egalitarian free-for-all in which the lowliest teams get an annual opportunity to test their worthiness against the mightiest... The European Cup [he refused to acknowledge its new name] is now totally protected from that or, indeed, from any sort of uprising from the continent's footballing peasantry."

Of course, continued Corrigan, it was obvious to see why the format had been changed by UEFA, because "the bulk of the television revenue comes from the five main football countries and the financial blow of one or more of them not being represented in the finals is no longer to be risked."

Such fears were well founded. Since 1996 only Porto have won the Champions League from a country other than England, Spain, Italy and Germany. In contrast, between 1983 and 1993 clubs from nine nations lifted the European Cup.

On the other hand, the football served up by the Champions League is often magnificent – sporting theatre at its finest and of a far higher quality than the World Cup. As a result, qualifying for the Champions League has become for many clubs more important than winning their domestic cups. Liverpool, for example, won the 2012 Carling Cup and were runners-up in the FA Cup Final, but still sacked manager Kenny Dalglish at the end of the season. "The Carling Cup and the FA Cup don't generate the revenue and the success that is needed to keep investing," said Liverpool Managing Director Ian Ayre. "You have got to have continued progress in the league. If you don't do well in the league and you don't get into the Champions League, you are writing cheques from your own pocket, aren't you? That is not a sustainable way, going forward."

And who can blame Liverpool for chasing UEFA's euros? In the 2010–11 season a total of €754.1 million was allotted to the thirty two teams who qualified for the Champions League, with each club receiving a minimum €7.2 million. On top of that, win bonuses of €800,000 were distributed in the pools stage (plus €400,000 for every draw) and the clubs that reached round sixteen received a further €3 million.

The prize on offer for reaching the last four was €4.2 million and the two clubs that reached the final (Barcelona and Manchester United in this case) shared €14.9 million, with the victors taking home €9 million of that sum.

That's not a bad little earner in what is not a bad little competition. As then Manchester United manager Alex Ferguson said at the start of his side's 2011–12 European campaign: "I think the Champions League is the best competition in the world now. Better than the World Cup, better than the European Championship, it's a fantastic tournament."

Prawn sandwich

"Some people come to Old Trafford and I don't think they can spell football let alone understand it. As I've said, away from home our fans are what I would call the hardcore fans – but at home they have a few drinks and a prawn sandwich and don't realise what's going on out on the pitch."

Roy Keane, Manchester United captain, 8 November 2000

A valid point, or one man's prejudice against people who like prawns? It was a debate that raged for weeks in the wake of Keane's comments following United's 1-0 defeat of Dynamo Kiev in the 2000–01 Champions League. Since then the term "prawn sandwich brigade" has become a term of abuse for football's corporate supporter, the man or woman who sits in a plush box eating and drinking and doing everything but watching the match down below. Not only are real fans deprived of a chance to watch their team, went the gist of Keane's diatribe, but the corporate carousers were creating an atmosphere-free zone at Old Trafford.

The problem for Keane, 29 at the time, was that he had grown up in the 1980s, an era where stadiums were often dirty and dangerous, fans on the terraces swaying to and fro like a field of corn in the wind. It was also a time when watching football was cheap. In 1990, the year Keane signed for Nottingham Forest – and the year Lord Taylor published his report into the Hillsborough Disaster – a Manchester United fan could watch his heroes for as little as £3.50. A 2011 study by the Bank of England revealed that with cumulative inflation of 77.1 per cent since, those same fans who rocked on the United Road terraces would now be asked to pay £6.20 for the privilege of watching the newest vintage.

United are one of the cheaper clubs, however. Further south, Arsenal became the first club to break the £100 barrier, the first time an English club has charged three figures for a seat. According to the same Bank of England report, that represents 920 per cent inflation in the 20-odd years since the Taylor report.

But every club's at it these days. Less than a fortnight after winning the 2011–12 Premier League crown (their first for forty four years), Manchester City rewarded their long-suffering fans by increasing season-ticket prices by an average 9 per cent for the 2012–13 season, although City's most expensive price of £745 is still peanuts in comparison to the £1,955 that Arsenal fans have to pay if they want the best season-ticket seats in the Emirates. And to think the Gunners last won something in 2005.

The clubs' response to accusations of over-pricing is that supporters are now paying to sit in a state-of-the-art stadium watching the best players in the best league in the world. In other words: no one wants a return to the dark days of the 1980s when supporters were caged and treated, as Lord Taylor memorably said his report, like "prisoners of war". But Lord Taylor said something else in his report when he recommended the introduction of all-seater stadiums, something that has been conveniently forgotten by the clubs. Addressing the concerns of those fans who stood on the terraces for financial expediency more than for the atmosphere, he said: "Clubs may well wish to charge somewhat more for seats than for standing but it should be possible to plan a price structure which suits the cheapest seats to the pockets of those presently paying to stand."

"I do not think [Lord] Taylor saw the commercial revolution around the corner, beginning with the increase of television money," said Rogan Taylor in an interview with the *Guardian* in August 2011. Taylor, a Liverpool fan, was chairman of the Football Supporters Association when the report was published. "Of course, the grounds have improved out of all recognition, but the ticket price increases have not mostly been necessary to pay for that – they are now going into the arms race of escalating players' wages."

The two demographic groups most affected by the burgeoning cost of tickets are the old and the young. A 1983 report by the Sir Norman Chester Centre at Leicester University's found that 22 per cent of supporters at Coventry City were aged between 16 and 20. A similar study a decade later revealed that 25 per cent of Aston Villa fans were from the same age bracket. In 2007, when the Premier League conducted its National Fan Survey, the figure for 16 to 24 years old had slumped to 11 per cent.

And yet, as the Premier League boasted in a report in November 2011, "at the end of the first Premier League season, in 1992/93, the aggregate attendance was 9.75 million and 69.6 per cent of available seats were sold. By the 2010/11 season, the aggregate had increased to 13.4 million and an occupancy rate to 92.2 per cent. The clubs have worked hard to ensure that Premier League football is attractive and accessible." Further down the report it let slip that the "average age of an adult supporter is 41."

In an interview with the BBC in 2012 to mark the twentieth anniversary of the publication of *Fever Pitch*, Phil Dorward of the Premier League celebrated the fact that more women, children and people from ethnic minorities now attended matches. "In the mid-'80s we can say the crowd was white and male and that's about it," he said, adding: "Football hasn't gentrified, but the country has changed and football reflects that."

In other words, there's no longer prejudice in football. Everybody's welcome, provided you can pay through the nose for a ticket. "Lots of traditional working-class fans have stopped attending," said John Williams, a senior lecturer in football sociology at Leicester University. "The market is said to decide ticket prices, but it also excludes many poorer fans."

One result of Roy Keane's polemic on prawns was the emergence of a groundswell of support for a reintroduction of terracing. In 2001, the then Sports Minister Kate Hoey came out in favour of a "safe standing" area for 2,000 to 3,000 fans. But the plans have met with consistent resistance from the Premier League and its members. As recently as 2011 Manchester United refused to countenance the idea, saying: "The club agrees with the Government's consistent line over the last twenty years – that seating is a safer way to watch a football match than any possible configuration of standing."

Safer, and more acceptable to the prawn sandwich brigade.

Baseball cap

OBJECT
84

... as worn by American Malcolm Glazer, whose family owns Manchester United. We've chosen a cap for our eighty fourth object purely for practicality – were we to assemble the stereotypical headdress of all foreign owners of Premier League clubs we'd be able to set up our own millinery.

As of 2012–13, twelve of the twenty Premier League clubs were under – or part under – foreign ownership. Arsenal, Aston Villa, Liverpool and Sunderland were in the same American club as United, while Chelsea and Reading answered to a Russian. Fulham were under the care of an Egyptian, QPR a Malaysian and at West Ham a large chunk of the club is Icelandic-owned. New boys Southampton are Swiss-owned and reigning champions Manchester City are in the hands of Sheikh Mansour bin Zayed Al Nahyan. We've come a long way since William Sudell used the wealth from his cotton mills to turn Preston North End into the inaugural champions of the First Division (see object 10).

Or have we? After all, Sudell used the money from the mills (illegally as it turned out) to import the best players from Scotland and to fund ground improvements at Deepdale Park. He argued for professionalism and wholeheartedly supported the formation of the Football League because of the financial benefits it would clearly bring to Preston North End. In short, Sudell was as concerned with profit as he was with performance – and in that regard he's no different from Mansour bin Zayed Al Nahyan, just that Sudell was born in Preston and the Sheikh in Adu Dhabi.

The explosion of foreigners investing in British football has caused a fair share of comment, much of it negative, particularly at Manchester United where fans have long accused the Glazers of burdening the club with debts totalling £500 million following their takeover in 2005.

Across town, the purchase of Manchester City in 2007 by Thaksin Shinawatra, the prime minister of Thailand overthrown in a military coup a year earlier, caused little negative comment at first. Even when Human Right Watch (HRW) wrote to the Premier League in July 2007 warning them Thaksin is "a human rights abuser of the worst kind" there was a collective shrug of the shoulders. Amnesty International also expressed their concerns about whether Thaksin passed the League's "fit and proper person" test that all potential owners are required to undertake. "Thaksin did preside over some very serious human rights violations," said an Amnesty spokesperson. "If the Premier League wants to take any of that into account when making their decisions, we're happy to make our documents available to them."

But the Premier League didn't, and nor did Manchester City, not even when HRW claimed that under Thaksin 2,500 people were killed during one three-month period at the start of 2003.

The BBC opened a forum on its website, asking football fans their opinion if Thaksin was a suitable man to be running a Premier League club bearing in mind the allegations. One response from someone called "Webby" was fairly typical of the response: "Sorry but this is really boring me now... Let him without sin cast the first stone."

Thaksin duly took control of City, but the fans soon revolted; nothing to do with his past, mind; it's just he was unable to lift the club out of the doldrums. In September 2008 Thaksin sold the club to Sheikh Mansour bin Zayed Al Nahyan for a reported £200 million and the coach he'd hired – former England boss Sven Goran Eriksson – was delighted to see the back of him: "In the beginning it was good with Shinawatra," he said. "But he didn't understand football, he hadn't a clue."

Thaksin was subsequently convicted in his absence (he went on the run) of corruption by a Thai court and sentenced to two years in prison. In 2009 City stripped him of his title of honorary club president because he had become "an embarrassment they will no longer tolerate."

Fortunately for City – and for English football – the new owners have done much to erase those fifteen months of shame. It's estimated that Sheikh Mansour has ploughed around £1 billion into City since 2008, their investment bearing fruit in May 2012 as the club won their first League title since 1968.

That's a similar sum to the one Roman Abramovich has sunk into Chelsea over the last decade in his ultimately successful quest for the club to become champions of Europe. The Blues beat Bayern Munich to win the 2012 Champions

League and the front page of the *Observer* the following day summed up the feeling of Chelsea fans.

Above a photograph showing goalscoring hero Didier Drogba handing the trophy to Abramovich was the caption: "To a Russian, with love."

OBJECT 85

Pair of women's shorts

Sepp Blatter set the tone for his reign as FIFA president within forty eight hours of taking office back in 1998. On the subject of future World Cups he declared: "I think the evening games, particularly the final, should start earlier. Should start at 6p.m. local time. Having a 9p.m. kick-off is a bad thing. It means we cannot have a party on the day of the final."

See what I mean? Small wonder that it wasn't long before the doyen of British football reporters, Brian Glanville, was saying of Blatter: "he has fifty new ideas a day and fifty one of them are bad."

One might say – someone who has football's best interests at heart – that Blatter's worst idea was to stand for re-election as FIFA's president in 2010, which he won convincingly, by the way, garnering 186 votes out of a possible 208. It was a one-horse race, admittedly, his opponent having withdrawn the previous week in the face of corruption allegations, but as the old saying goes, "you can only beat what's in front of you". One wonders where the votes of the other twenty two delegates went...

But seeing as Blatter's contribution to football is discussed elsewhere (see object 63), we thought we'd use this object as an opportunity to explore some of those many ideas he's mooted in the last fifteen years. And we'll let you decide if the *Daily Mirror* was right to wonder, as it did in 2011, if it's more than a coincidence that Blatter's name "almost rhymes with 'Mad Hatter'."

1. While general secretary of FIFA, Blatter proposed ahead of the 1994 World Cup in the United States that matches should be split into four quarters, not to reduce the effect of the sweltering temperature on players, but "as an olive branch to the American broadcasting networks." Four quarters would mean more commercials and more money for FIFA. Hooray, and who cares about the fans.

2. In 1996 Blatter "mused about extending the width of the goal by half a metre, and adding 25cm of height to the frame." This would increase the number of goals scored and make the game more attractive to sponso... sorry, spectators.

3. In March 2010 Blatter held talks with Leandro Negre, president of the International Hockey Federation, to ask his opinion on the offside rule. Hockey did away with their offside rule and Blatter reportedly wanted to do likewise. "He asked me a lot of questions about it and how successful it was," Negre told Sky Sports. "He did seem very interested in how we had implemented it."

4. In an address to the Oxford Union in October 2013 Blatter told his student audience he preferred Barcelona's Lionel Messi to Cristiano Ronaldo of Real Madrid, suggesting the latter spends too much time "at the hairdresser". The Portuguese Federation and Ronaldo were furious, the player saying in a statement that Blatter "shows clearly the respect and consideration that FIFA has for me, for my club and my country". Blatter later apologised.

5. Having awarded the 2022 World Cup to Qatar, Blatter then suggested FIFA would break with tradition by staging the tournament "in the winter", at a time when the ferocious Arabian heat would be at its weakest. Never mind that this would play havoc with the domestic schedule of most participating nations. Blatter has suggested in the past that the European season run from February to November so the

winter months could be used for internationals.

6. One of the few ideas of Blatter's to have made it on to statute books is the absurd rule about players being booked if they remove their shirts while celebrating a goal. Despite having said in 2010 – in discussing his opposition to goal line technology – that football isn't about science but "emotions, passion", Blatter has done his best to outlaw the joyful and raw spontaneity of scoring a goal. So we now have the surreal sight of Sergio Agüero being booked for removing his shirt seconds after his goal had won Manchester City the 2012 Premier League title in arguably the most dramatic conclusion to a football championship ever seen.

7. In 2011 Blatter declared "there is no racism" in football. When told that, no, there was, and there was plenty of evidence to prove it, the smooth-talking Swiss suggested in that case it might be a good idea if "the one who is affected by it, he should say that this is a game. We are in a game, and at the end of the game, we shake hands."

8. Thought it can't get any worse? Oh, it can. We saved the barmiest of Blatter's ideas for last, an idea of such breathtaking crassness that you have to do a double take and ask yourself if he really said it, the president of FIFA, the most powerful man in football. In January 2004 Blatter suggested women's football would perhaps be more popular if "the women play in more feminine clothes like they do in volleyball. They could, for example, have tighter shorts."

OBJECT
86

Mobile phone

Even by the standards of Italian football, the scandal that erupted in 2006 was shocking, revealing a depth of corruption unimaginable to most Italian fans. It was orchestrated by

**one man, Luciano Moggi, the former Juventus general direc‑
tor, who with the help of his mobile phone corrupted the soul
of Calcio.**

Italy has a long history of betting, match-fixing and financial malpractice (there were five incidents in the twenty five
years before The Great Italian Football Scandal of 2006, or
Calciopoli, as it was dubbed) but never had one ensnared so
many venerable clubs.

Moggi was a "former deputy station master from a small
Tuscan town", who believed he was cut out for bigger things.
In 1973 he joined Juventus as a scout and gradually wheedled
his way into the affections of the Agnelli family, the owners
of the FIAT car company and Juventus football club. By 1994
Moggi was the general director of Juventus and together with
two other members of the board he formed the "Triad". The
Triad brought success to Juventus: seven Italian Serie A titles
and a Champions League crown (1996) between 1994 and
2006. "In an era of financial disaster," wrote the newspaper
La Stampa (a paper admittedly owned by FIAT), "the Triad is
a model of virtue."

Famous last words. The scandal broke in May 2006, but
the Italian judiciary had been on to Moggi for at least two
years, ever since an investigation into the Neapolitan mafia
– the *Camorra* – had uncovered evidence of an illegal betting
ring involving some of the biggest clubs and most powerful
men in football. According to John Foot, author of *Calcio: A
History of Italian Football*, as a result of the discovery magistrates involved in the investigation "ordered phone taps on
Moggis's six or so mobile phones."

For eight months a team of six transcribers typed out
100,000 conversations, and, says Foot, what they heard was
almost too incredible to be true. "Referees chatting with powerful club presidents, the same club presidents conversing
with those who selected and disciplined the referees, the vice-
president of the football federation joking with the same club

presidents. Everyone was friendly with Moggi – as long as they did his bidding."

As the pace of the investigation quickened and the net widened, it became obvious that Italian football was rotten to its core. Yet no one was really surprised. "It's exactly how we imagined it to be," said one gloomy Italian journalist.

By mid-May Turin magistrates revealed they were examining the books of seventy one clubs, and on the nineteenth of the month Moggi's house was raided by tax police. The media was hooked, with one paper, *La Repubblica*, splashing coverage of the case over eleven pages while another, *La Gazzetta dello Sport*, crowed that Moggi had been cast out by his former friends and associates and is "shut up inside his home with his six silent mobiles which don't ring any more."

Four clubs were at the heart of the scandal: Juventus, Fiorentina, Lazio and AC Milan, the latter of which was owned by Silvio Berlusconi, the Italian prime minister. The case went to court in July 2006 with the Italian Football Federation's prosecutor Stéfano Palazzi laying out the charges on the same day Italy beat France in Germany to win the World Cup.

Palazzi called on the four clubs to be thrown out of Serie A, which they were when the court announced its verdict. Milan, Lazio and Fiorentina were demoted to Serie B but Juventus were despatched even further, to Serie C, and also stripped of their 2005 and 2006 Serie A titles.

All four appealed and three were reinstated to Serie A; Juventus made it back into Serie B – the first time in its once glorious history that the club played a season outside the top-flight.

Moggi received his comeuppance in November 2011 when the former Juventus general director (already banned for life from involvement in football) was sentenced to five years and four months in prison. Not that he actually saw the inside of a cell, owing to the complexity of Italian law. Various members of Moggi's network of fixers also received prison sentences; the length varied but the whine didn't: all of them were the victims of a miscarriage of justice. "I have never done anything wrong or committed any sporting fraud," stated the 74-year-old Moggi, adding with the nerve for which he is known: "I will have faith in justice and will pursue this in every form. This is football, the road is hard and difficult, but I am not afraid."

He appealed his conviction and lost, the verdict being announced in April 2012. In the same month another Italian football scandal broke, police announcing that they were investigating allegations of match-fixing in 2010–11 involving Bari of Serie A. As of early 2014 more than 50 people have been arrested in the ongoing investigation with Lazio captain Stefano Mauri and Juventus coach Antonio Conte both receiving bans for failing to report match-fixing.

Giovanni Trapattoni, the widely respected Italian coach who took Ireland to the 2012 European Championships, said of the latest allegations: "We give an ugly image of our football. As an Italian, the first feeling is that we are mocked abroad, we are always linked to illicit dealings and are considered mafia members."

Wag sunglasses

A pair of branded sunglasses might, at first glance, appear an odd inclusion in our history of football, but this oversized object represents the enormous cultural shift that has taken place over the last twenty years. It's a shift that has given the game glamour, and the Oxford English Dictionary a new entry – the word "WAG".

Of course, there was a time when a Wag was what they called the team joker. He was the one who thought it a hoot to urinate in the dressing room bath, or shave off half the goalkeeper's moustache while he was asleep at the back of the bus.

The said goalkeeper would then return home to face the wrath of his wife, his missus, 'er indoors, whatever they used to call footballers' partners back in the old days. These were a breed of women who chose to stay out of the limelight, leaving fame to their husbands while they saw to the family. Like hedge fund managers, footballers' wives were known to exist but no one had ever actually seen one.

Take Norma Charlton, for example, to whom Sir Bobby has been married for fifty one years. While Charlton was spearheading the England attack during the 1966 World Cup finals he spoke to his wife for ten minutes each day on the phone. "I urged Norma to travel down to see all our games," recalled Sir Bobby in his autobiography, "but she said it wasn't practical because of the arrangements she had to make for the care of the children."

The wives of the England squad did travel to London for the final, and afterwards returned with their men to the team hotel in Kensington to celebrate their victory over West Germany. Also there were David Corbett and Pickles, the dog who had discovered the stolen World Cup (see object 33) a few months before. Corbett remembered that he and players' wives were in a separate room to the players. "The women weren't allowed upstairs," he said. "They made a fuss of the dog but God they were upset. 'Our husbands win the World Cup and the FA banish us down here!' they said."

Perhaps it was the sexism so prevalent in the game back then that made the women tough. On one occasion Norma took the great Bill Shankly to task about the 4-3-3 system he was employing at Liverpool, while Barbara Clough was cut from a similar cloth. She wasn't a football fan – Brian reckoned that during his time in charge of Derby County in the 1960s his wife had seen a total of ten League matches – but when her husband became embroiled in a bitter dispute with the Derby board in 1973 she formed The Protest Movement. "Barbara called the players' wives and had them bring their husbands to yet another meeting," recalled Clough in later years. Barbara was instrumental in persuading her husband to leave Derby, telling him that he could do better. Within six years Clough had guided Nottingham Forest to European Cup glory.

In contrast, the modern footballer's wife doesn't do protests, and she doesn't really do movement; well, it's not easy what with the surgically enhanced breasts, the collagen lips and the botoxed face.

The collective noun for these women is WAGS (wives and girlfriends), a word first coined by the *Sunday Telegraph* in 2002 but which really captured the public's imagination during the 2006 World Cup in Germany. England, as usual, underperformed on the pitch but their Wags were world-beaters in the shops and bars of the small spa town of Baden-Baden. They quaffed £30,000 of champagne, ran up six-figure hotel bills and shopped till they dropped. In one afternoon alone six Wags spent £57,000 on clothes in less time than it took England to be dumped out of the tournament by Portugal. So, while the women stocked up on Prada, Gucci and Christian Dior, the men were brought down by Figo, Petit and Cristiano Ronaldo.

On the back of the Baden-Baden behaviour the Wags became celebrities in their own rights; one brought out her own perfume, another published a book and a third released a Christmas DVD, something to do with legs, bums and tums. As a result becoming a WAG is seen as a career move by an increasing number of young women, the *Guardian* sighing that nowadays "many girls can name more wives and girl-friends of footballers than female politicians." The paper wasn't impressed. The desire of the twenty first century woman to be a WAG, they declared, brought "to mind a sort of 1950s womanhood: they seem to be expected to come when called and, equally, to stay away when they're not wanted."

Come when called... Who is the *Guardian* trying to kid? Look what happened to Bobby Charlton when he called his wife during the 1966 World Cup. Norma might not have been a feminist in the modern sense of the word but she was far more her own woman than Cheryl, Coleen or Carly. She was also perhaps more content, despite the fact her husband earned in a career what a Wayne or an Ashley picks up in a month. For as Alison Kervin, author of *A Wag's Diary* says of her subjects: "I just feel desperately sorry for them... Some of those I met found it very, very difficult living in somebody else's shadow."

So the pair of oversized sunglasses deserve their place in our history of football for few objects so stylishly symbolise the journey the footballer's wife has made in the last half a century. Perhaps for one or two WAGS they are worn to hide the sadness of their vacuous existence, but for most the glasses shield their eyes from the shine of their silver Mercedes.

Beckham Buddhist statue

OBJECT 88

Before we get down to business, or should that be Buddha, with our next object let's take a trip back to the past, to 1892 to be precise, when Charles Edwards dipped his pen in his ink and bemoaned what had become of the modern footballer in an article for The *Nineteenth Century:* "In their respective neighbourhoods they are the objects of the popular adoration. They go to the wars in saloon

carriages. Their supporters attend them to the railway station to wish them 'God speed', and later in the evening meet them on their return... they are better known than the local members of parliament. Their photographs are in several shops, individually and grouped. The newspaper gives woodcuts of them and brief appreciative biographical sketches. Even in their workaday dress they cannot move in their native streets without receiving ovations enough to turn the head of a prime minister."

So there you have it, unequivocal proof that nothing much has changed, apart from the woodcuts. The first of the Ten Commandments may have forbidden idolatry, but if football had been around in Moses' time they would have probably inserted a clause about it being acceptable on a Saturday afternoon. And of all the footballers that have been idolised over the centuries (three so far and counting) few have received as much worship as David Beckham. The man is a God, literally.

It was back in 2000 when the then Manchester United and England midfielder learned that he'd been immortalised in a Buddhist temple in Thailand. "Football has become a religion and has millions of followers," explained the temple's head monk Sangkarak Chan. "So to be up to date, we have to open our minds and share the feelings of millions of people who admire Beckham."

The 30cm high statue of Beckham was, explained the *London Evening Standard*, situated in "a spot normally reserved for angels." Is there a difference? Covered in gold leaf, Beckham sat at the foot of the main Buddha image in Bangkok's Pariwas Temple alongside 100 other minor deities. Sculptor Thongruang Haemhod explained that he hoped his work would survive for many years so that future Manchester United fans could worship "Becks". "We want the people of this and the next generation to know what was going on in the year 2000," said Haemhod.

Perhaps the most surprising aspect of the whole story was

why David Beckham should be such a hit in Thailand, hardly known for being a hotbed of football. The year 2000, however, was when the craze for English football – or at least the Premier League – began to gather momentum worldwide. More and more foreign players were coming into the Premier League (the last time a Premier League team fielded an all-England XI was Aston Villa in February 1999) and television coverage was expanding into the Far East.

To cash in on this increasing popularity, in 2003 the Premier League launched the biennial Barclays Asia Trophy – a tournament featuring three Premier League teams against local teams that has been held variously in Malaysia, Thailand, Hong Kong and China.

In 2012 the Premier League launched its "Premier League Trophy Tour" throughout Asia, North America and Africa and, according to its website "global fan following of the Premier League is 1.46 billion – or 70 per cent of the world's estimated 2.08 billion football fans." During the 2010–11 season 750,000 of these foreign fans came to England to attend Barclays Premier League matches.

Such diligence is paying off. According to a 2011 survey by a leading global sports market research company, three of the five best supported clubs in the world are English: Arsenal in fifth place with 113 million fans; Chelsea fourth with 135 million supporters and Manchester United in top spot with 354 million fans, a whopping 84 million more than Barcelona in second.

To cater for this need, the Premier League signed a deal in April 2012 with Talksport which will see the radio station broadcast all 380 Premier League matches for the next four seasons in three languages – English, Spanish and Mandarin. "My favourite statistic is that 54 per cent of adults [in the UK] consider themselves a fan of the Premier League," said Scott Taunton, chief executive of TalkSport. "The only country higher is Indonesia, where 56 per cent of people say they are fans. There are 230 million Indonesians and 60 million Brits.

Suddenly we are into markets that are huge. In China 650 million people claim to be Manchester United fans."

Beckham left United for Real Madrid in 2003, a move that reportedly doubled the number of replica Real shirts sold in the Far East. When he visited Japan shortly after signing for the Spanish club, Beckham was mobbed wherever he went. "God save the new king!" gushed one television reporter.

One day a deity, the next a king... Brand Beckham was unstoppable. Even now in retirement, the boy from east London continues to be the face of British football, travelling to the Amazon in 2014 to film a documentary for the BBC to coincide with their coverage of the World Cup in Brazil.

Back in May 2012, when Beckham was playing for LA Galaxy, he and his teammates were invited to the White House for a photo opportunity with Barack Obama. The President of the United States singled out the Englishman for praise and quipped it's "a rare man who can be that tough on the field and also have his own line of underwear".

Asked later how he felt about meeting the leader of the free world, Beckham replied: "It was one of the best moments of my life. I had such a busy week and I arrive at the White House to meet the President and the First Lady, and he gives me a lot of stick and gives my underwear a plug; it was perfect."

Just goes to show no one can brand it like Beckham.

French phrase book

OBJECT
89

FRENCH Phrase Book

For the holidaymaker and traveller abroad
Over 1,400 carefully chosen phrases
Over 1,500 useful words

travel · accommodation · eating and dr...
shopping · sightseeing

Before we introduce our next object, here's a stat with which to impress your friends: when the inaugural Premier League season kicked off in August 1992 there were

only eleven non-British players involved. Nine years later, on 26 December 1999, Chelsea played Southampton fielding eleven non-British players: Two Frenchmen, two Italians, a Nigerian, a Romanian, a Dutchman, a Brazilian, a Spaniard, a Uruguayan and a Norwegian. They were managed by an Italian.

So in fact we could have chosen an Italian phrase book, or a Spanish or... but no we made do with French. Partly because France has provided English football with two of the most influential figures in the game: Manchester United's Eric Cantona and Arsenal manager Arsène Wenger.

But how did the transformation take place, from eleven foreign players in a total of twenty two clubs to eleven foreign players in just one starting XI, and all within the space of seven years?

The money that came into the Premier League in the wake of the lucrative deal with BSky B was obviously a huge factor, making available to clubs funds that once they could only have dreamed about. There was another reason, however, one that came about in December 1995 when the European Court of Justice made its judgement that, as we have seen, came to be known as the "Bosman Ruling".

As well as reforming the transfer system, the ruling also "forced the abandonment of all citizenship restrictions on team composition".

As ESPN's Jon Carter commented in a 2011 article reflecting on the ruling: "The game was radically changed and, for the first time, more was spent on foreign stars than home-grown players – £182 million compared to £158.2 million – in England in 1999."

By the year 2000, BSkyB had increased its broadcasting contract with the Premier League to £1.1 billion and clubs had even more money at their disposal with which to buy big foreign stars. And no one bought foreign stars as enthusiastically as Arsène Wenger. When French midfielder Samir Nasri arrived at Arsenal from Marseille in 2008, he was delighted to find that "everybody speaks French, with the Swiss players, the Africans, the French lads and... the boss [Wenger] talks in French when he has discussions with players and only speaks English in team meetings." Asked if that had helped him settle in at the Emirates, Nasri replied: "I have settled in very well. I do not feel that I am in a foreign country with all the French speakers around."

The following year only four of Arsenal's twenty seven-man squad were born in the UK, compared to nineteen out of the 21-strong squad of 1989–90. In a match against Portsmouth in 2009 both Arsenal and their opponents fielded starting XIs without one English player among the fifteen nationalities represented.

It didn't go down well with one of the English managers in the Premier League, the then boss of Blackburn Rovers Sam Allardyce. "For the national team in the future it is looking very, very bleak," he said in response to the all-foreign affair. "The Premier League and the FA really need to get together and start immediately on how they are going to address this situation."

That was a little rich coming from Allardyce. Prior to taking over at Blackburn he'd spent seven years in charge of Bolton Wanderers, a club who maintained their existence in the Premier League by importing talented if little-known foreigners. In 2005 there were sixteen nationalities in the Bolton squad, including a Mexican, an Omani and a Japanese midfielder. Asked to explain himself to the *Observer* Allardyce replied: "We have to go out and cover every corner of the globe for new players. And we will look in as many countries as possible because it's getting so hard to find players to play at the top level." According to the *Observer* Allardyce "was taken by the professionalism of his overseas players. He was also surprised by the bargains that could be struck abroad."

The downside to the number of non-English players in the Premier League is the decline in the standard of the national team. During his time coaching England in the 2000s Sven-Göran Eriksson (a Swede and the first non-Englishman in the post) lamented the lack of options available to him in team selection, saying: "There are too many foreign players but I don't think there is anything you can do about that. You have to accept it."

The overwhelming majority of English football fans certainly have, placing more store on how their club performs than their country. Sam Allardyce's foreign contingent helped Bolton qualify for the 2005–06 UEFA Cup, and as the *Observer* noted wryly: "those still uncomfortable with the proliferation of overseas professionals, just ask the Bolton fans how much it means. They are pinching themselves at the prospect of their first ever European adventure."

Allez les Trotters, as the French might say.

Wad of euros

Forgive us but we couldn't get our hands on the full £86m required for our next object, so instead of the whole sum that Real Madrid paid Tottenham Hotspur for the services of midfielder Gareth Bale in the summer of 2013 we'll make do with a thick wad of cash. But you get the picture.

The transfer was a world record, surpassing that established by Real four years earlier when they paid Manchester United £80m for Cristiano Ronaldo. Bale doesn't appear to be burdened by being the most expensive player in football, scoring regularly for his new club in his first season in Spain.

One man who can't have been pleased with Bale's transfer

is UEFA president Michel Platini. In the wake of Ronaldo's then record transfer, the Frenchman warned: "These excessive transfers are happening almost every day. These transfers are a serious challenge to the idea of fair play and the concept of financial balance in our competitions."

In September 2009, three months after Platini's declaration, UEFA introduced their Financial Fair Play regulations covering 660 top division clubs in fifty three European countries. Citing "repeated, and worsening, financial losses" among a number of European clubs, and the global economic downturn, UEFA unveiled the FFP regulations:

"They include an obligation for clubs, over a period of time, to balance their books or break-even. Under the concept, clubs cannot repeatedly spend more than their generated revenues, and clubs will be obliged to meet all their transfer and employee payment commitments at all times. Higher-risk clubs that fail certain indicators will also be required to provide budgets detailing their strategic plans."

The FFP regulations began their three-year implementation in the summer of 2011, with clubs being allowed to record maximum losses of £39.5 million in total over the following three years, but only if this sum is subsided by a club owner with the money sunk into the club permanently in return for shares. If owners are unable or unwilling to subside the £39.5 million debt, then the maximum loss allowed is £4.4 million. This figure will fall to £26.4 million from 2014 to 2017, after which UEFA expects all its members to be in the black. The Club Financial Control Panel, comprising eight independent experts and led by former Belgium Prime Minister Jean-Luc Dehaene, was set up to manage the FFP regulations.

UEFA also announced strict penalties for those clubs that fail to meet the regulations. Clubs could have prize money withdrawn and be banned from dipping into the transfer market with the ultimate penalty the risk of being thrown out of European competition. Players might also be suspended if it was found their signings had contributed to the club's debt.

Then, in November 2011, Manchester City announced record annual losses of £195 million – mainly as a result of their transfer dealings – and they and a number of top clubs began to get twitchy as they examined the FFP small print. There was talk of the clubs launching a legal challenge to the regulations so they could carry on buying with impunity. UEFA reacted with alarm and held a series of meeting with officials from the European Commission [EC] to make sure the regulations were legally watertight. In March 2012 UEFA and the EC issued a joint statement, confirming "that UEFA's Financial Fair Play regulations are fully consistent with EU State Aid policy." Joaquín Almunia, vice-president of the EC and the commissioner for competition added: "The UEFA rules will protect the interests of individual clubs and players as well as football in Europe as a whole... there are questions whether the FFP rules can work, but the UEFA/EC joint agreement means there will be no room for clubs to manoeuvre their way out of the framework."

All of which is bad news for the likes of Manchester City, one of the biggest spenders in European football, who since Sheikh Mansour took control of the club in 2008 have spent £712m on transfer fees alone. Their losses for the year to May 2013 were £52m, an eye-watering sum given the FFP rules, but still peanuts compared to what Real Madrid paid for Gareth Bale.

Vuvuzela

It measures approximately 65cm, costs £1.50 and produces a single note (B flat for the musically-minded among you) at a decibel range somewhere between 115 and 127. And rarely has an object divided the football world like the vuvuzela during the 2010 World Cup in South Africa. On the one side there were thousands of African and European football fans blowing the plastic trumpet for all their worth during matches, egged on by FIFA.

On the other side was an equal number of football fans whose enjoyment of the matches was ruined by having the trumpet blown in their ears; not to mention the players, broadcasters, referees and armchair fans whose lives – for various reasons – were made a misery during four painful weeks. As US broadcaster ESPN declared midway through the tournament: "the plastic horns have become a major sub-plot of the World Cup."

The story of how the vuvuzela came to dominate the headlines during the 2010 World Cup distracted from the major plot of the tournament – the fact that for the first time in eighty years an African country was playing host to the world's greatest footballing extravaganza. Ten years earlier, in 2000, South Africa had controversially lost out to Germany by one vote in their bid to stage the 2006 tournament. In that same year, Neil van Schalkwyk, a plastics toolmaker from Cape Town, designed a plastic horn that he began selling to supporters at local football matches. He called it "Boogie Blast", his inspiration being the homemade metal horns fashioned by fans from old drink cans. In an interview in 2004, van Schalkwyk described how "ardent football supporters... started calling it the vuvuzela, like, collectively, people started calling it that. It means pump it up, lift it up. It is a slang name for lifting spirits."

It was Nelson Mandela who saw how the vuvuzela could raise South Africa's chances of winning the bid to host the 2010 World Cup. Ordering a batch of the horns to be taken to Zurich in May 2004, the 86-year-old Mandela and the South African delegation serenaded FIFA officials before they sat down to decide which of the five African nations should be granted the honour of hosting their continent's first World Cup six years hence.

South Africa beat Morocco by fourteen votes to ten, leaving Mandela so happy he told reporters "I feel like a young man of 15." The country's president, Thabo Mbeki, was more sober in his reaction, declaring on television that "Africa's time has come. We want to ensure that, one day, historians will reflect upon the 2010 World Cup as a moment when Africa stood tall and resolutely turned the tide on centuries of poverty and conflict."

Not all the world seemed won over at the prospect of an African country hosting football's showpiece event. There were dire warnings in sections of the European press about the crime rate in South Africa, while in September 2006 former West German captain Franz Beckenbauer wittered on condescendingly about the organisation for the 2010 World Cup being "beset by big problems...but these are not South African problems – these are African problems. People are working against rather than with each other." Then in stepped Sepp Blatter to promise he would "explain the value of the World Cup" to the Organising Committee. Well he would know.

As it turned out, the 2010 World Cup went off without a hitch. The stadiums were built on time, the crime wave never materialised, the organisation was impeccable and there were shocks on the pitch, as both finalists from the 2006 tournament – Italy and France – failed to win any games and were eliminated at the pool stage. The only grumble of complaint (apart from the ball) concerned the vuvuzela. Actually it wasn't a grumble, it was like a giant global groan... but it still wasn't enough to drown out what South African newspaper *Cape Argus* described as the "dreaded vuvuzela". They weren't alone. Described variously as sounding like a "buffalo breaking wind", "a swarm of angry hornets" or, in the words of the *Daily Mail,* "the industrial whine of plastic Globo-trash", vuvuzelas were the bane of broadcasters' lives. Eventually several of them took measures to filter out the vuvuzela.

The players found them just as distracting. Portugal's Cristiano Ronaldo admitted "it is difficult for anyone on the pitch to concentrate [and] a lot of players don't like them", while Spain midfielder Xabi Alonso called on FIFA to "ban those things... it is not nice to have a noise like that." To which FIFA president Sepp Blatter responded by saying people should "not try to Europeanise an African World Cup... that is what African and South Africa football is all about – noise, excitement, dancing, shouting and enjoyment... would you want to see a ban on the fan traditions in your country?"

But not for the first time Blatter's finger was off the pulse. "Part of our culture?" declared Mondli Makhanya, the former editor-in-chief of the *Johannesburg Sunday Times.* "Balderdash! Singing is very much a part of South African culture. During apartheid, we sung in the worst of times. When people were protesting, we sang. When people were being shot, we sang. We sing vociferously at funerals; we sing vociferously at weddings. What this instrument has done is to take something away from the football culture."

Meanwhile, an argument had erupted about who had actually invented the vuvuzela, with Neil van Schalkwyk's claim being disputed by one Freddie Maake, who said he'd come up with the idea thirty years earlier, and then the insistence of the Nazareth Baptist Church that their deceased founder, Isaiah Shembe, deserved the credit.

All of which was immaterial to the correspondent of the *Africa News* who, on 17 July 2010, wrote in glowing terms of how the World Cup had been a credit to all Africans.

"It did all the things that all the Afro-pessimists said could not be done: it designed and created stadia as good as any in the world; it managed the logistics of a hideously complex event; it administered a remarkable security operation that prevented any major crime incidents from tainting the tournament."

However, continued the paper, there was one dark cloud hovering over the Rainbow Nation – the vuvuzela.

"This long trumpet, we were told, is authentically African, the sound of the savannah, of celebration, of fervour... [but] far from enhancing the first World Cup held on African soil, came close to ruining it... Culture, eh? If this is our culture, we should dump it. Straight red card. Who made money out of the vuvuzelas? Why, the Chinese, of course. China's factories quickly churned out more than a million of the misbegotten trumpets, and cleaned up at the World Cup."

Corner flag

OBJECT 92

If our last object, the vuvuzela, was an acquired taste, then the same could be said about its successor – the goal celebration, represented for our purposes by a corner flag. Why a corner flag? Because during the 1990 World Cup it was the object of Roger Milla's affection every time the Cameroon striker celebrated one of the four goals he scored in the tournament. As one newspaper related, Milla serenaded the flag with "a hip-shaking salsa" in exuberant delight at each goal.

Before Milla sashayed onto the scene, celebrating a goal resembled a communal love-in, much to the irritation of the sport's ruling bodies. In 1975 the English Football League told all clubs that "kissing and cuddling should be stopped and players continuing to act in this way should be charged with bringing the game into disrepute."

FIFA issued a similar message in 1982 when it stated that the "exuberant outbursts of several players at once jumping on top of each other, kissing and embracing, should be banned from the football pitch."

This was nothing new. Goal celebrations had been exercising the minds of the men in suits since as far back as 1923, when England played France in a friendly in Paris. After the 4-1 win to the visitors, England captain Charlie Buchan was given a "severe reprimand" by the Football Association for having shaken the hand of one of his goalscorers. Do it again and you'll never play for England, the FA told Buchan, because "hand-shaking was one of those things that wasn't done."

Nor was dancing, but the 38-year Milla changed all that in 1990 with the dance that he's always insisted was improvised, a spur of the moment reaction to the ecstasy of scoring. Ten years later the *Observer* noted that: "Celebrations really came of age at the 1990 World Cup, where Roger Milla's grinding hips, an expression of joy which would today be considered restrained, inspired argument the world over. Professional footballers... watched and learned."

They learned fast, and imaginatively. At the 1994 World Cup Bebeto scored Brazil's second goal in the win against Holland and celebrated by running to the camera and rocking an imaginary cradle. His wife, watching back home, had just given birth to a boy called Matheus (who in 2011 signed for Brazilian side Flamenco). The celebration was immortalised the same year when it was included in the first official FIFA video game to be released.

Bebeto, like Milla, later claimed it was all off-the-cuff, not something that could be said of Jürgen Klinsmann's reaction to scoring his first goal for Spurs at the start of the 1994–95 season. The German arrived in England with a reputation for diving (see object 81) so what did he do when he scored the winner in the 4-3 win over Sheffield Wednesday on his debut? He did a mock dive towards the Tottenham fans. "Teddy Sheringham [his teammate] told me that when I got my first goal we should both dive, so we did it," said Klinsmann later. "It was a joke, really. I won't be doing it anymore." A joke, and a masterstroke from the German, a self-parody that won over the Spurs fans in a stroke.

By the time of the 1996 European Championships, goal celebrations were beginning to get out of hand, prompting FIFA to call for restraint and urging players to dispense with "choreographed celebrations". Fat chance. When England beat Scotland at Wembley in Euro '96 Paul Gascoigne celebrated his goal with the "dentist's chair", a re-enactment of an infamous act of debauchery in a Hong Kong nightclub during a pre-tournament tour.

Two years later, playing for Rangers against Celtic in the Old Firm match, Gazza celebrated a goal by pretending to play the flute in front of the Celtic faithful. This highly emotive sectarian gesture cost Gascoigne a £20,000 fine and led to death threats from terrorist groups.

Gascoigne wasn't the last player to get carried away in the act of scoring a goal. A few months after Gazza's flute faux pas, England striker Robbie Fowler was slapped with a £60,000 fine – and a four-match ban – for pretending the goal line was a line of cocaine.

More recently, Everton striker Tim Cahill celebrated a goal for Everton in 2008 by imagining he was handcuffed, a gesture of solidarity for his brother who had been sentenced to six years in prison for blinding a man.

"Celebrations have become part of the DNA of sporting endeavour," said Martin Perry, a British sports psychologist who has studied the response of players to scoring a goal. "There's a clear need to express feelings, to reinforce the sense of superiority. Some players will practice their celebrations even before the game starts. They think it helps them perform better by giving them an incentive. But there's a danger. The contrary school of thought holds that celebrations lead to loss of concentration. The focus gets diluted."

Perry's findings were backed up by a report in the *American Journal of Sports Medicine* which studied injuries in the Turkish football league in 2004–05 and found that 6 per cent were caused by goal celebrations that went wrong.

Because for every Julius Aghahowa – the Nigerian striker who marked his goal against Sweden in the 2002 World Cup with seven consecutive back-flips – there's a Fabián Espíndola. He was the Argentine striker who celebrated a goal for Real Salt Lake in 2008 by attempting a back flip. It didn't come off and Espíndola tore his ankle ligaments. And then, to rub salt into Espíndola's very public wound, his goal was disallowed for being offside. "I'm embarrassed," he said later as he contemplated eight weeks on the sidelines. "I'm never going to do that again."

OBJECT
93

Packet of cigarettes

Frankly, we were spoiled for choice when it came to deciding our next object. We wanted something that would best symbolise the decadence, the extravagance, the opulence, the downright deranged world in which

the best-paid stars of the modern game live. Come on, if you earned £250,000 a week (what the president of the United States, the most important man in the world, earns in a year) wouldn't you lose touch with reality?

First we thought of the air rifle that England and Chelsea defender Ashley Cole used to shoot a student with at the club's training ground in 2011. Then there was the £1.5 million that Stoke City winger Matthew Etherington admitted to gambling away in 2009, or the fireworks left off by Manchester City striker Mario Balotelli in the bathroom of his mansion in 2011, causing damage worth £400,000. And not forgetting Manchester United's £4,000-a-head Christmas party in 2007 in which partners weren't invited but 100 handpicked young women from the city were, one of whom later claimed she'd been raped by a player, allegations that proved false.

In the end, however, we've gone for a packet of twenty Marlboro cigarettes, as smoked by Wayne Rooney. In 2010 a Manchester prostitute did a classic "kiss and tell" job on the England striker, revealing to the *News of the World* that he had paid her thousands of pounds for sex while his wife was pregnant. According to the young woman in question – Juicy Jen, to give her her stage name – after one bout of lovemaking Rooney fancied a post-coital cigarette. So he summoned a member of the five-star hotel staff, "demanding cigarettes [and] handing over £200 in exchange for a packet of 20 Marlboro".

"As much as I loved a ciggie, I would have drawn a line at paying 200 quid," remarked Jimmy Greaves, one of Rooney's predecessors in an England striker's shirt. "Two weeks' wages even at the peak of my earning!"

United fans were disgusted by the sordid revelations surrounding Rooney. Doesn't he know smoking is bad for the health?

Perhaps we're all deranged...

Larry the bird

As we near the end of our peregrination through more than 150 years of football progress, let us pause for a moment and reflect on some of the momentous moments in the sport's history: William McGregor's letter in 1888 suggesting the formation of a football league; the inaugural World Cup in 1930; George Eastham's challenge of the "retain and transfer" system in 1963. And when we have ceased to marvel at football's evolution let our eyes rest on our next object and let us ask ourselves: "How did we come to this?"

Object 94 is "Larry the Bird" or, as he's better known to an estimated 500 million users worldwide, the Twitter logo. Why, you may ask yourself is the logo included in our history? The answer is simple: to emphasise the coarseness in the modern game, a microcosm, one might argue, of society as a whole in the twenty first century.

Before the advent of Twitter in 2008, footballers kept their opinions to themselves, or at least to within the confines of the dressing room. If they were ever forced to appear before a journalist, games were invariably of two halves and victories left them over the moon.

Football might have been the game of the people but its protagonists were rarely seen or heard by those people; instead they preferred to retreat behind the imposing iron railings of their mock-Tudor mansions. When it was a revealed a few seasons back that Tottenham defender Benoit Assou-Ekotto occasionally rode the London Underground there was widespread astonishment: what, he slums it with the rest of us! Well, sometimes, when he's not driving one of his six classic American sports cars he keeps in a museum near Heathrow Airport.

Then came Twitter, and suddenly the clever marketing men and women at football clubs up and down the country saw an opportunity for players to reconnect with the game's lifeblood – you and me.

Among the first to take up the tweet were some of the biggest names in English football, including Wayne Rooney, Peter Crouch and Steven Gerrard. "Folks asking why I'm not on facebook," tweeted Rooney early on. "I prefer [Twitter] really 'cos it seems more of a community thing." In the three years from June 2009 to June 2012, the number of people following the England striker exploded from 3,000 to more than 4,000,000.

Peter Crouch didn't last quite so long, quitting the social network in August 2010 after allegations broke in the tabloids that he had cheated on his fiancée with a teenage prostitute. "Don't judge me for what I did," was Crouch's last imploring tweet before departing, like Captain Oates, into the great beyond.

Crouch lasted longer than Everton midfielder Darren Gibson, who opened his Twitter account in April 2011 when still with Manchester United. Rio Ferdinand welcomed his arrival to the twitterverse and told his followers to "show him some love tweeps!" Loathing not love was what Gibson received, with several United supporters heaping scorn on the Republic of Ireland international for his recent performances: "You are an abysmal excuse for a footballer. You're a one trick pony – a shit one at that. What Fergie sees in you I do not know" was fairly typical of the abuse. Gibson shut down his account after two hours and the following season left United for Everton.

If Gibson proved himself a little thin-skinned, some of his Premier League peers have shown themselves to be thick-headed in the twitterverse. Increasingly, clubs and governing bodies are realising that it does the game no good in encouraging players to speak their minds if those minds turn out to be smaller than the pea in the referee's whistle. Leicester

City defender Michael Ball was fined £6,000 by the FA for sending homophobic tweets to a soap actor, while Manchester United striker Federico Macheda had to stump up £15,000 in March 2012 after being found guilty of a similar offence. Newcastle's Nile Ranger and West Ham's Ravel Morrison have also fallen foul of the FA for homophobic comments on Twitter, while the powers-that-be took £15,000 out of Jason Puncheon's wages after the Crystal Palace midfielder used twitter to make derogatory comments about his former manager, Neil Warnock, in 2014.

A growing number of clubs are now assuming that responsibility, with Arsenal manager Arsène Wenger warning his players of the potential "negative repercussions" while former Manchester United boss Alex Ferguson expressed his dislike of the medium in characteristically blunt fashion. "There are a million things you can do with your life other than that," blasted Fergie. "Go to a library and read a book... I don't understand it but it is something that we, as a club, are looking at because there can be issues attached to it and we don't want that."

The FA, recognising that Twitter – rather like Sepp Blatter – is here to stay no matter how much they wish it wasn't, has started to run seminars "to educate players", while at the same time warning that there will be lengthy bans for anyone who breaches disciplinary rules with their tweets. "Participants are required to act in the best interest of the game and should be aware postings on social networking sites are likely to be subject to public and media scrutiny," ran an FA memo issued in the spring of 2012. "We are conscious the use of social networking sites can be positive but participants should exercise caution."

But will footballers ever be able to exercise caution with the same diligence they exercise their bodies? Not according to neuropsychologist Dr David Lewis, who believes Twitter and footballers is a potent brew: "Sportspeople tend to be very emotional," Dr Lewis told the BBC in 2011. "They take offence, they're very sensitive and they tend to blast off in all directions when they're in an emotional state."

Or as the comedian Frankie Boyle commented: "Twitter has replaced muttering to yourself on the sofa."

And even millionaire footballers have sofas.

Teacup

Frankly, it's nothing short of a miracle that our next object is still in one piece. Not that it's particularly old or fragile or rare, just that this teacup had the good fortune to escape the wrath of Sir Alex Ferguson in the last forty years. The Glaswegian guv'nor, the most successful manager in the history of British football, has smashed as many teacups over the years as he has won trophies. And not just teacups. Tea trays, tea urns and, on one notorious occasion, even a football boot have been sent flying by Fergie during one of his infamous dressing room rants. "I do explode like a volcano at times," he once conceded. "And that gets rid of all the strain and tension. It's a violent emotion and I must release it fast."

Ferguson's way might not have been Matt Busby's way, the manager he supplanted as the most successful at Old Trafford, but his way has worked during a 39-year coaching career that began with East Stirling in 1974. From there Fergie – no mean striker in Scottish club football during the 1960s – took charge at St Mirren before moving to Aberdeen in 1978. Within seven years he'd turned the Dons into Scotland's dominant side, winning three League titles, four SFA Cups and beating Real Madrid in the final of the Cup Winners Cup in 1983.

He did it, says Archie Knox, his assistant manager, by giving the players "a winning mentality" and by instilling the fear of God into their souls. In one European tie in Romania Aberdeen came in at half-time trailing 2-0. Waiting for them was an urn full of tea and Ferguson, both near boiling point. "We were all petrified going into the changing room because we knew what was coming," recalled midfielder Neale Cooper. The Aberdeen captain Willie Miller remembered that Ferguson began with the teacups before turning his ire on the urn, giving it a "fore-arm smash". His players ran out of the changing room and turned the game around in the second half.

Ferguson moved to Old Trafford in November 1986, inheriting from his predecessor Ron Atkinson a club in crisis. Without a League title since 1967, United's only silverware since lifting the European Cup in 1968 had been three FA Cups. Club chairman Martin Edwards later explained why he hired a man with no experience of English football: "He struck me as the young Turk of British football who was destined for success... I also knew of his reputation as the manager of a small club who had taken on the two big clubs in Glasgow [Rangers and Celtic] and come out on top. It seemed to me that the qualities it had taken to do that were just what we needed at Old Trafford."

But Ferguson struggled at first, overshadowed at every step by the spectre of Busby. Three mid-table finishes in his first four seasons in charge did little to convince the United faithful that Ferguson had a future. When they lost 5-1 to Manchester City in October 1989 the United fans serenaded their manager with chants of "Ferguson out". A few weeks later bookmakers William Hill began taking bets on Ferguson's future, quoting odds of 7-4 that he would be dismissed before the opening League match of 1990–91. "He's in the hands of his own results," said a William Hill spokesman. "We don't think it's in bad taste – it's probably the least of his pressures, nothing compared to the press vilification."

What saved Ferguson's skin was success in the 1990 FA Cup Final against Crystal Palace, followed the next season by victory in the Cup Winners' Cup, achieved by a squad long on experience.

The 1992–93 season was when United began their march to the summit of English football. In November 1992 Ferguson paid Leeds United £1.2 million for Eric Cantona, the volatile Frenchman with a reputation for doing his own thing. Ferguson also blooded three of the United youth academy – David Beckham, Gary Neville and Nicky Butt – having previously eased a skinny Welshman called Ryan Giggs into the side. Looking back on that period at United Ferguson explained: "I have had my problems at Old Trafford. Three years after I came here we came to a standstill despite spending a considerable sum of money on new players, but we got through, our youth policy began to pay off and we haven't really looked back since."

In November 2011 Ferguson celebrated twenty five years in charge of United, and others looked back on what he'd achieved in that time: twelve League titles, two Champions League crowns, five FA Cups and four League Cups, with the 1999 Treble his crowning achievement. He'd turned Manchester United into the most dominant club of any era in English football, resisting challenges to his supremacy from Arsenal and Chelsea and rising above the financial bickering behind the scenes at the club.

How had Ferguson achieved such omnipotence – and during an era when for the first time in football the power balance between player and manager shifted dramatically in favour of the former? Archie Knox, who worked with Ferguson at United until 1991, says his "uppermost quality has always been his drive and desire. Winning is a drug for him, being on top, be it football or tiddlywinks."

He's also a canny reader of men, the only manager to get the best out of Eric Cantona and one who has proved similarly adept at handling the temperamental Wayne Rooney.

The small band of players whose egos outgrew Ferguson's control – Ruud van Nistelrooy, Jaap Stam, and Roy Keane – were moved on.

Even Beckham got the boot – literally – as Ferguson grew ever more exasperated with the England star's celebrity lifestyle. Matters came to a head in February 2003 when the United manager kicked a football boot in frustration after his side had lost 2-0 to Arsenal. The boot hit Beckham in the face. That summer Beckham joined Real Madrid.

Fergie finally retired in May 2013, the same month that Manchester United clinched their 13th Premier League title under the Scot. In all he won 38 trophies during his 27 years at Old Trafford; the number of teacups he smashed during that time is anybody's guess.

One pound coin

OBJECT 96

One of the clubs Alex Ferguson appeared for as a player was Rangers, enjoying a couple of years at Ibrox in the late 1960s. It wasn't a time when the Glasgow club was at its strongest, seriously second best to rivals Celtic who won the European Cup in 1967 and clinched nine consecutive League titles between 1966 and 1974. Still, compared to where Rangers are now, the swinging sixties weren't so bad.

We've chosen to represent the fall from grace of Rangers with a £1 coin – what Scottish businessman Craig Whyte paid for the club in May 2011 when he bought it from David Murray, owner of Rangers for the previous twenty three years. Whyte paid a pound because when he took charge of Rangers they were approximately £18 million in debt (though the bulk of his sum was soon paid off).

Then Her Majesty's Revenue & Customs (HMRC) came calling, demanding £49 million in unpaid tax, and forcing Murray to put the club into administration in February 2012, declaring that the tax bill could reach as much as £134 million. As the Scottish Football Association declared Whyte unfit to hold a position in football – fining Rangers £160,000 and imposing a one season transfer ban – administrators Duff & Phelps unveiled a series of wage cuts among playing staff to reduce the club's costs.

Events then moved rapidly during the summer of 2012 with a consortium headed by Charles Green taking control of the club and the HMRC then forcing Rangers into liquidation in June. Green reformed the Ibrox club as Newco Rangers, but at a meeting of Scottish Premier League clubs in July it was decided to reject their application to join the SPL as a punishment for their past financial mismanagement. Instead the new-look Rangers were consigned to Division Three in the 2012–13 season. Since then they have climbed steadily back towards the top of Scottish football, winning consecutive promotions so that come the 2014–15 season Rangers will be in the Championship, one league below the SPL and their long-awaited chance for revenge against those clubs that voted against them.

Royal Mint commemorative 50p coin

The offside law, where do you start? Not with this 50p coin, released in early 2012 by the Royal Mint in a cack-handed attempt to bolster their street cred. The coin was one of twenty nine minted to celebrate the London Olympics, each representing a different Olympic sport. The fifty pence coin has football, or more precisely, a simplified version of the offside law that has been baffling folk for nearly 150 years.

The coin depicts a player about to pass to one of two team-mates, with the first (on the left) marked as offside and the second (level with the defender) onside. In launching the football 50p the Royal Mint slapped itself on the back, a spokes-woman lauding the "unusual and eye-catching" design and saying the half a million coins now in circulation had already "generated significant interest from collectors and sports fans."

And, as she quickly discovered, the Referees' Association, who were soon blowing their collective whistle and accusing the Royal Mint of getting ahead of itself. Reporting on the contretemps, the *Guardian* said the coin's diagram "appears to illustrate the offside law as it was until 1995, when it was overhauled by the International FA Board to reduce the number of stoppages in matches. The revision to the law meant that any player in an offside position when the ball is played is no longer automatically penalised."

In other words, it's not an offence in itself to be in an offside position. Mal Davies, a member of the Referees' Association said the Royal Mint's mistake was "embarrassing" and explained that since 1995 guidelines issued to assistant referees instruct them to wait and see whether a player in an offside position becomes involved in active play, either by "interfering with play, or interfering with an opponent, or by gaining an advantage by being in that position."

By now the Royal Mint, not to mention many of the people in possession of the coins, were becoming confused. Which, let's be honest, isn't the first time as far as the offside law goes.

The *Guardian* came to the rescue of those people trying to make sense of the 50p: "That means that if the midfielder on the coin passes to the striker on his left, but the striker chooses not to play the ball or interfere with an opponent, he is not offside and play continues."

The Royal Mint began backtracking like a top-class defender, saying the coin was there "to provoke discussion", but that went down as well as a cold meat pie at half-time with Mal Davies. "On parks pitches it will just encourage players to keep pressurising officials to blow the whistle immediately any time a player is in an offside position and to abuse them when they don't," he complained. "It's always good to see attempts to explain the Law to a wider audience, and the coin looks good – but unfortunately it takes us back to the last century and just confuses the issue even more."

Plus ça change, and all that. As Davies alluded, the offside law has been irritating the hell out of people ever since Henry Malden and his chums assembled in a study at Cambridge in 1848 (see object 1). On that occasion they agreed that "if the ball has passed a player and has come from the direction of his own goal, he may not touch it till the other side has kicked it, unless there are more than three of the other side before him. No player is allowed to loiter between the ball and the adversaries' goal."

This "more than three" (i.e. four) was reduced by the Football Association in 1866 to three (which still didn't satisfy Queen's Park (see object 6)) and that's how the offside law remained until 1925, when three became two, much to the delight of Herbert Chapman (see object 32).

The offside law as it stands today is fairly simple to follow if a little too big to fit on the back of a fifty pence coin. Sit up straight and pay attention:

A player is in an offside position if:
he is nearer to his opponents' goal line than both the ball and the second-last opponent

A player is not in an offside position if:
he is in his own half of the field of play or
he is level with the second-last opponent or
he is level with the last two opponents

A player in an offside position is only penalised if, at the moment the ball touches or is played by one of his team, he is, in the opinion of the referee, involved in active play by:
interfering with play or
interfering with an opponent or
gaining an advantage by being in that position.

Old sponge

OBJECT
98

"The magic sponge has been a familiar sight on sports fields up and down the nation for generations. No matter how great or small the injury, no matter what the sport, it seemed there were no limits to its supposedly miraculous healing powers. But now its very existence is being threatened by health and safety considerations."

The *Western Mail* feared for the future of the sponge in its edition of 23 July 2004. More magical than Paul Daniels, sponges had been healing broken fingers, bloodied noses and even bruised egos since time immemorial. How could it get a red card?

According to an article in the *Observer* in 2003, "the wondrous sponge first appeared on the scene just after the formation of the Football League in 1888" as clubs realised they needed to look after their players if they wished to challenge for the title.

As football became more regulated and practices such as "hacking" and "charging" were outlawed so serious injuries decreased. In an article titled "Football Mania", written for The *Nineteenth Century* in October 1892, Charles Edwards reported that "on the subject of accidents, it is gratifying to be able to say emphatically that with the progress of scientific [sic] Association football injuries to players are becoming more and more rare." According to Edwards there were plenty of mild sprains and strains during the course of an average season, but "for these Anti-Stiff and embrocations of many kinds are ready to do effective service". In one match, remarked Edwards, a "player's leg was broken midway between the ankle and the knee-cap [and] the snap of the bone was audible fifty yards away. But though it was an unfortunate affair, the sufferer was comforted by the sympathies of the public."

Sympathy from the player's club was another matter. For most of the nineteenth century clubs regarded players as pieces of meat, to be discarded if rotten. In 1902 the Manchester City and Wales full back Di Jones suffered a gash in a pre-season training session; the wound became infected and Jones died a few days later. At an inquest to discover whether City were responsible for his death the club blamed Jones for his death, saying he had insisted on walking off the pitch unaided. The coroner agreed, declaring in his summing up: "are football clubs to supply a medical staff on their field?

I don't think there is any obligation on them to do that."

But according to Neil Carter of the International Centre for Sports History and Culture at De Montfort University at Leicester, "because of a rise in the number of injuries clubs began to insure themselves against claims from players who would lose time off work from football injuries, leading some clubs to establish more formal medical arrangements." Middlesbrough, in 1898, were one of the first, taking out insurance on its players who held everyday jobs. Carter says the policy included a clause stipulating "that a player shall at once retire from the field and have the injuries immediately attended to and he shall not resume play without the permission of a duly qualified surgeon or medical man, etc."

In the inter war years and throughout the 1950s British football swore by the sponge as the remedy for all ailments, and even the death of Sunderland goalkeeper Jimmy Thorpe in February 1936 didn't shake the game out its complacency. Thorpe died after being targeted by Chelsea players in a bad-tempered affair that left him with broken ribs and a badly bruised head. He died a few days later, *The Times* attributing his death to the "rough usage of the opposing team".

On continental Europe there was a more enlightened attitude to sports medicine, to which British clubs began to be exposed in the wake of the launch of the European Cup in 1955. Even so, *Charles Buchan's Football Monthly* ran an article by Bill Croft in its February 1956 edition titled "Yugoslavia have a Doctor on the bench!" The exclamation mark said it all: they're soft overseas.

But three months later Manchester City goalkeeper Bert Trautmann broke his neck playing against Birmingham in the FA Cup Final. Incredibly, the German was allowed to play on for the remaining fifteen minutes of the match and only when he had an x-ray several days later was it discovered he'd dislocated five vertebrae in his neck, the second of which had fractured.

Gradually, British clubs began to take the issue of sports

medicine more seriously – prompted in part by the scrapping of the maximum wage in 1961 which markedly increased the value of players.

In the 1961–62 season there were a series of meetings between clubs and medical experts to discuss how medical assistance to players could be improved. The following year Alf Ramsey appointed Alan Bass as the first England squad doctor, but many other clubs simply hired enthusiastic amateurs – many of whom were ex-professional players – who had little or no sports injuries training. According to Neil Carter: "A goalkeeper who played during the 1960s and 1970s for clubs throughout the league... commented that 'physiotherapy didn't seem that sophisticated and attention to injuries on the field seemed clumsy at times – magic sponge and strong smelling salts seemed the answer to most problems!'"

In 1981 the Football League stipulated that it was the "responsibility of the home club to ensure that a qualified medical practitioner was in attendance throughout the match", but it wasn't until the advent of the Premier League in 1992 that clubs really began to hire the top medical experts to safeguard the wellbeing of their players. Yet despite this Chelsea lodged a complaint with the FA and the Premier League in 2006 in the wake of a fractured skull sustained by goalkeeper Petr Cech. The delay in hospitalising Cech led Chelsea coach Jose Mourinho to slam the medical facilities: "My goalkeeper was in the dressing room for thirty minutes waiting for an ambulance," said Mourinho. "This is something English football has to think about. This is much more important than football."

As a result of Chelsea's complaints the FA and Premier League introduced new measures in 2007, which included the "requirement for every game to have an ambulance on standby for players and officials... and made it compulsory for clubs to provide two paramedic stretcher-bearers, with a club doctor and physiotherapists on the team benches, as well as a qualified 'crowd doctor' on standby."

According to a report in the *Guardian* in March 2012 these changes "may have saved Fabrice Muamba's life", the Bolton player who suffered a cardiac arrest during an FA Cup tie against Tottenham at White Hart Lane a few days earlier. Muamba's heart stopped beating for seventy eight minutes yet thanks to the prompt action of the medical team, who gave him fifteen defibrillator shocks, the 23-year-old survived.

Not even the magic sponge could have pulled that one off.

Microchip

OBJECT 99

Finally, Big Brother is watching football! It would have been helpful if FIFA had sanctioned the use of goal line technology in 1984, the year that George Orwell's seminal novel was set (think of all the countless controversies it could have prevented), but football's governing body finally entered the twenty first century in July 2012 when the International Football Association Board (IFAB) voted in favour of using technology for "instantaneous decisions" during matches.

The case for some form of goal line technology began gathering pace after the 2010 World Cup in South Africa. A shot from England's Frank Lampard hit the underside of the German bar and bounced down two feet over the goal line. It was a goal, clearly, and just about everyone in the stadium knew it – except the three match officials. Of course, the Germans had little sympathy for the English; why should they after they suffered a similar injustice against England during the 1966 World Cup Final. What goes around comes around, or in this case what goes over the line sometimes doesn't.

Faced with such an embarrassing error in the sport's showpiece tournament, FIFA President Sepp Blatter apologised to England and conceded the time might have come to "reopen the file of technology". Previously, FIFA had favoured leaving decisions to "human beings" but with a host of other top sports – including rugby, cricket and tennis – embracing twenty first century technology there was no escaping the grasp of modernity.

Or so we thought. Then, in the summer of 2011, the second most powerful man in football – UEFA president Michel Platini – came out in favour of remaining stuck in the past. "In my opinion technology isn't good for football," said the former French international, whose only defence seemed to of the "in my day" variety. "Football was managed by just one man for 100 years and it was impossible to appreciate everything that happened on the pitch, so sometimes he would make decisions without having seen what went on. Now if a referee doesn't see something it's because he's not very good."

What Platini failed to appreciate is that a) the technology is now available to make split-second decisions and b) for the first century of football there was little at stake, other than a sportsman's natural desire to win. Football's now awash with money – and don't FIFA and UEFA know it – and an incorrect decision over a goal could have huge financial ramifications.

One measure introduced by UEFA in a desperate attempt to placate those calling for goal line introduction was the appearance of two additional referees in Champions League and Europa League matches. Their job was to provide the referee with four extra eyes but even with their presence mistakes have continued to be made.

FIFA, meanwhile, grudgingly agreed to trial two systems over a four month period during the 2011–12 season, their proviso stating that they must provide 100 per cent reliability, accuracy and speed of "the decision-making process". The first system, Hawk-Eye, involves the use of numerous cameras to track the ball in flight. Software then "calculates the ball's location for each frame by identifying the pixels that correspond to the ball through at least two cameras. The margin of error for the system is 3.6mm."

The second system uses a microchip inserted in the middle of the ball and sensors inside the posts and crossbar. Magnetism then determines if the ball has crossed the line.

Trials of both worked well, and in May 2012 Hawk-Eye cameras were used for the first time in a competitive match in Britain when AFC Totton played Eastleigh FC in the Senior Hampshire Cup Final. The following month the cameras were seen at Wembley when England played Belgium, the first occasion goal line technology was used in an international match. Though Hawk-Eye wasn't required in the hosts' 1-0 victory, England manager Roy Hodgson said of its presence: "It is another advance technologically and one which I hope will prove successful and will at least banish some of the ghosts of the past."

Ironically, a couple of weeks later England were the beneficiaries of football's failure to embrace technology in their Euro 2012 clash with the Ukraine. Defending a 1-0 lead in the second half England cleared the ball off the line and no goal was given by the officials, not even by the fourth referee who – on the instructions of UEFA – was standing right by the goal for just such an event. Yet television replays showed that the ball was clearly over the line before John Terry hoofed it back out. "Devic scored a goal and I don't know why it wasn't allowed," muttered Ukraine coach Oleg Blokhin later, adding: "What can I say? There are five referees on the pitch and the ball was half a metre over the line."

The technology was used for the first time at FIFA's Club World Cup in Japan in December 2012 and will be fully operational at the 2014 World Cup – though only the match referee will be told of the verdict, with spectators unable to see replays on stadium big screens. "It is a historic day for international football," said Sepp Blatter, adding that he was sure his pal

Platini would come round to the idea of goal line technology. "He cannot go against history and this is new history. I am sure he is smart enough to realise that something has happened today in football."

FIFA Ballon d'Or

So here we are, we've come to the end of our journey, and what started with an old school bench is ending with the Ballon d'Or. A golden ball; it feels somehow appropriate that we blow the full-time whistle admiring such an object. It symbolises the glamour, the extravagance and, dare we say, the gaudiness of modern football. To think when we started all those objects ago football had no rules, no money and no clubs, and now look at it. At times it feels like it's showbiz first and sport second.

And yet the first recipient of the Ballon d'Or couldn't have been more old school. Stanley Matthews of plain old Blackpool won it first in 1956, beating Alfredo Di Stéfano into second place. One wonders what Stan made of it all; a player who'd earned £1 a week when he started his career with Stoke City a quarter of a century earlier.

The award was the idea of Gabriel Hanot, the French journalist responsible for the European Cup, as a way of honouring the continent's finest player. Journalists voted for the winner and only European players at European clubs were eligible, explaining why Pelé nor any other of the great Brazilians from the '60 and '70s feature in the list. Nonetheless there are some names to conjure with on the winners' rostrum: Lev Yashin (the only goalkeeper to be honoured), Eusebio, Bobby

Charlton, George Best, Franz Beckenbauer, Johan Cruyff, the first player to win a hat-trick of Golden Balls, and Michel Platini, the first player to win three consecutive titles (1983 to 1985).

FIFA stole the Golden Ball in 2010, merging the award with their own World Player of the Year which had been inaugurated in 1991 and was voted for by coaches and captains of international teams. Rechristened the FIFA Ballon d'Or (who says the sport's governing body is run by control freaks?), the trophy was won by Lionel Messi in 2009, 2010, 2011 and 2012, thereby equalling Platini's record of a quarter of a century earlier, before Cristiano Ronaldo broke the Argentine's winning streak in 2013. According to former Manchester United manager Alex Ferguson, Messi now bears comparison with the best players from history. "Critics have always questioned whether players like Pelé from the '50s could play today," said Ferguson. "The answer to that is great players would play in any generation. Lionel Messi could play in the 1950s and the present day, as could Di Stéfano, Pelé, Maradona, Cruyff because they are all great players."

Messi's genius is in his goalscoring (in 2011–12 he broke Gerd Müller's thirty-nine-year-old record of sixty seven goals in a single season) that has helped Barcelona dominate Europe in recent years. Winners of the Champions League in 2009 and 2011, the Catalan club have also won three consecutive Spanish League titles starting in 2009.

As a result, the Argentine striker has been enriched with more than just medals. According to a report published in 2013 by Forbes, Messi is the world's best-paid footballer on $41m – the previous year of which $21m was in endorsements and sponsorship, not bad for a player who turned 27 in June 2014. Lionel Messi has the world at his feet, yet it appears that those feet are also firmly on the ground. In collecting his fourth Ballon d'Or the modest Argentine said: "The fourth award that I have had is just too great for words. I would like to recognise my other colleagues from

Barcelona... I would also like to recognise all of my friends in the Argentinian national team. Everyone that has worked with me, coaches and staff."

Because great as he undoubtedly is Messi knows he'd have nothing – no millions, no medals, no golden balls – without the help of his teammates. There may be more stars in football's firmament than ever before but the game is still essentially no different to the one that Charles Alcock did so much for a century ago. And it seems fitting to end our history of football with what Alcock wrote in 1906, words that have as much resonance today as they did then:

> The whole secret of success in football lies, it is almost superfluous to add, in the measure of a team's combination. A club eleven composed of entirely mediocre players will generally make a good show against, if it does not actually beat, a coalition of members of different bodies of vastly superior capacity individually. There is no royal road to football, and the first lesson that a young footballer must take to heart and learn thoroughly is unselfishness... A selfish player, one who enters a football field with the idea of contributing purely to self-glorification, will very soon find himself out in the cold, and his place filled by one who is more capable of advancing the general well-being of his side. Combination is the only possible way to the attainment of anything like perfection of working in a football team, and the sooner the tyro recognizes the importance of mastering this first lesson, the sooner will he be on the way to advancement.

Here's to the next 150 years of the Beautiful Game.

Appendix: The 1863 Football Association Rules

1 The maximum length of the ground shall be 200 yards; the maximum breadth shall be 100 yards; the length and breadth shall be marked off with flags; and the goal shall be defined by two upright posts, 8 yards apart, without any tape or bar across them.

2 A toss for goals shall take place, and the game shall be commenced by a place-kick from the centre of the ground by the side losing the toss. The other side shall not approach within ten yards of the ball until it is kicked off.

3 After a goal is won, the losing side shall be entitled to kick off, and the two sides shall change goals after each goal is won.

4 A goal shall be won when the ball passes between the goal-posts or over the space between the goal-posts (at whatever height), not being thrown, knocked on, or carried.

5 When the ball is in touch, the first player who touches it shall throw it from the point on the boundary line where it left the ground in a direction at right angles with the boundary line, and the ball shall not be in play until it has touched the ground.

6 When a player has kicked the ball, any one of the same side who is nearer to the opponent's goal-line is out of play, and may not touch the ball himself, nor in any way whatsoever prevent any other player from doing so until he is in play; but no player is out of play when the ball is kicked off from behind the goal-line.

7 In case the ball goes behind the goal-line, if a player on the side to whom the goal belongs first touches the ball, one of his side shall be entitled to a free kick from the goal-line at the point opposite the place where the ball shall be touched. If a player of the opposite side first touches the ball, one of his side shall be entitled to a free kick at the goal, only from a point fifteen yards outside the goal-line, opposite the place where the ball is touched, the opposing side standing within the goal-line until he has had his kick.

8 If a player makes a fair catch, he shall be entitled to a free kick, providing he claims it by making a mark with his heel at once; and in order to take such kick he may go as far back as he pleases, and no player on the opposite side shall advance beyond his mark until he has kicked.

9 No player shall run with the ball.

10 Neither tripping nor hacking shall be allowed, and no player shall use his hands to hold or push his adversary.

11 A player shall not be allowed to throw the ball or pass it to another with his hands.

12 No player shall be allowed to take the ball from the ground with his hands under any pretence whatever while it is in play.

13 No player shall be allowed to wear projecting nails, iron plates, or gutta-percha on the soles or heels of his boots.

Definition of Terms

A Place Kick is a kick at the ball while it is on the ground, in any position which the kicker may choose to place it.

A Free Kick is the privilege of kicking the ball, without obstruction, in such manner as the kicker may think fit.

A Fair Catch is when the ball is caught, after it has touched the person of an adversary, or has been kicked or knocked on by an adversary, and before it has touched the ground or one of the side catching it; but if the ball is kicked behind the goal-line, a fair catch cannot be made.

Hacking is kicking an adversary.

Tripping is throwing an adversary by the use of the legs.

Holding includes the obstruction of a player by the hand or any part of the arm below the elbow.

Touch is that part of the field, on either side of the ground, which is beyond the line of flags.

Bibliography

Athletics and Football, Montague Shearman (Longmans Green & Co, 1887)
The Ball is Round: A Global History of Football, David Goldblatt
    (Penguin, 2007)
Beastly Fury: The Strange Birth of British Football, Richard Sanders
    (Bantam Press, 2009)
British Society 1914-1945, John Stevenson (Penguin, 1984)
Calcio: History of Italian Football, John Foot (Harper Perennial, 2007)
Clough: The Autobiography, Brian Clough (Corgi, 1995)
The Day a Team Died, Frank Taylor (Souvenir Press, 1983)
Edward Elgar: Memories of a Variation by Dora Penny Powell
    (Geoffrey Cumberlege, 1946)
The End of the Terraces: The Transformation of English Football, Anthony King
    (Continuum, 2002)
Engineering Archie, Simon Inglis (English Heritage, 2005)
Fever Pitch, Nick Hornby, (Gollancz, 1992)
Fields of Glory, Gavin Mortimer (Andre Deutsch, 2001)
Firsts, Lasts & Onlys Football, Paul Donnelley (Hamlyn, 2010)
Football: The Association Game, Charles Alcock (George Bell & Sons, 1906)

Football: The First Hundred Years: the Untold Story, by Adrian Harvey (Routledge, 2005)
Football Grounds of Britain, Simon Inglis (Harper Collins, 1996)
Football Nation, by Andrew Ward and John Williams (Bloomsbury 2010)
Football in Sun and Shadow by Eduardo Galeano (Fourth Estate, 2003)
Football is My Business, Tommy Lawton (Sporting Handbooks, 1947)
Gazza: My Story, Paul Gascoigne with Hunter Davies (Headline, 2005)
German Football: History, Culture, Society, Alan Tomlinson (Routledge, 2005)
God is Brazilian, Josh Lacey (Tempus, 2005)
The Heart of the Game, Jimmy Greaves (Little, Brown, 2005)
A History of British Football, Percy Young (Arrow Books, 1974)
A History of Marlborough College, A.G Bradley (John Murray, 1923)
History of the World Cup, Brian Glanville (Faber & Faber, 2010)
How They Stole the Game, David Yallop (Constable, 2011)
Inverting the Pyramid: A History of Football Tactics, Jonathan Wilson (Orion, 2008)
The Leaguers: The Making of Professional Football in England, 1900–1939, Dr. Matthew Taylor (Chicago University Press, 2007)
A Lifetime in Football, Charles Buchan, (Mainstream, 2011)
Metatarsals and Magic Sponges: English Football and the Development of Sports Medicine, Neil Carter (International Centre for Sport, History and Culture, 2007)
My England Years, Bobby Charlton (Headline, 2009)
Pelé: The Autobiography, Pelé (Simon & Schuster, 2006)
The Road to Wigan Pier, George Orwell (Mariner Books, 1972)
Sir Alex: The Story of 21 Remarkable Years at United, David Meek and Tom Tyrrel (Orion, 2007)
Sport and Leisure Cultures, Alan Tomlinson (Palgrave Macmillan, 2002)
The Sunday Times Illustrated History of Football, Chris Nawrat and Steve Hutchings, (Octopus Publishing Group, 1998)
The Victorians and Sport, Mike Huggins (Hambledon Continuum, 2004)
William Sudell: Football's First Northern Hero?, Neil Carter (International Centre for Sport, History and Culture, 2007)

Journals and Newspapers

Africa News
The Athletic News
Birmingham Mail
Boston Herald
Cape Argus
Charles Buchan's Football Monthly
Chemistry and Industry journal
Chicago Tribune
Daily Express

Daily Herald
Daily Mail
Daily Mirror
Daily Record
Daily Star
Daily Telegraph
L'Équipe
The Field
France Football

Glasgow Herald
The Graphic
Guardian
The Historical Journal
Independent
Independent on Sunday
Irish Times
Kingston Gleaner
Lincolnshire Echo
Liverpool Echo
Liverpool Post
London Evening Standard
LA Times
Mail on Sunday
Manchester Daily Dispatch
News Chronicle
New York Times

The Nineteenth Century
North Eastern Daily Gazette
Observer
Preston Herald
The People
Soccer and Society
Southern Daily Echo
Sporting Life
Sun
Sun and Central Press
Sunday Times
Sunday Telegraph
The Times
Western Mail
When Saturday Comes
World Soccer
Yorkshire Post

Websites

http://bleacherreport.com
http://blogs.reuters.com/soccer/tag/diving/
http://footballspeak.com
http://footysphere.com/
http://fourfourtwo.com–
http://shm.oxfordjournals.org
http://soccernet.espn.go.com
http://www.aljazeera.com
http://www.attackingsoccer.com
http://www.cottontown.org/
http://www.elgar.org
http://www.financialfairplay.co.uk
http://www.gersnetonline.co.uk
http://www.gringoes.com/
http://www.nj.com/soccer-news/
http://www.queensparkfc.co.uk
http://www.shankly.com/
http://www.soccerballworld.com
http://www.talksport.co.uk

http://www.thecelticwiki.com
http://www.tottenhamhotspurs.tv
http://www.victorianlondon.org/entertainment/football.htm
http://zaire1974.blogspot.fr
https://twitter.com/
www.arsenal.com
www.bbc.co.uk/sport
www.deloitte.com
www.fifa.com
www.liverpoolfc.com/
www.manutd.com/
www.premierleague.com
www.richardlindon.com
www.scottishfa.co.uk/
www.thefa.com
www.uefa.com
www.worldsoccer.com
www.wsc.co.uk

Image credits

Unless otherwise specified, all images credited below are reproduced under Creative Commons licences (see here for more info: http://creativecommons.org/licenses/by/2.0/).

© = Copyright (all rights reserved)
TM = Trademark, ® = Registered Trademark
(cc sa) = Creative Commons share-alike licence (see here for more info: http://creativecommons.org/licenses/by-sa/2.0/)

1 Ell Brown; 2 Lionel Allorge (cc sa); 4 Paul Hudson; 5 Ben Sutherland; 7 Kate Ter Haar; 8 Tony Hall; 9 Peter Houghton; 10 Chris Hills; 11 Carl Clifford; 12 © The Old Fashioned Football Shirt Company Ltd. Image appears courtesy of TOFFS. Visit their website, www.toffs.com, for this and other retro football shirts.; 13 Carlos Úbeda; 15 Jimmy Baikovicius (cc sa); 16 State Records New South Wales; 18 Flickr user "Mr Littlehand"; 19 Matthew Wilkinson; 20 ® FIFA. Please note that the reproduction of this image is in no way intended to convey FIFA's endorsement of this book or the material contained herein.; 21 Matt Preston (cc sa); 22 The Living Room Antiques, Kenmore; 23 This public domain image appears courtesy of the Library of Congress.; 24 © Nick Sheerin; 26 The author of this public domain image is unknown.; 27 Christian Kadluba (cc sa); 30 Flickr user "woody1778a"; 31 M. Rehemtulla for QUOI Media Group (cc sa); 32 Chris Applegate (cc sa); 33 Ben Sutherland; 34 Ilker Ender; 35 David Holt (cc sa); 36 Brett Weinstein (cc sa); 37 John Atherton (cc sa); 38 How can I recycle this (http://www.recyclethis.co.uk); 39 Sergio Calleja (cc sa); 40 Twitter user "Svadilfari"; 41 *Charles Buchan's Football Monthly* "Issue No. 1" front cover is used with permission from www.footballmonthlyarchives.co.uk; 43 Mary Keogh; 44 © Nick Sheerin; 45 Henry Leirvoll (cc sa); 46 Marco Tedaldi (cc sa); 47 Ben Sutherland; 48 Meghan E. Patterson; 49 © The Old Fashioned Football Shirt Company Ltd. Image appears courtesy of TOFFS. Visit their website, www.toffs.com, for this and other retro football shirts; 50 Andrew Michaels; 51 René Clausen Nielsen (cc sa); 52 Daniel Weir (N.B. image not to be re-used for commercial purposes); 53 Celso Flores; 54 Jo Naylor; 55 TM © The National Aeronautics and Space Administration. Please note that the reproduction of this image is in no way intended to convey NASA's endorsement of this book or the material contained herein; 56 Vivodefutbol. com; 57 Michael Caviglia (cc sa); 58 © The Old Fashioned Football Shirt Company Ltd. Image appears courtesy of TOFFS. Visit their website, www. toffs.com, for this and other retro football shirts; 59 © The Old Fashioned Football Shirt Company Ltd. Image appears courtesy of TOFFS. Visit their website, www.toffs.com, for this and other retro football shirts; 61 James Lee; 62 John Johnston; 63 Bryan Alexander; 64 Daniel Richardson; 65 Flickr user Fréderic; 66 Manos Radisoglou; 68 Wonderlane (www.wonderlane.com); 69 © Nick Sheerin; 70 © Rolf Kosecki / Corbis; 71 Todd Ehlers; 73 Andrew

Frog; **74** thebittenword.com; **75** Flickr user "enigmachck"; **76** Motohide Miwa; **77** Andrew Malone; **78** Flickr user "avlxyz" (cc sa); **79** Mike Gifford (cc sa); **80** Wikimedia Commons user "gongo"; **81** Jeff Keacher; **82** Flickr user "El Ronzo"; **83** Flickr user "emma.maria"; **84** © Janine Lamontagne / iStockphoto; **85** © adidas. Image of "adidas Women's Coast Shorts W E72897" reproduced courtesy of adidas. The Trefoil logo is a registered trade mark of the adidas Group used with permission; **86** Tom Godber (cc sa); **87** Flickr user "Queenbeeofbeverleyhills"; **88** © Richard Paknam. Richard's blog on Buddhism can be found at www.thaibuddhist.com; **90** www.2012. taxbrackets.org/; **91** David Ambrocik; **92** Paul Haeder; **93** Jintae Kim; **94** © ® Twitter. Please note that the reproduction of this image is in no way intended to convey Twitter's endorsement of this book or the material contained herein; **95** Flickr user "star5512" (cc sa); **96** Andrew Michaels; **97** © Crown Copyright. Image appears by kind permission of the Royal Mint; **98** Steven Depolo; **99** Flickr user "yellowcloud"; **100** Wikimedia Commons user Laslovarga.

Acknowledgements

I'd like to thank Sandy Tyrie, curator, Scottish Football Museum, for clearing up the confusion surrounding the Scottish badge in the formative years. I'm grateful, too, to all the staff at the British Library in King's Cross, and the British Newspaper Library, Colindale, for their efficiency and endeavour in locating countless books, journals and newspapers stretching back 150 years.

In addition I would like to express my thanks to the following publishers for their permission in allowing me to quote from their books: English Heritage, *Engineering Archie: Archibald Leitch – Football Ground Designer* by Simon Inglis [2005]; Bantam, *Beastly Fury: The Strange Birth of British Football* by Richard Sanders [2010]; Orion, *Inverting the Pyramid: The History of Football Tactics* by Jonathan Wilson [2008]; Constable & Robinson, *How They Stole The Game* by David Yallop [2011]; Penguin, *The Ball is Round: A Global History of Football* by David Goldblatt [2006] and Neil Carter, Senior Research Fellow at the International Centre for Sports History and Culture at De Montfort University at Leicester, who kindly allowed to quote from his excellent essays "Metatarsals and Magic Sponges: English Football and the Development of Sports Medicine" and "William Sudell: Football's First Northern Hero".

Finally, thanks to Pete Ayrton, Ruthie Petrie and Nick Sheerin at Serpent's Tail for giving shape to the book in a way I know Pete wishes Arsène Wenger could do with the Arsenal back four.